GERMAN LUFTWAFFE

IN WWII

ORDER OF BATTLE

GERMAN LUFTWAFFE

IN

WWII

CHRIS McNAB

amber
BOOKS

First published in 2009 by
Amber Books Ltd
Bradley's Close
74–77 White Lion Street
London N1 9PF
United Kingdom
www.amberbooks.co.uk

ISBN: 978-1-906626-20-4

Project Editor: Michael Spilling
Design: Hawes Design
Picture Research: Terry Forshaw

Printed in Thailand

PICTURE CREDITS
AKG Images: 91
Art-Tech/Aerospace: 41, 60
Art-Tech/MARS: 16, 30, 78
Cody Images: 6, 40, 54, 96, 110, 146, 164, 176

All Artworks: Art-Tech/Aerospace

MAPS
Cartographica: 29, 35, 46/47, 71, 77, 85, 105, 113, 126, 129, 141, 145
Patrick Mulrey: 21, 39, 64, 82, 94, 107, 108, 132, 156, 157, 162, 170
All maps © Amber Books

CONTENTS

The Pre-War
Luftwaffe

Under the terms of the Versailles Treaty, Germany was prohibited from operating military aviation. Yet by 1939, Hitler had managed to oversee the development of a tactically powerful *Luftwaffe*, albeit one with significant long-term weaknesses.

He 111 and He 115 production. The former would become the key German medium bomber of World War II.

In retrospect, it is all too apparent how mistakes made in the development of the *Luftwaffe* between 1933 and 1939 would be paid for in the blood of Germany's pilots, soldiers and civilians in the years 1939–45. As it emerged into the light of the post-Versailles world, the Nazi leadership was faced with fundamental decisions about the nature of its military aviation arm. In short, it had to decide between a tactical air force, one geared to short-/medium-range operations in support of land forces manoeuvres, or a strategic air force designed for long-range actions against an enemy's national infrastructure. As we shall see in this book, the *Luftwaffe* was brilliantly developed in the short term, the talents of its pilots and the quality of its machines implanting instant respect amongst the Allies. In the long term, however (and a fact becoming apparent even by the autumn of 1940), the *Luftwaffe* would never be capable of the awesome strategic reach later demonstrated by Britain's Bomber Command or the US Eighth Air Force, both of which gutted the heart of a largely impotent Germany in the later years of World War II.

The story of the *Luftwaffe* reads very much like that of a hero in a classical tragedy. At first, there is a rise to greatness. When unleashed against Poland in 1939, then much of Western Europe in 1940, the *Luftwaffe* generally stood head and shoulders above the rest. Obsolescent enemy air forces were massacred; ground troops were terrorized by a professionally executed ground-attack campaign. Such results led to hubris, at least in Hermann Göring, the *Luftwaffe*'s chief, who overestimated the air force's ability. This hubris was dented by defeat in the Battle of Britain and progressively eroded by the inability to maintain air supremacy against the British, Soviets and American aircraft as the war developed.

Then came the downfall. The Allies unleashed such an aerial arsenal against the *Luftwaffe* that by the end of the war its resistance was almost suicidal. This book gives some of the facts and figures about the *Luftwaffe*'s journey from dominant force to ragged survivors. While there is no defending the German regime collectively, as individuals the *Luftwaffe* pilots demonstrated truly inspiring courage and talent.

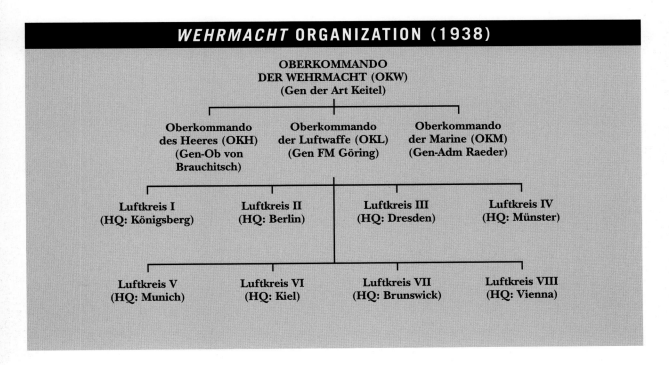

WEHRMACHT ORGANIZATION (1938)

OBERKOMMANDO DER WEHRMACHT (OKW)
(Gen der Art Keitel)

Oberkommando des Heeres (OKH) (Gen-Ob von Brauchitsch)

Oberkommando der Luftwaffe (OKL) (Gen FM Göring)

Oberkommando der Marine (OKM) (Gen-Adm Raeder)

Luftkreis I (HQ: Königsberg)

Luftkreis II (HQ: Berlin)

Luftkreis III (HQ: Dresden)

Luftkreis IV (HQ: Münster)

Luftkreis V (HQ: Munich)

Luftkreis VI (HQ: Kiel)

Luftkreis VII (HQ: Brunswick)

Luftkreis VIII (HQ: Vienna)

Building the *Luftwaffe*

From 1933, all of Hitler's armed forces were committed to massive programmes of expansion and professionalization. The aviation arm was no exception, although economic limitations would restrict its development and combat power.

The initial post-World War I obstacle to the development of German combat aviation was the Versailles Treaty. Although the treaty gave Germany provision for a small defensive army and navy, known as the *Reichswehr*, no allowance was made for combat aviation. Thus the Imperial Air Service was disbanded, its aircraft destroyed and the training of military aviators and building of military aircraft banned.

Secret programmes

Although the Versailles Treaty was theoretically stringent, it was weakly enforced. Furthermore, the Weimar government managed to implement air force training under the cover of civilian operations. Flying clubs offered basic aviation training in gliders and light aircraft, and the pilots could then step up to flying for civil air transport companies. The most famous of these was *Deutsche Luft Hansa Aktiengesellschaft*, formed in January 1926. *Lufthansa* (the one-word name was adopted in 1933) gradually established air routes between Germany and Spain, the Far East and the Americas. As well as providing travel opportunities, however, *Lufthansa* also facilitated pilot experience in what would become key *Luftwaffe* military aircraft types – the Junkers Ju 52 and Ju 86, the Heinkel He 111 and the Focke-Wulf Condor. More direct military training was provided to German pilots at a secret base at Lipetsk in Russia. Steadily, Germany was rebuilding its air force.

Birth of the *Luftwaffe*

The German *Luftwaffe* officially declared its existence in May 1935. By this time, however, it already existed in everything but name, presided over since 1933 by the Minister of Aviation, Hermann Göring, and eventually ordered according to eight *Luftkreise* (Air Districts) under the overall command of the *Oberkommado der Luftwaffe*. Göring, a World War I fighter ace himself, was prone to thinking in tactical rather than strategic terms, and to looking at problems with a fighter pilot's dash rather than a commander's logic.

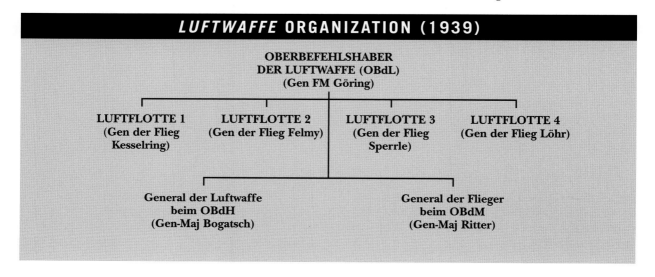

LUFTWAFFE ORGANIZATION (1939)

OBERBEFEHLSHABER
DER LUFTWAFFE (OBdL)
(Gen FM Göring)

| LUFTFLOTTE 1 (Gen der Flieg Kesselring) | LUFTFLOTTE 2 (Gen der Flieg Felmy) | LUFTFLOTTE 3 (Gen der Flieg Sperrle) | LUFTFLOTTE 4 (Gen der Flieg Löhr) |

General der Luftwaffe
beim OBdH
(Gen-Maj Bogatsch)

General der Flieger
beim OBdM
(Gen-Maj Ritter)

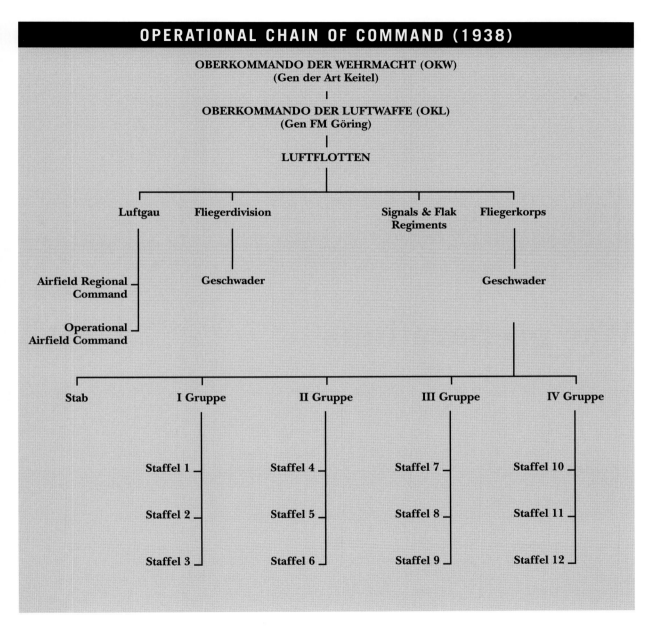

OPERATIONAL CHAIN OF COMMAND (1938)

OBERKOMMANDO DER WEHRMACHT (OKW)
(Gen der Art Keitel)

OBERKOMMANDO DER LUFTWAFFE (OKL)
(Gen FM Göring)

LUFTFLOTTEN

| Luftgau | Fliegerdivision | Signals & Flak Regiments | Fliegerkorps |

Airfield Regional Command — Geschwader — Geschwader

Operational Airfield Command

| Stab | I Gruppe | II Gruppe | III Gruppe | IV Gruppe |

Staffel 1	Staffel 4	Staffel 7	Staffel 10
Staffel 2	Staffel 5	Staffel 8	Staffel 11
Staffel 3	Staffel 6	Staffel 9	Staffel 12

Yet where Göring did succeed was in securing finance for his nascent *Luftwaffe* during times in which all the services were clamouring for funding. From 1935, when German rearmament declared itself openly in defiance of a largely impotent or careless wider world, Göring's position as one of Hitler's key figures gave him serious muscle in acquiring scant resources. Nevertheless, one point often overlooked in the *Luftwaffe*'s pre-war history is that aviation development was forever limited by the dearth of indigenous raw materials in Germany. The country had coal aplenty, but rubber, most metals and fuel were all expensive imports. While some historians have rightly pointed out that the *Luftwaffe* fatally ignored developing strategic aircraft in favour of tactical aircraft, the fact remains that a large strategic air force was not viable economically. In any case, most German authorities were focused purely on the issues of short-term survival – war across the German frontiers was a present possibility in Hitler's mind. Despite the economic restrictions, production of key types such as the Messerschmitt Bf 109 and Bf 110, the Junkers Ju 87, the Dornier Do 17 and the Heinkel He 111 accelerated at a decent rate. By May 1935, the *Luftwaffe* had some 2000 aircraft, and it would add thousands more over the next four years.

Commanding the *Luftwaffe*

In command of the *Luftwaffe* was Göring as its commander-in-chief and the Minister of Aviation. He was assisted in his command role by three key figures. From 1933, Göring's State Secretary for Aviation was Erhard Milch, a former *Lufthansa* director who now became responsible for developing German aircraft production. Hans Jeschonnek became chief of the *Luftwaffe* General Staff in February 1939, and had responsibility for operational matters. Jeschonnek was mentally invested in dive-bombing, and was a vocal figure in opposition to the development of a strategic, high-altitude bomber force. The director of the technical office was Ernst Udet, a former World War I fighter ace. He took responsibility for overseeing the *Luftwaffe*'s aerial arsenal, including pushing the design and production of new types. As a testament to the grevious burdens of *Luftwaffe* office, both Udet and Jeschonnek would go on to shoot themselves, Udet in 1941 and Jeschonnek in 1943.

War preparations

By the second half of the 1930s, Germany's newborn air force was undergoing preparations for war. It also had the opportunity to gain some combat experience even prior to the invasion of Poland in September 1939.

In the four years from 1935, when the German military air arm stepped publicly out from the shadow of the Versailles Treaty, to the moment when Germany invaded Poland, the *Luftwaffe* transformed itself into the world's leading air force. Production figures for aircraft alone indicated that Germany was a rapidly militarizing nation: in 1938 German factories wheeled out 5235 aircraft, of which 3350 were combat types; the following year, the production figures rose to 8295 aircraft, 4733 of them combat types. The *Luftwaffe* was soon ready for war.

War and doctrine

As the *Luftwaffe* grew, it faced a fundamental question – what type of air force did it want to be? We have already seen something of the disagreement between those who inclined towards a strategic force and those who pushed for a more tactical concentration. If anything, these arguments sharpened in the second half of the 1930s, but were practically, if not satisfactorily, resolved.

On the strategic side of the divide were figures such as Dr Robert Knauss and General Walther Wever. In 1933, Knauss, a future *Luftwaffe* general then with *Lufthansa*, had published a well-respected report that advocated a powerful four-engine bomber force as the core of the new air arm. He argued that the ability to strike deep into the industrial zones of potential foes such as Poland and France would give the German homeland enhanced long-term security.

Wever, the first chief of the *Luftwaffe* General Staff, added to the debate with his own 1935 report. Somewhat more balanced than Knauss's, it recognized the need for a potent support element in the *Luftwaffe* while acknowledging that strategic bombing could have a critical effect. Knauss's arguments were never widely adopted by the military, and Wever's influence was curtailed by his death in 1936.

LUFTFLOTTEN OPERATIONAL AREAS

ICELAND

NORWAY

FINLAND

DENMARK

UNITED
KINGDOM

Luftflotte 2

Luftflotte 1

POLAND

SOVIET
UNION

FRANCE

Luftflotte 3

Luftflotte 4

ITALY

YUGOSLAVIA

ROMANIA

GREECE

September 1939

Just prior to the German invasion of Poland, the *Luftwaffe* was organized into four *Luftflotten* (Air Fleets), each commanded by a *General der Flieger* (the equivalent of an RAF air marshal or a lieutenant-general in the USAAF). Each *Luftflotte* contained a complete mix of fighters, ground-attack aircraft, bombers and reconnaissance and transport aircraft, and its operations covered a designated area of territory.

The map here shows the territories covered by *Luftflotten* 1–4, prior to the great expansion in operational zones brought about by the conquest of Poland and Western Europe. *Luftflotte* 1 and *Luftflotte* 2 controlled northeast and northwest Germany respectively, while *Luftflotte* 3 and *Luftflotte* 4 took on the southwest and southeast areas of the country. *Luftflotte* 4 also had jurisdiction over Austria and Czechoslovakia.

A combination of industrial issues in the production of sufficient aero engines and problems in bomber design caused the argument for a strategic air force to steadily attenuate. Moreover, there were increasingly influential voices pushing for a tactical air force. Hans Jeschonnek was short-termist in outlook, while Ernst Udet actually felt that all bombers should be capable of dive-bombing in support of the army. Furthermore,

from 1936 the tactical thinkers combat-tested their theories. Between 1936 and 1939, the *Luftwaffe* committed several major units to combat operations on the Nationalist side in the Spanish Civil War. Although the conflict illustrated something of the power of strategic raids against cities, *Luftwaffe* officials noted that actually hitting industrial targets from high altitude and breaking civilian morale was extremely difficult,

11

THE *SCHWARM*

The *Schwarm* (swarm) was the central tactical formation of the German fighter arm, and one that gave it a signal advantage over enemy fighters (particularly British aircraft) flying in the outdated 'V' formation (known by the Germans as the *Kette*). In the *Schwarm*, four aircraft flew in two pairs, each pair consisting of a leader and a wingman. The leader of each pair focused on looking out for enemy aircraft ahead, while the wingman looked to the rear. The aircraft in the second pair, which followed behind the first pair, were staggered up in height, so that at least one aircraft would be able to spot an enemy attack out of the sun. The *Schwarm* rejected rigid formation flying in favour of a looser, more responsive approach. Properly executed, the system had the advantage that all the pilots spent more time looking for enemy aircraft, rather than concentrating on formation flying.

Second Wing

Second Lead

Lead

Wing

whereas aircraft such as the He 111, Bf 109, Do 17 and Ju 87 proved their worth in more accurate close-support roles.

The Spanish Civil War helped tip the balance in favour of a tactical air force. However, it should also be recognized that the *Luftwaffe* was primarily destined for an offensive role. Since Germany was planning to gain territory through conquest, a tactically minded air force was more appropriate, at least in the short term. Strategic bombing, meanwhile, had greater relevance for the Allies, because for a long time it was essentially the only way to strike at German territory.

Structured for war

In terms of its immediate pre-war organization, the *Luftwaffe* was divided into four *Luftflotten* (Air Fleets) in September 1939, each with its own territorial combat jurisdiction. In turn, the *Luftflotten* were divided into *Fliegerkorps* or *Fliegerdivisionen*, then into *Geschwader*

(similar to the unit designated a 'wing' in the USAAF or a 'group' in the RAF). Each *Geschwader* was subdivided into three *Gruppen*, then further into three or four *Staffeln*, the equivalent of Allied squadrons and each consisting of 9–16 aircraft.

Types of units

In terms of operational types, there were four principal categories of combat *Geschwader* at the beginning of World War II. The *Kampfgeschwader* (KG) operated medium bombers, the *Stukageschwader* (StG) flew dive-bombers (Ju 87s), the *Zerstörergeschwader* (ZG) mainly used twin-engined attack aircraft and the *Jagdgeschwader* (JG) had single-seat fighters. Each *Luftflotte* had a balanced composition of aircraft types, from fighters down to transports. With highly trained crews, and having the benefit of some combat experience, the *Luftwaffe* had plenty of confidence for the forthcoming conflict.

AIRCREW READINESS (AUGUST 1938)

In August 1938, the *Luftwaffe* had a total of 3714 authorized crews on its books. As is so often the case with military data, the figures need unpacking somewhat. Training output lagged behind operational requirements, so only 1432 crews were fully operational, whereas 1145 had a partially operational status. Nevertheless, in terms of fully operational crews, it was the all-important fighter and medium-bomber forces that were best supported.

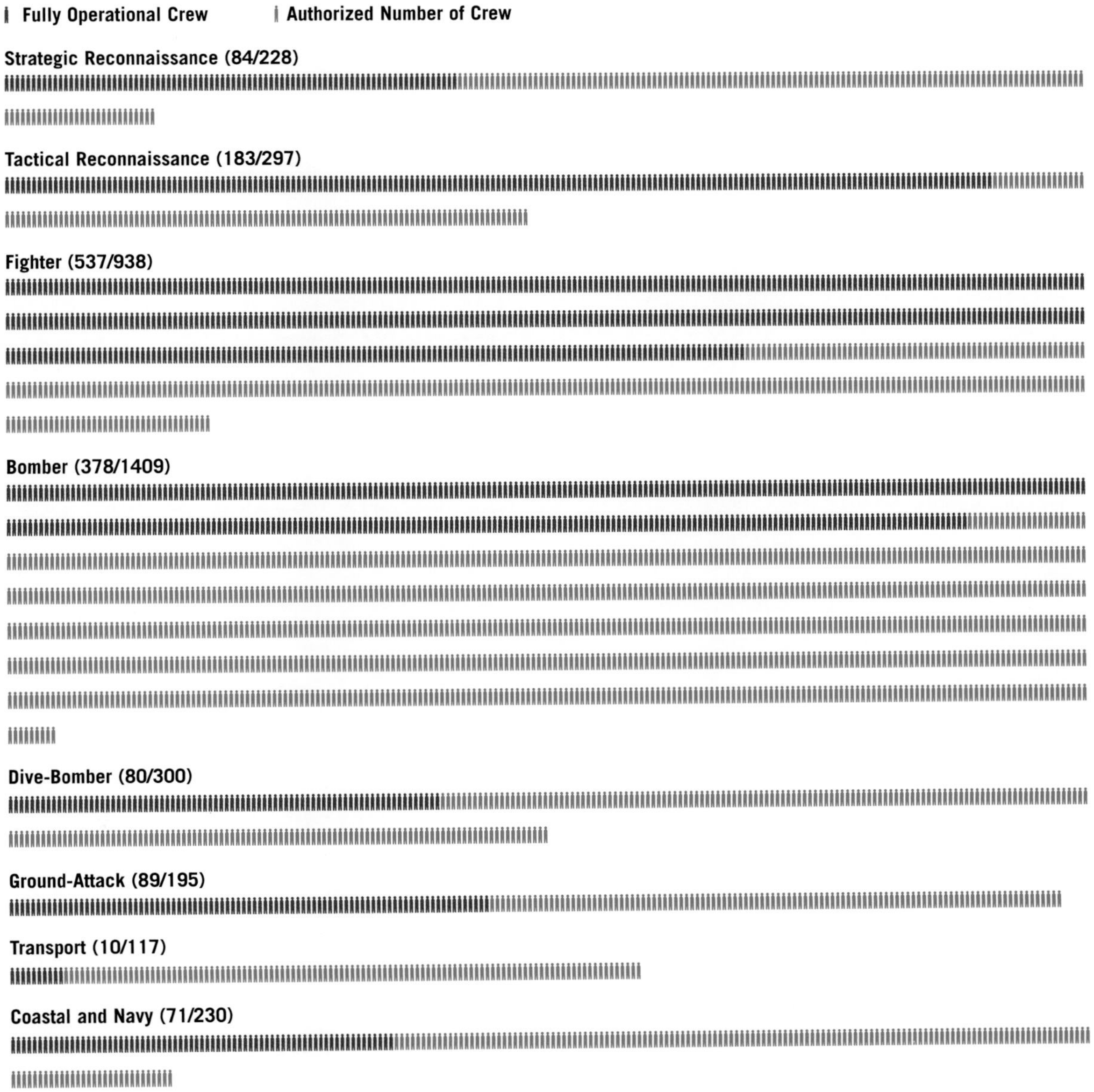

| Fully Operational Crew | Authorized Number of Crew

Strategic Reconnaissance (84/228)

Tactical Reconnaissance (183/297)

Fighter (537/938)

Bomber (378/1409)

Dive-Bomber (80/300)

Ground-Attack (89/195)

Transport (10/117)

Coastal and Navy (71/230)

GESCHWADER, GRUPPE AND STAFFEL (SEPTEMBER 1939)

The *Luftwaffe* flying organization revolved around the *Geschwader*, which at the beginning of the war had a strength of 94 aircraft. Four of these belonged to the *Stab* (HQ) unit, and the remainder were divided between three *Gruppen* of 30 aircraft each. The *Gruppen* each contained three *Staffeln*, and each *Staffel* had nine aircraft, the *Gruppe Stab* of three aircraft making up the 30. The *Staffel*, as the *Luftwaffe's* smallest operational unit, was the tip of the spear. At all times during the war, but especially as the war progressed, the difference between the theoretical and actual strength of a unit could be marked. Furthermore, as time went on, *Geschwader* often expanded to include a fourth *Gruppe*.

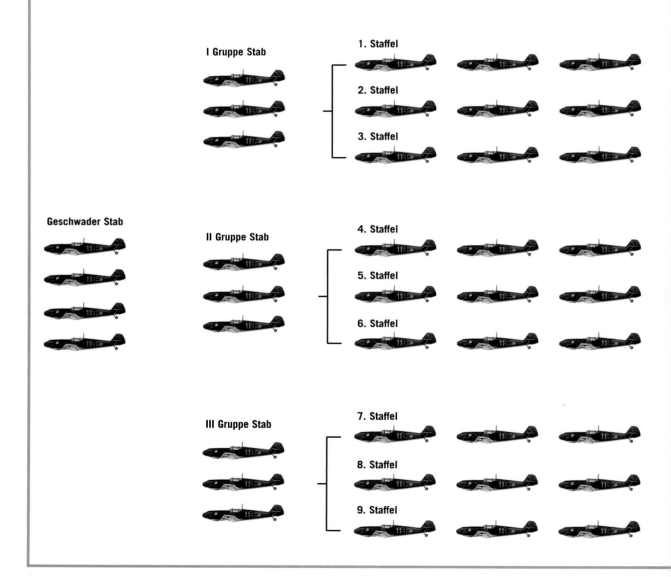

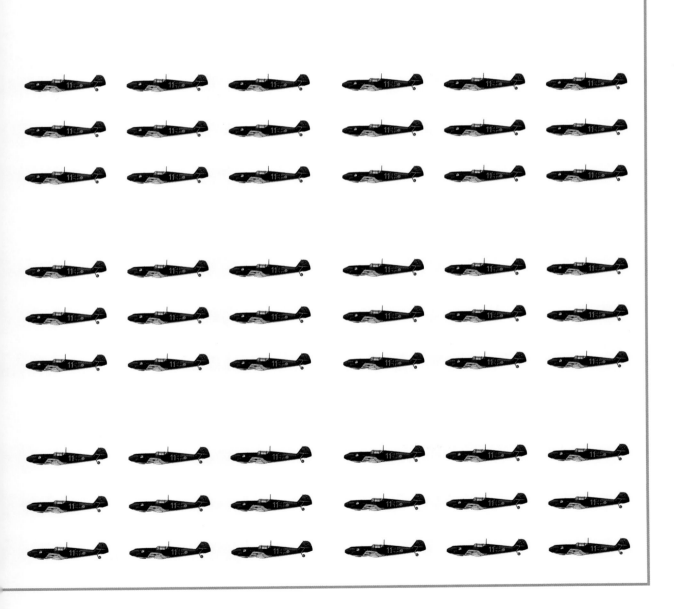

Invasion of Poland: 1939

The German invasion of Poland was a textbook example of a new form of warfare – *Blitzkrieg*. It was also an operation that convinced Hitler and other Nazi leaders about the supremacy of the *Luftwaffe* on the world stage.

Three Ju 87 Stuka dive-bombers fly in close formation. In Poland they proved themselves to be accurate ground-attack aircraft.

The rapid success achieved in the invasion of Poland took the world's breath away. Once German forces crossed the Polish border on 1 September 1939, it took the *Wehrmacht* and *Luftwaffe* only 28 days to bring the country to its knees, and add the first chunk of territory to the German *Reich*.

The land campaign ran as follows. Attacking from northern Germany and East Prussia was Army Group North, split into the Fourth Army under General von Kluge and the Third Army under General von Küchler. This force would form the northern half of a huge pincer movement, driving south towards and beyond Warsaw, along the Vistula and Bug Rivers. Attacking from Silesia in the west was Army Group South, led by von Rundstedt and consisting of the Eighth Army (Blaskowitz), the Tenth Army (Reichenau) and the Fourteenth Army (List). Army Group South would cut a broad swathe westwards, encircling Warsaw in cooperation with Army Group North, while also cutting off major Polish armies in pockets along the border lands. It was a brilliantly conceived operation reliant upon two factors: speed of advance and the technical and tactical superiority of the German forces.

Proving the *Luftwaffe*

The ground campaign worked to perfection. The armoured and infantry units swept across the borders and quickly punctured or bypassed the main Polish defences. By 8 September the army units were already hammering on the doors of Warsaw, while numerous Polish Army groups were surrounded and captured or destroyed. On the 17th, Soviet forces also joined the Germans in their enterprise, pushing across the eastern frontiers while the Polish Government fled abroad. Although the government had gone, vigorous Polish resistance nevertheless continued in Warsaw until 27 September, at which point came total national collapse. Poland was carved up for occupation between Germany and the Soviet Union.

The invasion of Poland was a textbook example of the new German style of combined-arms warfare, and it also helped to establish the *Luftwaffe*'s early war reputation as a premier tactical support arm. If anything, the success of *Luftwaffe* operations in Poland seemed to prove that those who argued for a tactical air force prior to the war

had been right all along. The Polish Air Force itself was decimated in just a few days, its obsolete collection of biplanes and other vintage aircraft being no match for the Messerschmitt Bf 109 fighter cover. Those aircraft that were not destroyed in the air were mopped up on the ground, either by fighter strafing runs or by bombing runs from Dorniers, Heinkels and Stukas. By utilizing efficient ground-to-air radio communications, the *Luftwaffe* was able to 'prepare the ground' ahead of the land forces' advance.

Future illusions

There is no denying the genuine brilliance of the *Luftwaffe* operation in 1939. The *Luftwaffe* proved a new concept in the close operational relationship between air and land power, and helped bring an entire country to its knees in less than a month.

Yet in hindsight there were reasons for caution, or at least questions unanswered. What must be borne in mind is that the Germans established air superiority against a clearly inferior air force, one that was particularly deficient in fighters (although not in the bravery of its pilots). That deficiency gave *Luftwaffe* medium bombers and dive-bombers a relatively safe environment in which to operate, with some notable exceptions. In later theatres, when the question of air superiority was either in doubt or decided in the Allies' favour, bombers became vulnerable and losses were high, especially once their fighter cover was preoccupied with survival. Even in Poland, we should not imagine that the operation was a walkover for the *Luftwaffe*. Although the Polish Air Force was technically inferior, its pilots committed every resource to the defence of their country, making the campaign a contested one, although the outcome was never in doubt.

Opening shots

Of course, the Poland campaign had far greater global implications. It put Germany on track to a Europe-wide, and ultimately worldwide, conflict; one in which the short-term thinking behind the design of the *Luftwaffe* would be found wanting. Yet for the time being, and essentially from September 1939 to the middle months of 1940, the *Luftwaffe* would reign supreme in the skies over Europe.

Ready for battle

At the opening of its campaign in Poland, the *Luftwaffe* fielded some 4161 aircraft of all types. This vast force was arrayed against the Polish Air Force, most of whose 800-odd aircraft were obsolete. The *Luftwaffe* was ready for battle, albeit against an opponent that had no means for offering decisive resistance.

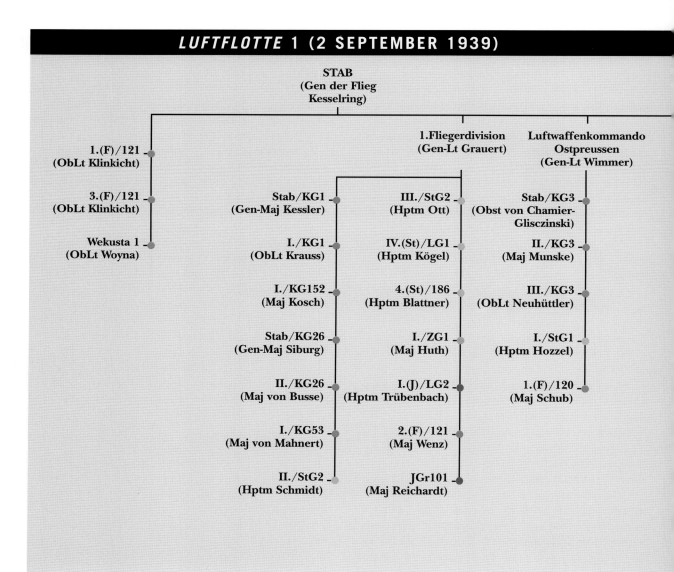

LUFTFLOTTE 1 (2 SEPTEMBER 1939)

STAB
(Gen der Flieg
Kesselring)

1.(F)/121
(ObLt Klinkicht)

3.(F)/121
(ObLt Klinkicht)

Wekusta 1
(ObLt Woyna)

1.Fliegerdivision
(Gen-Lt Grauert)

Luftwaffenkommando
Ostpreussen
(Gen-Lt Wimmer)

Stab/KG1
(Gen-Maj Kessler)

III./StG2
(Hptm Ott)

Stab/KG3
(Obst von Chamier-
Glisczinski)

I./KG1
(ObLt Krauss)

IV.(St)/LG1
(Hptm Kögel)

II./KG3
(Maj Munske)

I./KG152
(Maj Kosch)

4.(St)/186
(Hptm Blattner)

III./KG3
(ObLt Neuhüttler)

Stab/KG26
(Gen-Maj Siburg)

I./ZG1
(Maj Huth)

I./StG1
(Hptm Hozzel)

II./KG26
(Maj von Busse)

I.(J)/LG2
(Hptm Trübenbach)

1.(F)/120
(Maj Schub)

I./KG53
(Maj von Mahnert)

2.(F)/121
(Maj Wenz)

II./StG2
(Hptm Schmidt)

JGr101
(Maj Reichardt)

The *Luftwaffe* entered the Polish campaign in 1939 with its 4000-plus aircraft numerically weighted towards fighter and bomber types. Just under 1200 of its aircraft were fighters – Bf 109s – to provide air cover, while roughly the same number were medium-bomber types, He 111s and Do 17s. Some 366 aircraft were dive-bombers: both Ju 87As and Ju 87Bs formed into nine *Geschwader*. (The Ju 87B had a far more powerful

Junkers Jumo 211 engine than the Ju 87A's Jumo 210Ca.) This relatively small number of dive-bombers can be something of a surprise when considering the impact the Stukas had both on the Polish forces and in the world's media.

Facing them was the Polish Air Force, which had a paper strength of some 800 aircraft, although only just over 400 were actually operational. In terms of fighter

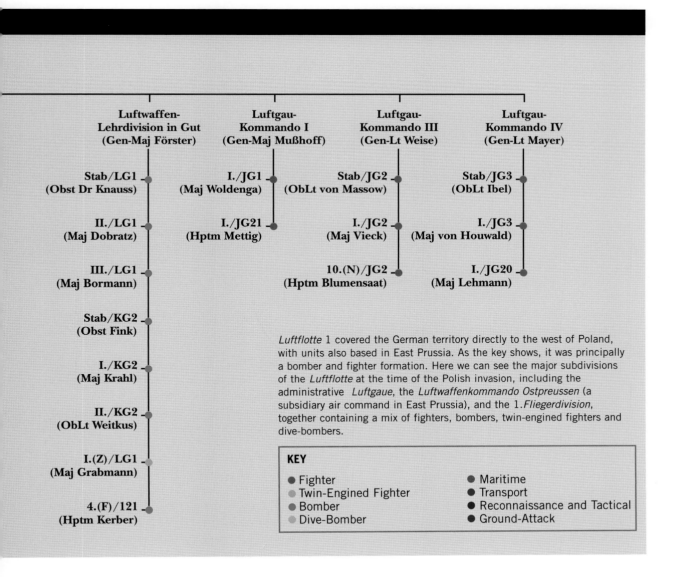

Luftwaffen-Lehrdivision in Gut
(Gen-Maj Förster)

Luftgau-Kommando I
(Gen-Maj Mußhoff)

Luftgau-Kommando III
(Gen-Lt Weise)

Luftgau-Kommando IV
(Gen-Lt Mayer)

Stab/LG1
(Obst Dr Knauss)

I./JG1
(Maj Woldenga)

Stab/JG2
(ObLt von Massow)

Stab/JG3
(ObLt Ibel)

II./LG1
(Maj Dobratz)

I./JG21
(Hptm Mettig)

I./JG2
(Maj Vieck)

I./JG3
(Maj von Houwald)

III./LG1
(Maj Bormann)

10.(N)/JG2
(Hptm Blumensaat)

I./JG20
(Maj Lehmann)

Stab/KG2
(Obst Fink)

I./KG2
(Maj Krahl)

II./KG2
(ObLt Weitkus)

I.(Z)/LG1
(Maj Grabmann)

4.(F)/121
(Hptm Kerber)

Luftflotte 1 covered the German territory directly to the west of Poland, with units also based in East Prussia. As the key shows, it was principally a bomber and fighter formation. Here we can see the major subdivisions of the *Luftflotte* at the time of the Polish invasion, including the administrative *Luftgaue*, the *Luftwaffenkommando Ostpreussen* (a subsidiary air command in East Prussia), and the 1.*Fliegerdivision*, together containing a mix of fighters, bombers, twin-engined fighters and dive-bombers.

KEY

● Fighter
● Twin-Engined Fighter
● Bomber
● Dive-Bomber
● Maritime
● Transport
● Reconnaissance and Tactical
● Ground-Attack

UNIT STRENGTH – *LUFTFLOTTE* 1 (SEPTEMBER 1939)				
Luftwaffe Unit	Base	Type	Str	Op
LUFTFLOTTE 1				
1.(F)/121	Stargard-Klützow	Do 17P/F	12	10
3.(F)/121	Stargard-Klützow	Do 17P/F	12	7
Wekusta 1	Stargard-Klützow	He 111J	3	3
1.FLIEGERDIVISION				
Stab/KG1	Kolberg	He 111H	9	9
I./KG1	Kolberg	He 111H	38	34
I./KG152	Pinnow-Plathe	He 111H	37	34
Stab/KG26	Gabbert	He 111H	6	5
II./KG26	Gabbert	He 111H	35	31
I./KG53	Schönfeld-Crössinsee	He 111H	31	31
II./StG2	Stolp-Reitz	Do 17P	3	3
		Ju 87B	35	34
III./StG2	Stolp-Reitz	Do 17P	3	3
		Ju 87B	36	34
IV.(St)/LG1	Stolp-Reitz	Do 17P	3	3
		Ju 87B	39	37
4.(St)/186	Stolp-West	Ju 87B	12	12
I./ZG1	Mühlen I	Bf 110C	34	27
I.(J)/LG2	Malzkow/Lottin	Bf 109E	42	33
2.(F)/121	Schönfeld-Crössinsee	Do 17P/F	11	10
JGr101	Lichtenau	Bf 109E	48	48
LUFTWAFFENKOMMANDO OSTPREUSSEN				
Stab/KG3	Elbing	Do 17Z	9	7
II./KG3	Heiligenbeil	Do 17Z	38	36
III./KG3	Heiligenbeil	Do 17Z	39	30
I./StG1	Elbing	Do 17P	3	2
		Ju 87B	38	38
1.(F)/120	Neuhausen	Do 17P	12	11

UNIT STRENGTH – *LUFTFLOTTE* 1 (SEPTEMBER 1939)				
Luftwaffe Unit	Base	Type	Str	Op
LUFTWAFFEN-LEHRDIVISION				
Stab/LG1	Neuhausen	He 111H	9	8
II./LG1	Powunden	He 111H	39	34
III./LG1	Prowehren	He 111H	39	32
Stab/KG2	Jesau	Do 17Z	9	9
I./KG2	Gerdauen	Do 17M	36	33
II./KG2	Schippenbeil	Do 17Z	39	37
I.(Z)/LG1	Jesau	Bf 110C	33	32
4.(F)/121	Jesau	Do 17P/F	12	11
LUFTGAU-KOMMANDO I				
I./JG1	Gutenfeld	Bf 109E	46	46
I./JG21	Gutenfeld	Bf 109D	39	37
LUFTGAU-KOMMANDO III				
Stab/JG2	Döberitz	Bf 109E	3	3
I./JG2	Döberitz	Bf 109E	41	40
10.(N)/JG2	Straussberg	Bf 109D	9	9
LUFTGAU-KOMMANDO IV				
Stab/JG3	Zerbst	Bf 109E	3	3
I./JG3	Brandis	Bf 109E	44	38
I./JG20	Sprottau	Bf 109E	37	36

Luftflotten.) In addition, the *Lehrdivision* – a kind of tactical development unit operating all the main types of combat aircraft – brought to the table an assortment of bomber and ground-attack types.

Ground work

Although the fighters would provide a critical ingredient in the air battle over Poland, the most significant element of the *Luftwaffe* campaign was the ground-attack forces. In total, the Germans brought together some 20 *Kampfgeschwader* of He 111s and Do 17s, plus a Stuka contingent arranged into five *Stukageschwader*. Messerschmitt Bf 109s and Bf 110s would also operate in a ground-attack role. Both aircraft had 20mm (0.78in) cannon as a component of their armament, and these were ideal for strafing soft-skinned and lightly armoured vehicles, plus exposed troop concentrations. There were particularly high expectations of the Stuka force. While

protection, the Poles were mostly flying the PZL P.11 and P.7A, neither a match for the Bf 109.

In terms of the organizational structure, the campaign against Poland was mainly in the hands of *Luftflotten* 1 and 4, and some units from the westward-looking *Luftlotten* 2 and 3 were also brought over for the campaign. (See opposite page for a map of the various

LUFTFLOTTEN 1 & 4 – **OPERATIONAL AREAS**

Luftflotte 2

EAST PRUSSIA

Luftflotte 1

POLAND

SOVIET UNION

Luftflotte 3

Luftflotte 4

HUNGARY

ROMANIA

ITALY

YUGOSLAVIA

BULGARIA

2 September 1939

At the beginning of World War II, the *Luftwaffe* was divided into four *Luftflotten*, or Air Fleets, each with a specific area of responsibility over the *Reich* and neighbouring territories. The operation against Poland in September 1939 was chiefly the domain of *Luftflotten* 1 and 4, under Generals Kesselring and Löhr respectively. The former formation (brown) operated out of northeastern Germany and over East Prussia, and the latter (orange) took responsibility for the southeast of the country.

Luftflotte 2 (green) and *Luftflotte* 3 (purple) mirrored the role of *Luftflotten* 1 and 4 over the western half of Germany. This division of air units would change dramatically over the coming years, expanding as Germany acquired more territory, then finally shrinking as the *Reich* was compressed by Allied gains in the final years of the war.

the effects of medium-bomber strikes against urban centres could not be predicted, the Stukas could deliver a decent bombload within its blast radius on an intended target. The Ju 87B could carry one 500kg (1102lb) bomb plus four 50kg (110lb) bombs; hence rolling waves of such aircraft could destroy an area of several acres in the path of advancing German armour and infantry. This capability was remarkable when

considering that the two-engined Do 17 had a bombload capacity of only 1000kg (2205lb). The Bf 109E fighter was itself capable of carrying four 50kg (110lb) bombs or one 250kg (551lb) weapon.

The time was now approaching for the *Luftwafffe* to prove itself in battle. With the force of two *Luftflotten* facing east on the morning of 1 September 1939, the *Luftwaffe* loosed the first shots of World War II.

I./KG1 (SEPTEMBER 1939)

In September 1939, I./KG1 of 1.*Fliegerdivision*, *Luftflotte* 1, brought to the order of battle a total of 38 operational Heinkel He 111s. If all these aircraft flew together on a single mission, they were capable of delivering 76,000kg (167,428lb) of bombs against an area target. Formed on 1 May 1939, KG1 would see action from the Polish campaign through to late 1944, serving purely in Eastern European theatres. Until September 1941, it flew He 111s, then took on Ju 88As before, finally, operating He 177s between June and August 1944.

Operational aircraft – 34 x He 111s

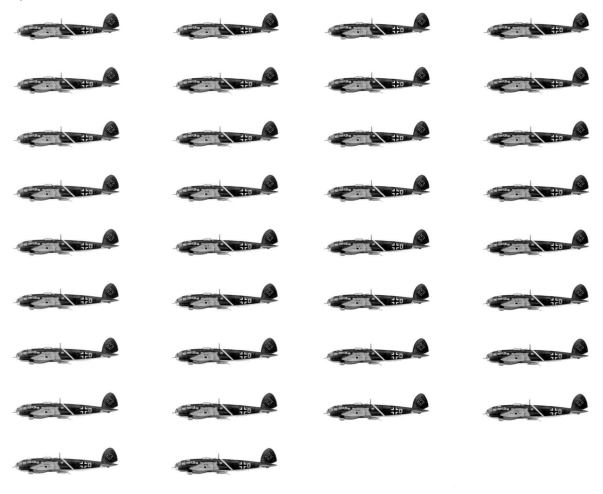

Tactical goals

While German fighters repelled the intrusions of Polish fighters, the ground-attack elements operated in conjunction with armoured units to hit the enemy ground forces from two dimensions.

Once the German invasion of Poland was launched on 1 September 1939, the *Luftwaffe* had two principal roles within the overall combined-arms *Blitzkrieg* doctrine. The first was to gain and maintain complete air superiority over the battlefield. Such a situation was essential to facilitate the second role: providing ground-support attacks in front of the advancing German armoured and infantry columns.

In this latter capacity, the *Luftwaffe* was to act essentially as a replacement for land artillery, selecting targets over the battlefield, reporting their positions to ground units using radio transmissions, then making strafing, level-bombing or dive-bombing attacks against the objectives to destroy or prepare them for the land forces' advance. Major objectives for the ground-attack missions included radio communications centres and infrastructure, transport hubs, airfields, concentrations of enemy troops or vehicles, supply convoys, supply dumps, and any other targets of opportunity that presented themselves.

Superior tactics

Blitzkrieg depended upon sound communications to maintain air strikes at the tip of rapid lines of advance. Air liaison detachments worked on the ground with armoured units, typically operating from lightly armoured vehicles such as the SdKfz 251 halftrack converted as a radio communications vehicle, and relaying messages between land and air. The system was not perfect – radio communications were frequently severed in the fog of war – and in such situations the *Luftwaffe* would resort to independent hunting. In addition, the heavy bomber units could strike at Poland's major cities, cutting into civilian morale and the country's industrial infrastructure.

UNIT STRENGTH – *LUFTFLOTTE* 2 (SEPTEMBER 1939)				
Luftwaffe Unit	Base	Type	Str	Op
LUFTFLOTTE 2				
1.(F)/122	Goslar	Do 17P	12	10
2.(F)/122	Münster	He 111H	11	10
Wekusta 26	Braunschweig	Do 17P	6	6
3.FLIEGERDIVISION				
Stab/KG54	Fritzlar	He 111P	6	6
I./KG54	Fritzlar	He 111P	33	30
II./KG28	Gütersloh	He 111P	35	34
1./KG25	Jever	Ju 88A	12	12
4.FLIEGERDIVISION				
Stab/KG55	Wesendorf	He 111P	6	6
I./KG55	Dedelstorf	He 111P	33	25
II./KG55	Wesendorf	He 111P	29	25
I./KG26	Lübeck-Blankensee	He 111H	36	32
Stab/KG27	Hannover-Langenhagen	He 111P	6	5
I./KG27	Hannover-Langenhagen	He 111P	35	31
II./KG27	Wunstorf	He 111P	36	32
III./KG27	Delmenhorst	He 111P	36	33
LUFTGAU-KOMMANDO XI				
II./JG77	Nordholz	Bf 109E	33	33
II.(J)/186	Kiel-Holtenau	Bf 109B/E	23	23
Stab/ZG26	Varel	Bf 109D	3	1
I./ZG26	Varel	Bf 109D	43	39
JGr126	Neumünster	Bf 109D	46	41
LUFTGAU-KOMMANDO VI				
Stab/JG26	Odendorf	Bf 109E	3	2
I./JG26	Odendorf	Bf 109E	44	43
II./JG26	Bönninghardt	Bf 109E	38	38
11.(N)/LG2	Köln-Ostheim	Bf 109D	9	9
I./JG52	Bonn-Hangelar	Bf 109E	48	38
II./ZG26	Werl	Bf 109D	48	45

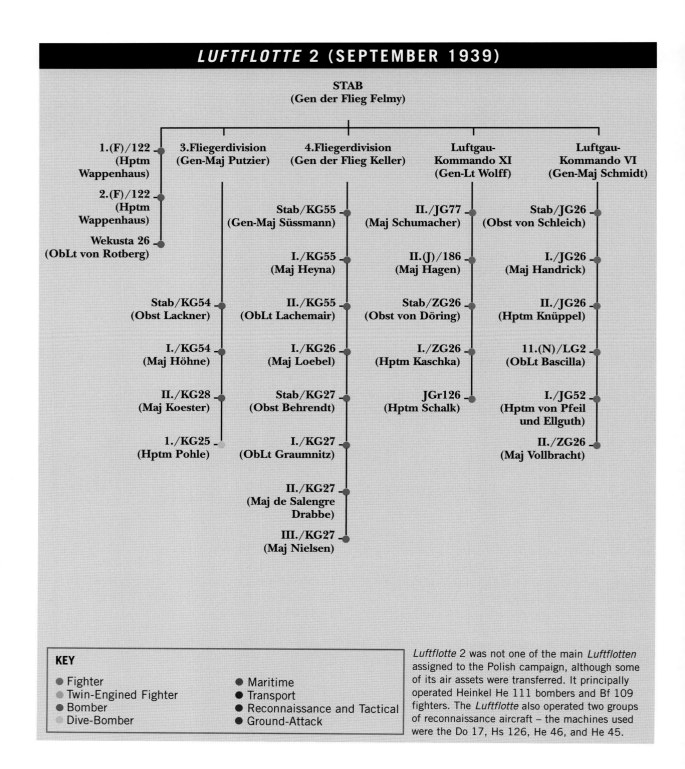

LUFTFLOTTE 2 (SEPTEMBER 1939)

STAB
(Gen der Flieg Felmy)

1.(F)/122
(Hptm
Wappenhaus)

2.(F)/122
(Hptm
Wappenhaus)

Wekusta 26
(ObLt von Rotberg)

3.Fliegerdivision
(Gen-Maj Putzier)

4.Fliegerdivision
(Gen der Flieg Keller)

Luftgau-
Kommando XI
(Gen-Lt Wolff)

Luftgau-
Kommando VI
(Gen-Maj Schmidt)

Stab/KG55
(Gen-Maj Süssmann)

II./JG77
(Maj Schumacher)

Stab/JG26
(Obst von Schleich)

I./KG55
(Maj Heyna)

II.(J)/186
(Maj Hagen)

I./JG26
(Maj Handrick)

Stab/KG54
(Obst Lackner)

II./KG55
(ObLt Lachemair)

Stab/ZG26
(Obst von Döring)

II./JG26
(Hptm Knüppel)

I./KG54
(Maj Höhne)

I./KG26
(Maj Loebel)

I./ZG26
(Hptm Kaschka)

11.(N)/LG2
(ObLt Bascilla)

II./KG28
(Maj Koester)

Stab/KG27
(Obst Behrendt)

JGr126
(Hptm Schalk)

I./JG52
(Hptm von Pfeil
und Ellguth)

1./KG25
(Hptm Pohle)

I./KG27
(ObLt Graumnitz)

II./ZG26
(Maj Vollbracht)

II./KG27
(Maj de Salengre
Drabbe)

III./KG27
(Maj Nielsen)

KEY

- Fighter
- Twin-Engined Fighter
- Bomber
- Dive-Bomber
- Maritime
- Transport
- Reconnaissance and Tactical
- Ground-Attack

Luftflotte 2 was not one of the main *Luftflotten* assigned to the Polish campaign, although some of its air assets were transferred. It principally operated Heinkel He 111 bombers and Bf 109 fighters. The *Luftflotte* also operated two groups of reconnaissance aircraft – the machines used were the Do 17, Hs 126, He 46, and He 45.

First *Blitzkrieg*

An immediate objective of the *Luftwaffe* was to crush the Polish Air Force, and so gain total air superiority. This it achieved, although the pluck of the Polish aviators ensured that it wasn't the walkover expected.

German land forces rolled across the Polish frontier at 04:45 on the morning of 1 September 1939. The *Luftwaffe* was immediately in action alongside them. In total, some 219 Ju 87s, 339 Bf 109s, 370 He 111s, 527 Do 17s, 82 Bf 110s and over 400 reconnaissance and transport aircraft were involved in the immediate air campaign. A primary target was the Polish Air Force's airbases, and it was hoped that Poland's air defence could be neutered even while on the ground.

The Polish Air Force at the time of the invasion was structured around two major brigades, the Pursuit Brigade (a fighter formation) and the Bomber Brigade; in addition there was a mix of fighter and reconnaissance aircraft spread between seven army commands. The aircraft wielded by the Poles were not all obsolete. They had some decent bombers in the PZL P.37 Los and the PZL P.23 Karas, but these were unfortunately few in number (36 and 50 respectively). The critical fighter force, however, was outdated (mainly PZL P.11s), and was outclassed by the Bf 109.

Historical accounts of the invasion of Poland often state that the Polish Air Force was practically destroyed on the ground by German surprise attacks. Certainly, a large number of aircraft were destroyed on the airbases, but the Poles managed to get enough aircraft off the ground to create some serious problems for the *Luftwaffe*. The Polish defence forces actually had in place an excellent observation post system across the country, which acted as a type of early-warning facility for airbases and targets further inland. When any observation post spotted a *Luftwaffe* aircraft, it relayed the position and heading information via radio or telephone back to the Pursuit Brigade headquarters, who then allocated air assets to make the intercept.

A major target for the *Luftwaffe* in Poland was, naturally, the capital Warsaw. The first bomber strikes against Warsaw went in at 06:00. These first raids were just a taste of what Warsaw had to come, but the strikes by He 111s, flying with Bf 110 escort, met with tougher than expected resistance. Warned by their observation posts, the Pursuit Brigade managed to put up over 50 fighters. They fell upon the bombers with determination. KG27 came out of the engagement particularly badly, losing six aircraft.

Retaliation

The Germans had learnt a salutary lesson – that you can never underestimate an enemy – and for the second mission, flown later that afternoon, the bombers were accompanied by both Bf 110s and Bf 109s. The Polish fighters were relatively solid aircraft, with decent manoeuvrability, but they had nothing approaching the power of the Bf 109. The PZL P.11, for example, had a top speed of around 420km/h (270mph), while a Bf 109E had a top speed of 570km/h (354mph) and bags more power in the climb and turn. Even the twin-engined Bf 110C had a superior performance, delivering a top speed of 560km/h (349mph) and packing a heavy armament of two 20mm (0.78in) cannon and six 7.92mm (0.31in) machine guns (two set in a rearward-facing turret). The early PZL P.7 aircraft had even less power and speed to play with, and had only two machine guns. The difference in performance, and the beefed-up German escort numbers, showed in the subsequent engagement. Four P.7s and three P.11s were shot down, although the Germans also lost two Bf 109s, making a total of three Bf 109 losses in Poland by the end of the first day.

Ground support

As the *Luftwaffe* was struggling over Warsaw, its ground-attack aircraft were delivering a harrowing offensive against Polish forces on the ground. The *Wehrmacht* soon came to appreciate the value of the ground strikes,

UNIT STRENGTH – *LUFTFLOTTE* 4 (SEPTEMBER 1939)				
Luftwaffe Unit	**Base**	**Type**	**Str**	**Op**
LUFTFLOTTE 4				
3.(F)/123	Schweidnitz	Do 17P	12	12
Wekusta 76	Schweidnitz	He 111J	3	3
2.FLIEGERDIVISION				
Stab/KG4	Oels	He 111P	6	6
I./KG4	Langenau	He 111P	27	27
II./KG4	Oels	He 111P	30	30
III./KG4	Langenau	He 111P	33	32
Stab/KG76	Breslau-Schöngarten	Do 17Z	9	9
I./KG76	Breslau-Schöngarten	Do 17Z	36	36
III./KG76	Rosenborn	Do 17Z	39	39
Stab/KG77	Grottkau	Do 17E/F	9	9
I./KG77	Brieg	Do 17E	37	37
II./KG77	Grottkau	Do 17E	39	39
III./KG77	Brieg	Do 17E	38	34
I./StG2	Nieder-Ellguth	Do 17P	3	3
		Ju 87B	38	37
I./ZG76	Ohlau	Bf 110C	35	31
3.(F)/122	Woisselsdorf	Do 17P	12	10
FLIEGERFÜHRER ZBV				
Stab/StG77	Neudorf	Ju 87B	3	3
I./StG77	Ottmuth	Do 17P	3	3
		Ju 87B	39	34
II./StG77	Neudorf	Do 17P	3	3
		Ju 87B	36	38
I./StG76	Nieder-Ellguth	Do 17P	3	3
		Ju 87B	36	28
JGr102	Groß-Stein	Bf 109D	45	45
Stab(J)/LG2	Nieder-Ellguth	Bf 109E	3	2
II.(S)/LG2	Altsiedel	Hs 123	39	39
1.(F)/124	Schloßwalden	Do 17P	11	10
LUFTGAU-KOMMANDO VIII				
I./JG76	Ottmütz	Bf 109E	51	45
I./JG77	Juliusburg-Nord	Bf 109E	48	43

especially when trying to break stubborn pockets of Polish resistance without adequate artillery support. For example, on 10 September the German Tenth Army faced one of its most serious challenges of the entire campaign, when it was counterattacked by a powerful Polish Army group near the Bzura River. The Poles managed to secure several bridgeheads on the banks of the river and even managed to sever the Tenth Army's main supply line.

Air bombardment

With a potential disaster looming for the Germans, it rested on the shoulders of the *Luftwaffe* to force a rescue. The *Luftwaffe* unleashed a rolling air bombardment of the Polish bridgeheads and troop concentrations. Here the Ju 87 came into its own. While the medium bombers pounded area targets, the Ju 87s could attack localized targets with some precision. Although the accuracy of dive-bombing can be exaggerated, there is no doubt that a Ju 87 could put a bomb fairly neatly on, say, a pontoon bridge structure or amidst a small park of vehicles. The German pilots improved their accuracy even further by releasing their bombs below the 914m (3000ft) altitude recommended as the minimum safe distance from the blast of their own bombs.

While the Stukas dropped their bombs, Bf 110s made horrifying strafing runs through the troops, while the Dorniers and Heinkels pounded large areas with high explosive. The effect on the Polish troops was catastrophic. They were unable to achieve any sort of manoeuvre freedom, casualties were horrendous and the horses used to move supplies and artillery went insane with the bomb blasts. In this way the Polish counterattack was crushed and reversed, and the Tenth Army was able to link up with the neighbouring Eighth Army and resume its advance.

From this point on, the *Luftwaffe* hammered at every Polish troop concentration it could, contributing to the surrender of hundreds of thousands of troops. Attack aircraft of *Luftflotte* 4 even made history by forcing the surrender of an entire army division purely through air power. The unfortunate unit was the Polish 7th Division, but other large Polish formations were soon to surrender following the German aerial pounding.

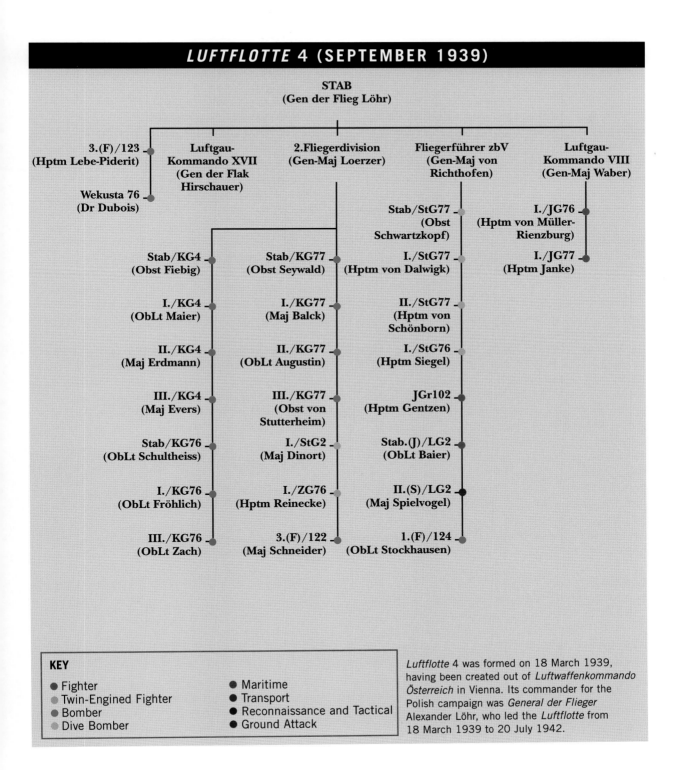

LUFTFLOTTE 4 (SEPTEMBER 1939)

STAB
(Gen der Flieg Löhr)

3.(F)/123
(Hptm Lebe-Piderit)

Wekusta 76
(Dr Dubois)

Luftgau-
Kommando XVII
(Gen der Flak
Hirschauer)

2.Fliegerdivision
(Gen-Maj Loerzer)

Fliegerführer zbV
(Gen-Maj von
Richthofen)

Luftgau-
Kommando VIII
(Gen-Maj Waber)

Stab/StG77
(Obst
Schwartzkopf)

I./JG76
(Hptm von Müller-
Rienzburg)

Stab/KG4
(Obst Fiebig)

Stab/KG77
(Obst Seywald)

I./StG77
(Hptm von Dalwigk)

I./JG77
(Hptm Janke)

I./KG4
(ObLt Maier)

I./KG77
(Maj Balck)

II./StG77
(Hptm von
Schönborn)

II./KG4
(Maj Erdmann)

II./KG77
(ObLt Augustin)

I./StG76
(Hptm Siegel)

III./KG4
(Maj Evers)

III./KG77
(Obst von
Stutterheim)

JGr102
(Hptm Gentzen)

Stab/KG76
(ObLt Schultheiss)

I./StG2
(Maj Dinort)

Stab.(J)/LG2
(ObLt Baier)

I./KG76
(ObLt Fröhlich)

I./ZG76
(Hptm Reinecke)

II.(S)/LG2
(Maj Spielvogel)

III./KG76
(ObLt Zach)

3.(F)/122
(Maj Schneider)

1.(F)/124
(ObLt Stockhausen)

KEY

● Fighter
● Twin-Engined Fighter
● Bomber
● Dive Bomber

● Maritime
● Transport
● Reconnaissance and Tactical
● Ground Attack

Luftflotte 4 was formed on 18 March 1939, having been created out of *Luftwaffenkommando Österreich* in Vienna. Its commander for the Polish campaign was *General der Flieger* Alexander Löhr, who led the *Luftflotte* from 18 March 1939 to 20 July 1942.

This is not to say, however, that the German ground-attack units had it all their own way. Ground-attack aircraft are most vulnerable when they climb out of their attack pattern, as during this time they lose much of their speed in the climb, as well as presenting a large top-profile target to an attacking aircraft. Polish Army and Pursuit Brigade fighters took advantage of this as much as possible, as long as they could evade the German fighter cover. In one action, for example, the Germans lost seven unescorted aircraft to the 142 *Eskadra*, the Poles suffering no losses during the attack.

Handling the bombers

From 1–3 September, the principal opponents of the Germans in the air were the Polish fighter and ground-attack units. On the 3rd, however, the Polish Bomber Brigade's P.23s and P.37s began operations against the German lines of advance. The lumbering Polish bombers were prime targets for the German fighters, but at first several raids did get through to their targets, imposing delays and casualties on several key Panzer units. The German commanders could not accept such delays, so portions of the *Luftwaffe* fighter arm were actually diverted to providing top-cover sorties over the advancing troop formations. This was exhausting but essential work, and it paid off – by 17 September, only 19 per cent of the Polish Bomber Brigade's aircraft were still flying, and these surviving machines escaped out to Romania. The Polish Army's aviation units also flew P.23s in similar ground-attack roles (although they were originally intended for reconnaissance). By 17 September, just 25 per cent of these aircraft were left, and they too fled to Romania.

Dominance

By mid-September, it was obvious to both the Germans and the Poles that the *Luftwaffe* had achieved air superiority. On the ground also, the campaign was gathering pace and inevitability. On 19 September, with the Soviets also advancing from the east on two fronts, 100,000 Polish soldiers in the Bzura pocket were overwhelmed and became prisoners of the Germans. Three days later, the Soviets took Lvov. Yet still Warsaw held out, and now the *Luftwaffe* was beginning to employ a very different form of warfare.

Warsaw had come in for attention from the *Luftwaffe* already in the campaign, but on 25 September the attacks grew to a new crescendo. On that day, 400 *Luftwaffe* bombers dumped thousands of tonnes of bombs on the city. The *Luftwaffe* claimed that it was mainly targeting military locations, but in actuality it was little more than a terror raid. The attack could have been worse, for by this time Göring had already diverted large numbers of medium bombers back to the western borders of Germany, fearing an attack from Britain or France. In their place, Ju 52s, by this time mostly employed in the transport role, were filled with huge numbers of incendiary bombs, these being literally pushed out of the cargo bay by the aircrew. The measure was crude, but it worked. The smoke from the burning city rose 5500m (18,000ft) over Warsaw, and a general Polish surrender came on 28 September.

Evaluation

While the invasion of Poland had been an undoubted success for the *Luftwaffe*, it was not without cost. The *Luftwaffe* lost some 230 aircraft to Polish aviators and anti-aircraft fire, with over 500 aircrew either dead, missing or taken (for a short time) prisoner.

Invasion of Poland, 1–28 September 1939

1 September 1939 – German forces invaded Poland across the length of its eastern and southeastern border. The *Luftwaffe* commenced its attacks at 06:00, striking at airbases and Polish Army targets throughout the country. By 8 September, German units had reached as far as the outskirts of Warsaw, and began bombarding the city using artillery and air power.

On 17 September, the Polish situation was made even more critical when Soviet forces invaded Poland from the east. Polish resistance in the Bzura pocket collapsed on 19 September, and 100,000 men were taken prisoner. Most of the surviving Polish Air Force aircraft had, by this time, fled to Romania, leaving the *Luftwaffe* in total control of the skies. On 25 September, the *Luftwaffe* proved the point by delivering a massive bombing raid on Warsaw, this helping prompt the final Polish surrender on 28 September.

INVASION OF POLAND

Invasion of Poland
1–28 September 1939

- German advance
- Red Army advance
- Polish retreat
- German field work
- Polish defensive lines
- Polish positions
- German–Soviet demarcation line

LITHUANIA

Baltic Sea

Lablau
Kaunas
Wilno

XXXXX Army Group North
BOCK

Königsberg
Insterburg
Kalvarya
Suwalk

XXXXX Belorussian Front

East Prussia

XXXX 3 KUECHLER

Narew (elts)
Grodno

Lauemburg
Gdynia
Danzig
Elbing

Stulp

XXX I

XXXX 4 KLUGE

XXX XIX GUDERIAN

XXXX Pozmorze

XXX XXI

Allenstein

XXX

Wodrig

Baranowicze

Stettin

XXX II

XXX III

Schneidemuhl
Bydgoszcz

XXXX Modlin

Bialystok

XXXX Modlin and Narew (elts)

XXX XIX GUDERIAN

POLAND

Inowroclaw
Wloclawek
Vistula
Plack

Rozan

Landsberg

Poznan

XXXX Pozmorze

Warsaw

Siedlce

Bug

Brest-Litovsk

U S S R

Guben

Leszno
Glogau
Kalisz

XXXX Poznan

Lodz

Rock

Lodz

G E R M A N Y

XXX x

Breslau

XXX XIII

XXXX 8 BLASKOWITZ

XXX XVI

XXXX XI Oppeln

Czestochwa

Tomaszon

Radom

Kielce

Lublin

XXXX Cracov

XXXXX Ukrainian Front

XXX XIV HOEPPNER IV

Katowice

Oder

XXXX Carpathian

XXXX 10 REICHENAU

XXX XV

XXXX Cracow Vistula

Cracow

Tarnow

Rzeszow

XXX VII

XXX VIII

Nowy Targ

Nowy Sacz

XXXX Carpathian

Przemysl

Sambor

Dniester

Prague

Kutna Mora

Protectorate of Bohemia-Moravia

Olamouc

Stanislowow

Brno

XXXXX Army Group South RUNDSTEDT

Znojmo

XXX XVII

Tregin

S l o v a k i a

Presov

Uzingorod

XXX XXII

XXX XVIII

R u t h e n i a

A U S T R I A

Trnava

XXXX 14 LIST

Zvolen

Vienna
Bratislavo

Miiskolc

1800
900
450
180
90
0 m

H U N G A R Y

Danube

Budapest

Tissa

Debrecen

0   100 km

0   100 miles

Denmark and Norway: 1940

In the invasion of Denmark and Norway, the *Luftwaffe* not only confirmed its talent for air combat, it also demonstrated its skill with an emerging form of warfare – the airborne assault using paratroopers and airlanding tactics.

The view from the nose-cone of a Heinkel He 111 as its flies over the icy landscape of Norway.

Following its successful struggle over Poland, the *Luftwaffe* entered a relatively long period of rest. Dubbed the 'phoney war', the period between October 1939 and April 1940 saw relatively little military action on the part of Germany, although the Soviet invasion of Finland in November 1939 ensured that large amounts of blood was spilt in the interim. Yet by the end of March 1940, Hitler had his sights set on two Scandinavian targets – Denmark and Norway.

German control of the northern territories was critical in Hitler's mind to protect essential imports of metal ores through Narvik; imports at risk from the potential depredations of the British Royal Navy. Furthermore, control of the northern territories would bring new opportunities for basing U-boat and *Luftwaffe* units. Regarding the latter, if the *Luftwaffe* had airbases in Denmark and Norway, they would be able to strike across the North Sea at northern British targets, and would have a more effective operational radius against British shipping.

Ground and air

The *Luftwaffe*'s operation against Denmark and Norway would be radically different from its part in the invasion of Poland. Air superiority was even less of a question over Scandinavia than it had been over Poland, but the *Luftwaffe* had another major focus. For the first time in military history, airborne assault tactics were to gain operational testing.

It should always be remembered that the *Luftwaffe* was much more than just its aviation. Thousands of personnel also served in land-based roles, including flak crews and also as paratroopers – the *Fallschirmjäger*. Developed during the interwar years, the *Luftwaffe*'s airborne forces would act as some of the Third Reich's most elite ground troops.

Operation *Weserübung*

The use of paratroopers as vertically deployed combat troops was pioneered by the Soviets and Italians during the 1920s and 1930s. Göring himself witnessed some Soviet trials, and in 1935 established his first airborne formations.

From the start, Göring was keen to retain the *Fallschirmjäger* under *Luftwaffe* jurisdiction, despite the competing interests of the *Heer* (Army), *Sturmabteiling* (SA) and *Schutzstaffel* (SS). By October 1935, he had established the foundations of an airborne regiment within the air force, and by May 1936 the Hermann Göring parachute battalion was established. On 1 April 1938, the battalion became I.*Bataillon, Fallschirmjäger-Regiment* 1 (I./FJR 1), and in early 1939 the regiment acquired a second battalion (brought in from the army), a third battalion being formed just before the onset of war. The *Heer* (Army) had also been training up airborne assault forces, although they focused primarily on airlanding – the direct landing of troops by transport aircraft – rather than on paratroopers. The division chosen for this training was 22.*Infanterie-Division*. All the paratrooper forces came, from 1 July 1938, under the

AIRCRAFT STRENGTH – OPERATION *WESERÜBUNG*		
Luftwaffe Unit	**Type**	**Str**
X.FLIEGERKORPS		
Fighters	Bf 109E	38
Bombers	He 111H	94
	He 111P	95
	Ju 88A	125
	Ju 88C-2	6
	Bf 110C	64
	He 115B/C	35
Stuka	Ju 87R	39
Maritime	Fw 200B/C	8
	Ju 52/See	13
Transport	Ju 52	536
	Ju 90	11
	Ju G-38	1

overall control of 7.*Fliegerdivision* (7th Airborne Division), commanded by a *Luftwaffe* officer, *Generalleutnant* Kurt Student. Although the division was essentially a land forces unit, it rested under *Luftwaffe* authority. It would be these troops, and the aviators who supported them, who would make such a critical contribution to the forthcoming campaign in Denmark and Norway.

Air resources

The German air assets utilized for the invasion of Denmark and Norway were substantial. All aircraft devoted to the operation were under the umbrella of

X.*Fliegergkorps*, commanded by *Generalleutnant* Hans Geisler. This force contained nearly 300 bombers, 100 fighters and 39 dive-bombers, and also over 500 transport aircraft (principally Ju 52s) for the resupply and airborne operations.

The two attacks would go in simultaneously, but for clarity we will here treat them separately. Both operations would, unlike the Polish campaign, rely on naval power, which was central in deploying German forces to key points around the convoluted Scandinavian coastline. The *Luftwaffe*'s principal roles would be to achieve air superiority, protect the shipping where necessary and possible, deliver airborne assaults against

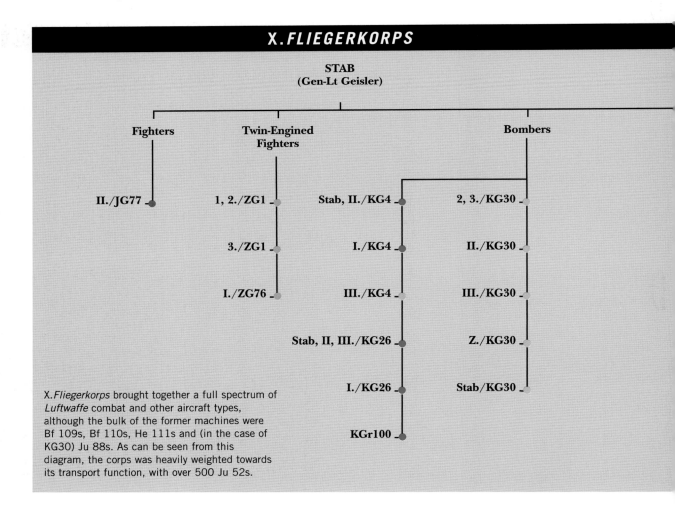

X.FLIEGERKORPS

X.*Fliegerkorps* brought together a full spectrum of *Luftwaffe* combat and other aircraft types, although the bulk of the former machines were Bf 109s, Bf 110s, He 111s and (in the case of KG30) Ju 88s. As can be seen from this diagram, the corps was heavily weighted towards its transport function, with over 500 Ju 52s.

key locations and provide ground support to German land forces.

Overrunning Denmark

The *Luftwaffe* was not expecting serious opposition from Denmark. The country had only a small and largely obsolete air capability split between a Marine Air Force, Army Air Force and Air Training School. The ground invasion began around 04:00 on 9 April, and at first light around 05:30 the *Luftwaffe* ground-attack units swung into action. Two squadrons of Bf 110s caught large numbers of Danish aircraft on the ground, or just attempting to take off, at Vaerlose airfield and

unleashed a sequence of devastating strafing runs. Much of the Danish Air Force's combat strength was destroyed in those critical first minutes, thereby giving the *Luftwaffe* almost instant air superiority.

The smooth running of the aerial campaign was reflected by equal success in the airborne assault operations. For both the Norway and Denmark actions, FJR 1 was the main airborne assault force. The 4./FJR 1 (4th Company, FJR 1) was designated to the Denmark operations, and had several objectives, including the Masnedø fortress and the airbase at Aalborg. Deployed by Ju 52s in low-level drops, the paras landed fairly accurately around their targets. Such was the shock they

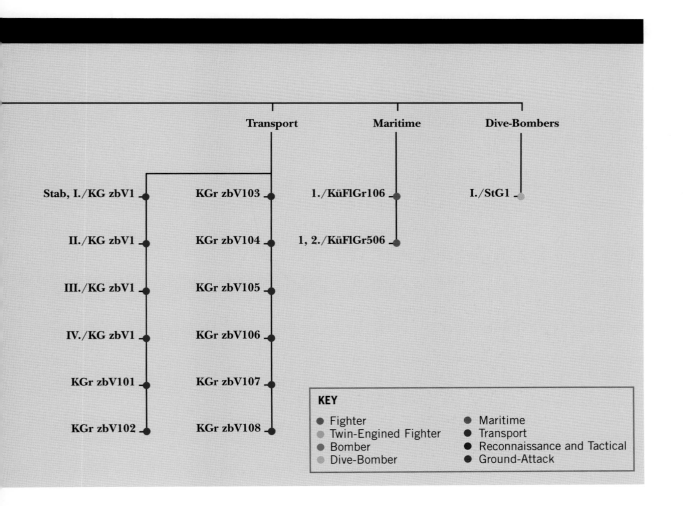

generated that most of their objectives were seized without firing a shot – the Danish troops simply fled when they saw the advancing paras. The paras would not have to wait long before spearhead German land units reached them to consolidate their gains.

With air superiority gained and the paras deployed, there remained little for the *Luftwaffe* to do over Denmark. Some units were required to strafe and bomb Danish units that put up tough localized resistance around Abild and Soelstad, but by the end of the first day Denmark had surrendered.

Norway

Norway would prove to be a tougher nut to crack for the Germans. Our focus here is the *Luftwaffe*, but it should be noted that the Norwegian campaign would see its harshest fighting between German and British naval forces and army units. The invasion went in on 9 April, with multiple naval assault groups delivering troops at vital points along the Norwegian coastline. As with Denmark, the critical *Luftwaffe* contribution was launching airborne assaults on key targets. This time, matters did not go so smoothly. The HQ and 2.*Kompanie* of FJR 1 were tasked with capturing Fornebu airfield, Oslo. The para drop was aborted due to fog, and a fighter force of Norwegian Gladiators from Fornebu subsequently claimed three He 111s and two Bf 110s for only one loss. (Many of these fighters, however, were subsequently destroyed by Bf 110 strafing runs on Norwegian airfields.)

Then German airlanding forces were flown straight onto the runway, expecting that the airfield was already in the hands of the paras. They were very roughly handled by Norwegian resistance. A critical situation was only retrieved when a flight of Bf 110s, low on fuel, themselves landed on the airfield and used their machine guns and cannon in a support role. By the end of the morning the airfield was secured.

Another airfield operation, against Sola-Stavanger, went much more amenably. The paras of 3./FJR 1 seized the airfield in a drop, and this allowed 250 transport aircraft to fly in 5000 more troops. Off Stavanger, German bombers also had success in sinking the Norwegian warship *Aegir*. Indeed, along the Norwegian coastline *Luftwaffe* bombing helped shine the path for

UNIT STRENGTH – X.*FLIEGERKORPS* (APRIL 1940)			
Luftwaffe Unit	Base	Type	Str
X.FLIEGERKORPS			
II./JG77	Husum	Bf 109E	38
1, 2./ZG1	Barth	Bf 110C	22
3./ZG1	Westerland	Bf 110C	10
I./ZG76	Westerland	Bf 110C	32
Stab, II./KG4	Faßberg	He 111P	42
I./KG4	Perleberg	He 111P	36
III./KG4	Lüneburg	He 111P	17
		Ju 88A	20
Stab, II., III./ KG26	Lübeck-Blankensee	He 111H	67
I./KG26	Marx	He 111H	36
KGr100	Nordholz	He 111H	27
2., 3./KG30	Westerland	Ju 88A	25
II./KG30	Westerland	Ju 88A	30
III./KG30	Westerland	Ju 88A	13
Z./KG30	Westerland	Ju 88C-2	6
Stab/KG30	Westerland	Ju 88A	1
Stab, I./KG zbV1	Utersen	Ju 52	56
II./KG zbV1	Schleswig-Stade	Ju 52	53
III./KG zbV1	Utersen-Hagenow	Ju 52	53
IV./KG zbV1	Hagenow	Ju 52	53
KGr zbV101	Neumünster	Ju 52	53
KGr zbV102	Oldenburg	Ju 52	53
KGr zbV103	Schleswig	Ju 52	53
KGr zbV104	Stade	Ju 52	53
KGr zbV105	Holtenau	Fw 200B/C	8
		Ju 90	11
		Ju G-38	1
KGr zbV106	Utersen	Ju 52	53
KGr zbV107	Fuhlsbüttel	Ju 52	53
KGr zbV108	Rantum-Hörnum	Ju 52/See	13
		He 59D	–
1./KüFlGr106	List/Sylt	He 115B/C	12
1., 2./KüFlGr506	List/Sylt	He 115B	11
		He 115C	12
I./StG1	Kiel-Holtenau	Ju 87R	39

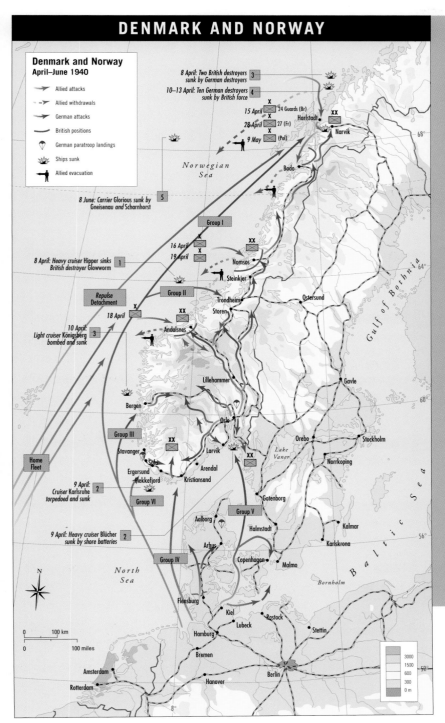

DENMARK AND NORWAY

Denmark and Norway
April–June 1940

Allied attacks
Allied withdrawals
German attacks
British positions
German paratroop landings
Ships sunk
Allied evacuation

8 April: Two British destroyers sunk by German destroyers 3

10–13 April: Ten German destroyers sunk by British force 4

X
15 April: 24 Guards (Br)
X
28 April: 27 (Fr)
X
9 May: (Pol)
Harlstadt
XX
Narvik

68°

Norwegian Sea

Bado

8 June: Carrier Glorious sunk by Gneisenau and Scharnhorst 5

Group I

16 April X
19 April X

XX
Namsos
Steinkjer

8 April: Heavy cruiser Hipper sinks British destroyer Glowworm 1

64°

Repulse Detachment

Group II

Trondheim
Ostersund
Storen

X
18 April
XX
Andalsnes

10 April: Light cruiser Königsberg bombed and sunk 3

Lillehammer

Gavle

Gulf of Bothnia

Bergen

Oslo

60°

Group III

XX

Stavanger
Sola
Ergersund
Flekkefjord
Larvik
Arendal
Kristiansand
XX

Orebo
Stockholm

Lake Vaner

Norrkoping

Home Fleet

9 April: Cruiser Karlsruhe torpedoed and sunk 2

Group VI

Gotenborg

Aalborg
Halmstadt
Group V

Kalmar

9 April: Heavy cruiser Blücher sunk by shore batteries 2

Arhus

Karlskrona

56°

Baltic Sea

Group IV

Copenhagen
Malmo

Bornholm

N

North Sea

Flensburg

0 100 km
0 100 miles

Kiel
Rostock
Lubeck
Stettin

Hamburg

Bremen

3000
1500
600
300
0 m

52°

Amsterdam

Berlin

Rotterdam

Hanover

8°

April–June 1940

At 05:00 on 9 April, German *Fallschirmjäger* were dropped at the unused fortress of Masnedø in Denmark and then at Aalborg airport. At 06:00, a battalion of infantry, which had been hidden in a merchant ship in Copenhagen harbour, emerged to seize the Danish king and his government.

Two divisions of the German XXI Infantry Corps crossed the border and moved into Jutland. Totally outmatched, the Danish Army put up little resistance except in North Schleswig, and there was a brief firefight for possession of the Royal Palace in Copenhagen.

At dawn on the same day, German troops were swarming ashore at Oslo, Bergen, Trondheim and even at Narvik, over 1610km (1000 miles) from the German mainland. German paratroopers seized Sola airport near Stavanger and dropped later on to Fornebu airport near Oslo, while the *Kriegsmarine* ferried the army formations across the Skagerrak and Kattegat.

Allied landings and naval actions in the north around Narvik briefly reversed the tide of German success, but the British and French troops were withdrawn at the end of May after reverses in France meant that they were more urgently needed there.

I./ZG76

Zerstörergeschwader 76 contributed Bf 110 units to the invasion of Denmark and Norway, and was subsequently based at Sola-Stavanger in Norway under X.*Fliegerkorps,* and then under the newly created *Luftflotte* 5. At full operational strength during the Denmark/Norway campaign, I./ZG76 comprised 32 Bf 110Cs. This aircraft was classified as a heavy fighter, as it boasted an armament of two 20mm (0.78in) cannon, four 7.92mm (0.31in) forward-firing machine guns and two 7.92mm (0.31in) machine guns set in the rear cockpit. It had a range of 775km (482 miles).

Operational strength – 32 x Bf 110Cs

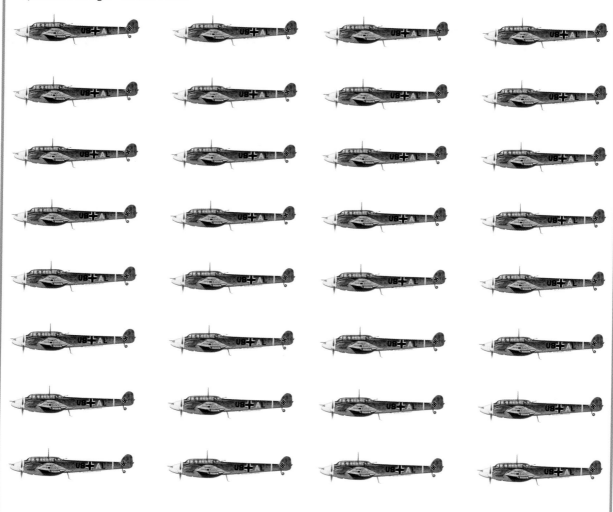

many of the German Army amphibious deployments. Yet the Norwegian campaign was only just beginning. The British had entered the war in earnest, and a large British landing at Namsos threatened to cut off German troops in Narvik. A company of FJR 1 was dropped in on 17 April to block Norwegian troops meeting the British advance. Eight of the 15 Ju 52s deploying them either got lost or were shot down. Only 61 men were left to fight, and they put up stout resistance against overwhelming odds until the survivors were forced to surrender four days afterwards.

Narvik would attract more paras later. On 15 May, I./FJR 1 (1st Battalion, FJR 1) was dropped in to reinforce the city, although it took 12 days for the men to fight through. They would remain there until the Allied evacuation was completed on 9 June. The initial fight had been hard, but the Norwegian campaign seemed to have proved the value of airborne assault.

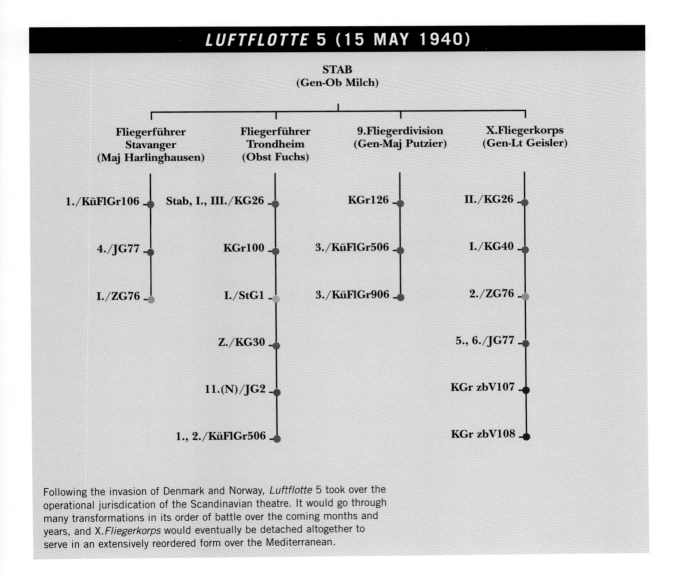

LUFTFLOTTE 5 (15 MAY 1940)

STAB
(Gen-Ob Milch)

Fliegerführer Stavanger (Maj Harlinghausen)	Fliegerführer Trondheim (Obst Fuchs)	9.Fliegerdivision (Gen-Maj Putzier)	X.Fliegerkorps (Gen-Lt Geisler)
1./KüFlGr106	Stab, I., III./KG26	KGr126	II./KG26
4./JG77	KGr100	3./KüFlGr506	I./KG40
I./ZG76	I./StG1	3./KüFlGr906	2./ZG76
	Z./KG30		5., 6./JG77
	11.(N)/JG2		KGr zbV107
	1., 2./KüFlGr506		KGr zbV108

Following the invasion of Denmark and Norway, *Luftflotte* 5 took over the operational jurisdication of the Scandinavian theatre. It would go through many transformations in its order of battle over the coming months and years, and X.*Fliegerkorps* would eventually be detached altogether to serve in an extensively reordered form over the Mediterranean.

Consolidation

With the 1940 invasion of Denmark and Norway, the *Luftwaffe* had once again proved that it could make a telling contribution to combined-arms warfare. Yet although Denmark fell in only one day, the *Luftwaffe* was committed to action over Norway for nearly two months.

The battle for Norway was one of the toughest engagements that the German forces, including the *Luftwaffe*, had to fight. The British and French (in the form of the Foreign Legion) had entered the fight in earnest, and the Royal Navy inflicted some devastating losses on the *Kriegsmarine* – between 10 and 13 April, a total of 10 German destroyers were sunk in British raids, plus numerous transport ships.

On account of this attrition, the *Luftwaffe* naturally aimed much of its attention against British warships, with some return. On 9 April, the British battleship *Rodney* was hit by an air-dropped bomb, although the thickness of its deck armour meant that there was only limited damage. On 17 April, the British cruiser *Sidney* was pounding Sola airfield with its heavy guns, but in payback it was almost completely wrecked by German air attacks. Two days later, the French cruiser *Emile Bertin* also suffered critical bomb damage.

UNIT STRENGTH – *SEEFLIEGERVERBÄNDE* (MAY 1940)				
Luftwaffe Unit	**Base**	**Type**	**Str**	**Op**
SEEFLIEGERVERBÄNDE				
2./KüFlGr106	Rantum	Do 18	9	4
3./KüFlGr106	Borkum	He 115B	8	8
		He 115C	4	2
KüFlGr406	Hörnum	Ha 139B	2	1
		Do 18	30	17
		Do 26	3	2
KüFlGr606	Kopenhagen	Do 17Z	33	27
1./KüFlGr706	Kopenhagen	He 59D	23	9
1./KüFlGr806	Kiel-Holtenau	He 111J	10	5
2., 3./KüFlGr806	Uetersen	He 111J	20	16
1./KüFlGr906	Aalborg-See	He 115B	9	4
2./KüFlGr906	Hörnum	Do 18	10	7

UNIT STRENGTH – *LUFTFLOTTE* 5 (MAY 1940)				
Luftwaffe Unit	**Base**	**Type**	**Str**	**Op**
FLIEGERFÜHRER STAVANGER				
1./KüFlGr106	Sola-Stavanger	He 115B	8	3
4./JG77	Sola-Stavanger	Bf 109E	12	8
1., 3./ZG76	Sola-Stavanger	Bf 110C/D	27	16
FLIEGERFÜHRER TRONDHEIM				
Stab, I., III./KG26	Trondheim-Vaernes	He 111H	75	58
KGr100	Trondheim-Vaernes	He 111H	28	13
I./StG1	Trondheim-Vaernes	Ju 87R	39	25
Z./KG30	Trondheim-Vaernes	Ju 88C-2	15	5
11.(N)/JG2	Trondheim-Vaernes	Bf 109D	11	6
1., 2./KüFlGr506	Trondheim-See	He 115C	17	7
9.FLIEGERDIVISION				
KGr126	Marx	He 111H	36	24
		He 111B	1	0
3./KüFlGr506	Norderney	He 111B	1	1
		He 115B	5	5
		He 111C	11	10
3./KüFlGr906	Norderney	He 111B	6	6
X.FLIEGERKORPS				
II./KG26	Aalborg-West	He 111H	36	7
I./KG40	Kopenhagen	Fw 200C	4	2
2./ZG76	Aalborg-West	Bf 110C	11	7
5., 6./JG77	Kristiansand-Kjevik	Bf 109E	28	20
KGr zbV107	Aalborg/Oslo	Ju 52	48	35
KGr zbV108	Hörnum/Aalborg /Bergen	Ju 52	11	8
		Ju 52/See	5	4
		He 59D	13	8
		Do 24	2	1
		Do 26	4	2
		Bv 138A	2	1

LUFTFLOTTE 5 OPERATIONAL AREA

NORWAY

Luftflotte 5

UNITED
KINGDOM

Luftflotte 2   Luftflotte 1

Luftflotte 3   Luftflotte 4

VICHY
FRANCE   ITALY

SOVIET
UNION

August 1940

Luftflotte 5 would be one of the fruits of German labour in Denmark and Norway. The conquest of the Scandinavian territories gave the *Luftwaffe* permanent bases in the far north of Europe. These were not only useful for conducting reconnaissance and anti-shipping flights over the North Sea, Baltic and Arctic waters, but the more southerly bases later gave opportunities to attack targets in northern England.

The aircraft types in use with *Luftflotte* 5 were the Messerschmitt Bf 109 (all *Luftwaffe* single-seat fighter units had switched to the Bf 109 by this stage of the war), the Heinkel He 111, the Junkers Ju 88, the Heinkel He 115 (for use in maritime operations in conjunction with the *Kriegsmarine*), the Ju 88 and, for reconnaissance purposes, the Henschel Hs 126, a two-seat single-engine aircraft with a range of 720km (447 miles).

Forcing evacuation

From the end of April, there was still another month of fighting ahead in Norway, but by now the *Luftwaffe* was starting to shift the campaign in Germany's favour. At this point Germany had complete air superiority, and it showed on the ground. The harbour facilities at Namsos and Steinkjer had been virtually bombed out of existence and British troops had lost freedom of movement. On 13 May, dive-bombers sank a British supply ship full of troops and armour. Such losses were unsustainable, and three weeks later the surviving Allies had fled Norway. By now, the *Luftwaffe* was riding high. It had made a signal contribution to two victorious campaigns, plus it had gained the combat experience to see it into future campaigns. The next objectives lay to the west of Germany – France and the Low Countries.

France and the Low Countries: 1940

By the end of June 1940, most of Europe was under the authority of Hitler's ever-expanding Third Reich. His armed forces, including his now battle-tested air force, began to look invincible.

A flight of Ju 52s over the Netherlands. This humble transporter was integral to German airborne assault tactics in the early years of the war.

Even with the familiarity that comes with the passage of time, there is no getting away from the brilliance of Germany's campaign in the West in 1940. The ground offensive, launched on 10 May, began with assaults into the Netherlands and Belgium, which forced the rapid surrender of those countries' governments and forces. Three German Army Groups containing 141 divisions took part, one of which, Army Group A, cut through the 'impassable' Ardennes to establish armoured bridgeheads on the River Meuse. These bridgeheads became the jumping-off points for a lightning German advance from France's eastern borders to its western coastline. Despite massive British intervention, which led only to the full-scale evacuation from Dunkirk between 27 May and 4 June, Marshal Philippe Pétain signed the German surrender terms on 22 June, signalling the fall of France and the end of Hitler's massive programme of westward expansion.

Battle proven

The campaign in the West was further proof of how formidable the *Luftwaffe* had become. What seemed to separate the German Air Force from its Allied counterparts was its tactical flexibility. Not only did fighter units put up protective screens over the advancing ground troops, achieving air superiority in the process, but ground-attack aircraft made Allied land-forces manoeuvres fraught with danger even behind the front lines. The precise deployment of German airborne troops resulted in the fall of major defences even before the arrival of the main German advances. The RAF, committed in force for the first time against the *Luftwaffe*, was ultimately unable to stop the tide and was pulled back to Britain to preserve its dwindling aircraft and aviators for the defence of Britain itself.

Tactical limitations

And yet, in the midst of the undoubted victory secured by Germany over Belgium, the Netherlands and France, there were also hints at the *Luftwaffe*'s limitations. The most important failure in the German air campaign was its inability to stop the British evacuation of most of its land army from the beaches of Dunkirk, despite *General der Flieger* Albert Kesselring's commitment of three *Fliegerkorps* to precisely that purpose.

HERMANN GÖRING (1893–1946)

A combat pilot during World War I, Göring won the *Pour le Mérite* and led the Richthofen Squadron.

• Appointed *Reich* Minister for Aviation in 1933, becoming commander-in-chief of the *Luftwaffe* in March 1935.

• Promoted to *Reichsmarschall* in July 1940, Göring's power nevertheless waned as the war progressed, partly from his vanity and self-indulgence, and partly as the military limitations of the *Luftwaffe* became clear.

• Arrested by Hitler in April 1945 after suggesting he take power; later escaped execution by the Allies for involvement in the Holocaust plans by taking cyanide.

The escape of the Allied forces proved that tactical air power did have significant limitations, and that the victories of the *Luftwaffe* achieved in Poland were not necessarily guaranteed in other theatres. This lesson would become critically clear to the German high command as 1940 played itself out.

The *Luftwaffe* looks west

While *Luftflotten* 1 and 4 had taken the lion's share of responsibility for the campaign in Poland, now *Luftflotten* 2 and 3 took centre stage. Together, these two formations would hurl nearly 3000 aircraft at the West.

The forces gathered for the assault on the West were truly impressive. The two major formations, *Luftflotte* 2 and *Luftflotte* 3, were commanded by Kesselring and

General der Flieger Hugo Sperrle respectively. The aircraft amassed included 850 Bf 109s, 350 Bf 110s, 1100 medium bombers, 400 Stukas and 500 transport aircraft.

LUFTWAFFE ORGANIZATION (MAY 1940)

OKL
(Gen FM Göring)

LUFTFLOTTE 1 (Gen der Flieg Stumpff)	LUFTFLOTTE 2 (Gen der Flieg Kesselring)	LUFTFLOTTE 3 (Gen der Flieg Sperrle)
Luftgau I	Fliegerkorps zbV2	I.Fliegerkorps
Luftgau II	IV.Fliegerkorps	II.Fliegerkorps
Luftgau III	VII.Fliegerkorps	V.Fliegerkorps
	Jafü 'Deutsche Bucht'	Jafü 3
	Jafü 2	

Luftflotten 2 and 3 were the principal formations utilized in the invasion of the West, although they received reinforcements from *Luftflotten* 1 and 4 and also took direct operational contributions from *Luftflotte* 5, usefully positioned just to the north of the main theatre of operations. At this stage of the war, the vast bulk of the *Luftwaffe* was concentrated in the West, with Poland requiring minimal occupation aviation.

The *Luftwaffe* had much to gain from the conquest of France and the Low Countries, but most especially the acquisition of operating bases from which to take the battle to the United Kingdom, separated from mainland Europe by a relatively narrow strip of sea.

In terms of immediate objectives, the *Luftwaffe* had its usual roles of ground support and aerial interdiction, added to which were some very specific objectives for airborne assault.

In Belgium, the premier target was the fortress of Eben Emael, in front of the Albert Canal, while in the Netherlands the *Fallschirmjäger* were tasked with capturing the Waalhaven and Valkenburg airfields and bridges at Moerdyk and Dordrecht, while the 22nd *Luftlande* Division would be used to assault the seat of the Dutch high command at The Hague. Airborne units had no significant objectives in France, however.

Neither France, Belgium nor the Netherlands had any comparable air power to resist the *Luftwaffe*. This, combined with a brilliant attack plan from the *Heer,* meant that the outcome of the invasion of the West was almost a foregone conclusion.

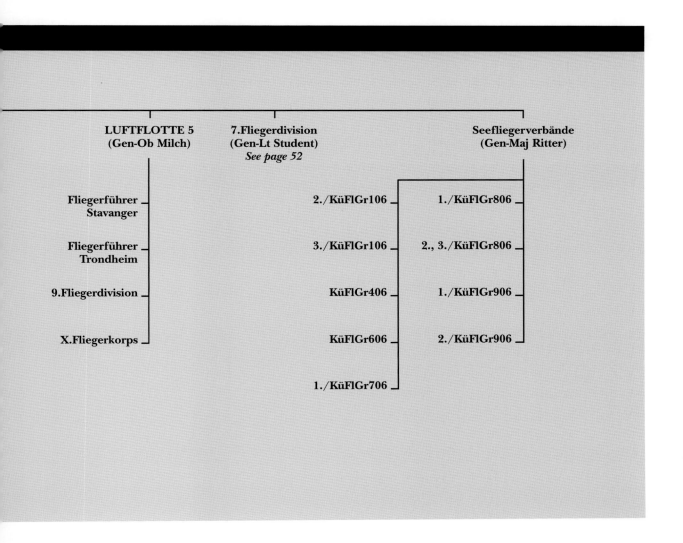

LUFTFLOTTE 5 (Gen-Ob Milch)	7.Fliegerdivision (Gen-Lt Student) *See page 52*		Seefliegerverbände (Gen-Maj Ritter)
Fliegerführer Stavanger	2./KüFlGr106		1./KüFlGr806
Fliegerführer Trondheim	3./KüFlGr106		2., 3./KüFlGr806
9.Fliegerdivision	KüFlGr406		1./KüFlGr906
X.Fliegerkorps	KüFlGr606		2./KüFlGr906
	1./KüFlGr706		

Belgium and the Netherlands

Although there was air combat over Belgium and the Netherlands, the German invasions of those countries are principally remembered for superbly executed airborne landings at key tactical and strategic locations.

The German invasion of the West was launched on 10 May 1940, and as usual the *Luftwaffe* was at the forefront of the attacks. Over the Netherlands, aircraft from *Luftflotte* 2 faced only 132 ageing aircraft of the Netherlands Army Air Service, and many of these were destroyed on the ground in initial strafing and bombing runs – the air force virtually ceased to exist in only four days of combat. Meanwhile, the German airborne assaults were encountering harder resistance. The bridges were seized in relatively short order, but there were heavy German casualties at the stubbornly defended Dutch airfields, where even the outclassed

Dutch fighters managed to shoot up many Ju 52s before the Bf 109s appeared on the scene. The final, controversial act of the campaign came on 13/14 May, when bombers of KG54 pounded Rotterdam to crush resistance, killing 800 civilians. Five days after the invasion, the Netherlands completely capitulated. Belgium suffered a similar fate. In one of the most brilliant operations of the entire war, German paras captured Eben Emael using precision glider landings, and Allied attempts to destroy bridges over the Albert Canal were ruthlessly smashed. Belgium surrendered on 28 May.

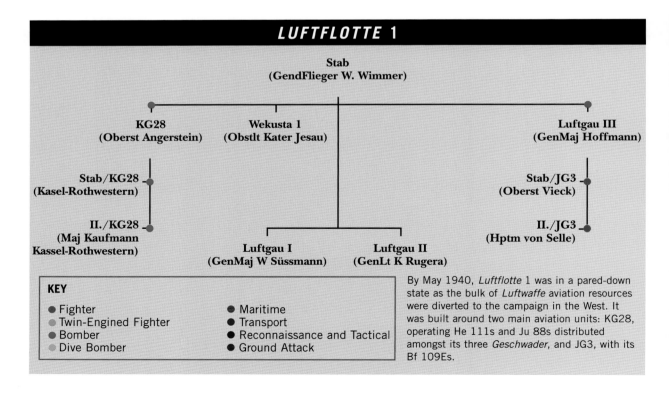

LUFTFLOTTE 1

Stab
(GendFlieger W. Wimmer)

KG28
(Oberst Angerstein)

Wekusta 1
(Obstlt Kater Jesau)

Luftgau III
(GenMaj Hoffmann)

Stab/KG28
(Kasel-Rothwestern)

Stab/JG3
(Oberst Vieck)

II./KG28
(Maj Kaufmann
Kassel-Rothwestern)

II./JG3
(Hptm von Selle)

Luftgau I
(GenMaj W Süssmann)

Luftgau II
(GenLt K Rugera)

KEY
- Fighter
- Twin-Engined Fighter
- Bomber
- Dive Bomber
- Maritime
- Transport
- Reconnaissance and Tactical
- Ground Attack

By May 1940, *Luftflotte* 1 was in a pared-down state as the bulk of *Luftwaffe* aviation resources were diverted to the campaign in the West. It was built around two main aviation units: KG28, operating He 111s and Ju 88s distributed amongst its three *Geschwader*, and JG3, with its Bf 109Es.

III./StG 51

The III.*Gruppe* of *Stukageschwader* 51 was part of *Luftflotte* 3 during the invasion of the West, belonging within I.*Fliegerkorps*. The only other Ju 87 units within *Luftflotte* 3 were *Stab* and II./StG 1 (which also contained Dornier Do 17s) and I.(St)TrGr186, these limited units indicating how few in number the Stukas were in the overall attack forces (some 400 aircraft out of an invasion force of 3500 aircraft).

Nominal strength – 39 x Ju 87Bs

The Fall of France

The German invasion of France would be the biggest operational test of the *Luftwaffe* to date. Not only were the distances covered great, but the *Luftwaffe* would face increasing resistance from the RAF.

The aviation resources available to France to face the German air onslaught were not comparable, but they were stronger than anything the *Luftwaffe* had faced to date. The *Armée de L'Air* had a total of 800 fighters, gathered into 24 groups of single-engined fighters (mainly Morane-Saulnier MS.406s, Curtiss Hav 75As and Dewoitine D.520s), plus six *escadrilles* of twin-engined fighters. The Royal Air Force would also throw in substantial support in the form of two squadrons of Gloster Gladiators and (eventually) 10 squadrons of Hawker Hurricanes, plus a collection of obsolete Fairey Battle and Bristol Blenheim bombers. Although the Bf 109 had the performance edge over most of the opponents, there was still the potential for some very serious losses amongst the *Luftwaffe* pilots, and the Allied threat was taken seriously. We should also

Invasion of the West
May–June 1940

→ German attacks

→ Allied counterattacks

⇢ Allied retreats

— Allied front lines

⊓⊔ Allied defensive lines

☂ German paratroop drops

✝ German glider assault

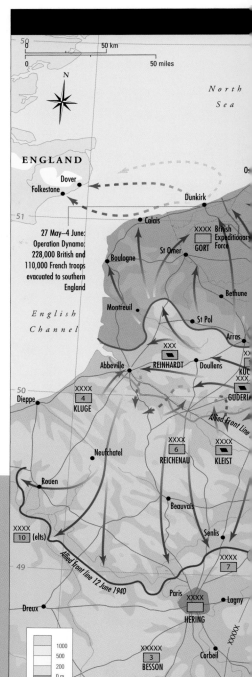

Invasion of the West, May–June 1940

10 May – German forces begin a massive invasion of Belgium, the Netherlands and France. Panzer, infantry and airborne assaults by Army Group B in the north rapidly overcome Belgian and Dutch defences, while a powerful thrust by Army Group A through the Ardennes forest gives the Germans bridgeheads on the Meuse by 14 May.
14 May – The Netherlands surrenders.
20 May – German Panzers reach the Channel coast at Noyelles. The Allies fall back to Dunkirk.
28 May – Belgium surrenders.
27 May–4 June – More than 300,000 British and French troops are evacuated from the beaches of Dunkirk.
10 June – German forces cross the Seine.
22 June – France surrenders.

INVASION OF THE WEST

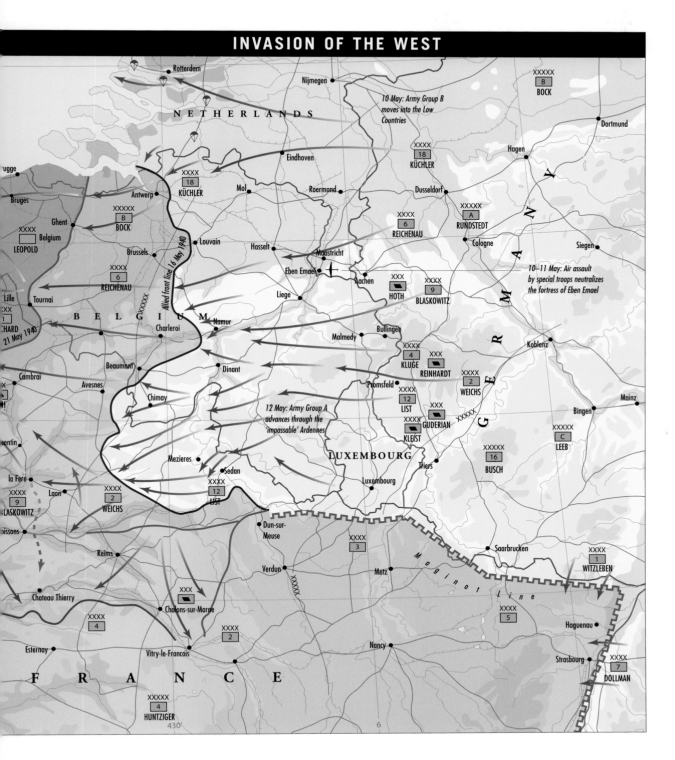

NETHERLANDS

Rotterdam

Nijmegen

10 May: Army Group B moves into the Low Countries

XXXXX
BOCK

Dortmund

Eindhoven

Hagen

XXXX
18
KÜCHLER

XXXX
18
KÜCHLER

Roermond

Dusseldorf

Mol

Antwerp

Bruges

Ghent

XXXXX
B
BOCK

XXXX
Belgium
LEOPOLD

Brussels

Louvain

Hasselt

Maastricht

Eben Emael

XXXX
6
REICHENAU

XXXXX
A
RUNDSTEDT

Cologne

Siegen

XXXX
6
REICHENAU

Aachen

Liege

XXX
HOTH

XXXX
9
BLASKOWITZ

10–11 May: Air assault by special troops neutralizes the fortress of Eben Emael

BELGIUM

Lille

Tournai

Charleroi

Namur

Malmedy

Bullingen

Koblenz

CHARD
21 May 1940

XXXX
1

Beaumont

Dinant

XXXX
4
KLUGE

XXX
REINHARDT

XXXX
2
WEICHS

Mainz

Cambrai

Avesnes

Chimay

Promsfeld

XXXX
12
LIST

XXX
GUDERIAN

Bingen

12 May: Army Group A advances through the 'impassable' Ardennes

XXXX
KLEIST

XXXXX
G E R M A N Y

XXXXX
C
LEEB

uentin

Mezieres

LUXEMBOURG

Thiers

XXXXX
16
BUSCH

la Fere

Sedan

XXXX
12
LIST

XXXX
9
LASKOWITZ

Laon

XXXX
2
WEICHS

Luxembourg

oissons

Dun-sur-Meuse

Reims

XXXX
3

Verdun

Metz

Saarbrucken

XXXX
1
WITZLEBEN

Chateau Thierry

Chalons-sur-Marne

XXX

Maginot Line

XXXX
4

XXXX
2

Vitry-le-Francois

Nancy

XXXX
5

Haguenau

Esternay

F R A N C E

Strasbourg

XXXX
7
DOLLMAN

XXXXX
4
HUNTZIGER

430'

6

acknowledge that apart from the Messerschmitt Bf 109, which would soon have a worthwhile competitor in the Supermarine Spitfire, the *Luftwaffe* was itself replete with vulnerable aircraft types. If caught without escorts, the Heinkel He 111 was a gift of a target for a determined fighter pilot, and the notorious Junkers Ju 87 was relatively easy to knock out of the sky if it could be caught on the climb. Essentially it was the combat experience of the *Luftwaffe* that gave it its true edge in the battle for France.

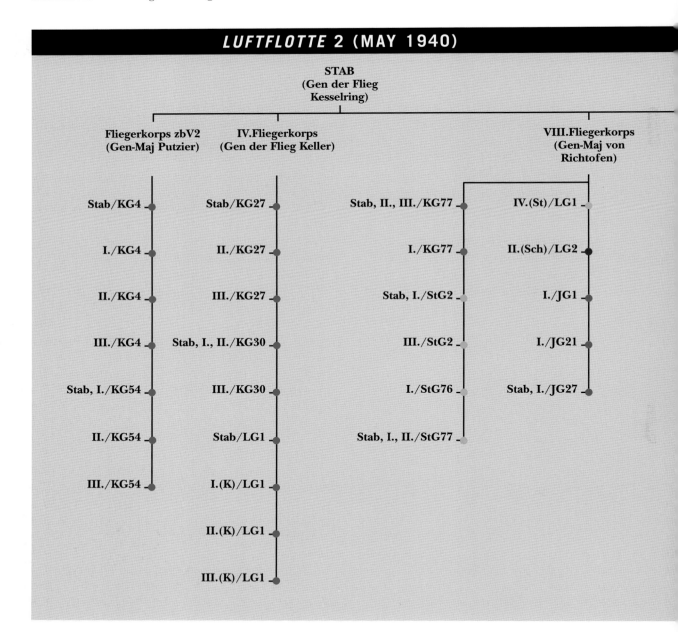

LUFTFLOTTE 2 (MAY 1940)

STAB
(Gen der Flieg
Kesselring)

Fliegerkorps zbV2 (Gen-Maj Putzier)	IV.Fliegerkorps (Gen der Flieg Keller)		VIII.Fliegerkorps (Gen-Maj von Richtofen)
Stab/KG4	Stab/KG27	Stab, II., III./KG77	IV.(St)/LG1
I./KG4	II./KG27	I./KG77	II.(Sch)/LG2
II./KG4	III./KG27	Stab, I./StG2	I./JG1
III./KG4	Stab, I., II./KG30	III./StG2	I./JG21
Stab, I./KG54	III./KG30	I./StG76	Stab, I./JG27
II./KG54	Stab/LG1	Stab, I., II./StG77	
III./KG54	I.(K)/LG1		
	II.(K)/LG1		
	III.(K)/LG1		

Once the *Luftwaffe* actually came to grips with the Allied aviators, what emerged was the complete tactical superiority of *Luftwaffe* fliers who had already honed their skills in combat. It was in France, therefore, that some of the great German fighter aces began to make

their names and establish their tallies. The legendary Adolf Galland accounted for 17 kills during the battle for France, including the shooting-down of three Hurricanes in one day. Even this was surpassed by the achievements of Wilhelm Balthasar, flying for the

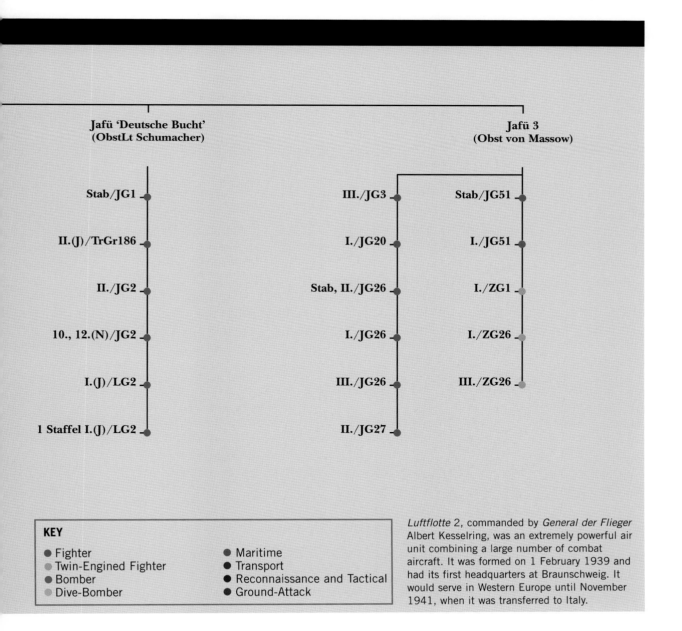

Jafü 'Deutsche Bucht'
(ObstLt Schumacher)

Jafü 3
(Obst von Massow)

Jafü 'Deutsche Bucht'	Jafü 3	
Stab/JG1	III./JG3	Stab/JG51
II.(J)/TrGr186	I./JG20	I./JG51
II./JG2	Stab, II./JG26	I./ZG1
10., 12.(N)/JG2	I./JG26	I./ZG26
I.(J)/LG2	III./JG26	III./ZG26
1 Staffel I.(J)/LG2	II./JG27	

KEY

● Fighter
● Twin-Engined Fighter
● Bomber
● Dive-Bomber
● Maritime
● Transport
● Reconnaissance and Tactical
● Ground-Attack

Luftflotte 2, commanded by *General der Flieger* Albert Kesselring, was an extremely powerful air unit combining a large number of combat aircraft. It was formed on 1 February 1939 and had its first headquarters at Braunschweig. It would serve in Western Europe until November 1941, when it was transferred to Italy.

UNIT STRENGTH – *LUFTFLOTTE* 2 (MAY 1940)				
Luftwaffe Unit	**Base**	**Type**	**Str**	**Op**
FLIEGERKORPS ZBV2				
Stab/KG4	Faßberg / He111D	He 111P	8 / 1	7 / 0
I./KG4	Gütersloh	He 111H	36	24
II./KG4	Faßberg	He 111P	35	28
III./KG4	Delmenhorst	He 111P / Ju 88A-1	23 / 37	12 / 21
Stab, I./KG54	Quackenbrück	He 111P / He 111D	42 / 1	37 / 0
II./KG54	Varrelbusch	He 111P	29	26
III./KG54	Vechta	He 111P	35	27
IV.FLIEGERKORPS				
Stab/KG27	Hannover-Langenhagen	He 111P / He 111D	41 / 1	29 / 1
II./KG27	Delmenhorst	He 111P	35	25
III./KG27	Wunstorf	He 111P	38	32
Stab, I., II./KG30	Oldenburg	Ju 88A-1 / He 111H	74 / 1	52 / 0
III./KG30	Marx	Ju 88A-1	30	20
Stab/LG1	Düsseldorf	He 111H / Ju 88A-1	5 / 1	4 / 0
I.(K)/LG1	Düsseldorf	He 111H	30	22
II.(K)/LG1	Düsseldorf	He 111H / Ju 88A-1	26 / 32	18 / 4
III.(K)/LG1	Düsseldorf	He 111H / Ju 88A-1	12 / 37	5 / 12
VIII.FLIEGERKORPS				
Stab, II., III./KG77	Düsseldorf	Do 17Z / Do 17U	77 / 1	55 / 1
I./KG77	Werl	Do 17Z	35	28
Stab, I./StG2	Köln-Ostheim	Ju 87B / Do 17M	43 / 6	36 / 5
III./StG2	Nörvenich	Ju 87B	38	27
I./StG76	Köln-Ostheim	Ju 87B	39	34
Stab, I., II./StG77	Köln-Butzweilerhof	Ju 87B / Do 17M	82 / 6	64 / 5
IV.(St)/LG1	Duisburg	Ju 87B	39	37
II.(Sch)/LG2	Lauffenberg	Hs 123A	49	38
I./JG1	Gymnich	Bf 109E	46	24

UNIT STRENGTH – *LUFTFLOTTE* 2 (MAY 1940)				
Luftwaffe Unit	**Base**	**Type**	**Str**	**Op**
VIII.FLIEGERKORPS				
I./JG21	Mönchen-Gladbach	Bf 109E	46	34
Stab, I./JG27	Mönchen-Gladbach	Bf 109E	43	32
JAFÜ 'DEUTSCHE BUCHT'				
Stab/JG1	Jever	Bf 109E	4	4
II.(J)/TrGr186	Wangerooge	Bf 109E	48	32
II./JG2	Nordholz	Bf 109E	47	35
10., 12.(N)/JG2	Hopstein	Bf 109D / Ar 68	31 / 36	30 / 13
I.(J)/LG2	Wyk-auf-Föhr	Bf 109E	32	22
1 Staffel I.(J)/LG2	Esbjerg	Bf 109E	16	10
JAFÜ 3				
III./JG3	Hopstein	Bf 109E	37	25
I./JG20	Bönninghardt	Bf 109E	48	36
Stab, II./JG26	Dortmund	Bf 109E	51	39
I./JG26	Bönninghardt	Bf 109E	44	35
III./JG26	Essen-Mühlheim	Bf 109E	42	22
II./JG27	Bönninghardt	Bf 109E / Bf 109C	43 / 1	33 / 0
Stab/JG51	Bönninghardt	Bf 109E	4	3
I./JG51	Krefeld	Bf 109E	47	28
I./ZG1	Kirchenhellen	Bf 110C	35	22
I./ZG26	Niedermendig	Bf 110C	34	11
III./ZG26	Krefeld	Bf 110C	37	30

Jagdgeschwader Richthofen. Between 10 May and 21 June, he shot down 22 enemy aircraft, a formidable tally to add to the successes of many other aces in the making. Also making an epic mark was the renowned Werner Mölders, the commander of III./JG53, who shot down 25 aircraft during the campaign in the West, although he himself was shot down (but survived)when jumped by a French fighter.

Forward bases

While the *Luftwaffe* fighter pilots might capture much of the historical press for the fall of France, there was also a great amount of work being done by the other elements of the German Air Force. The *Luftwaffe*'s

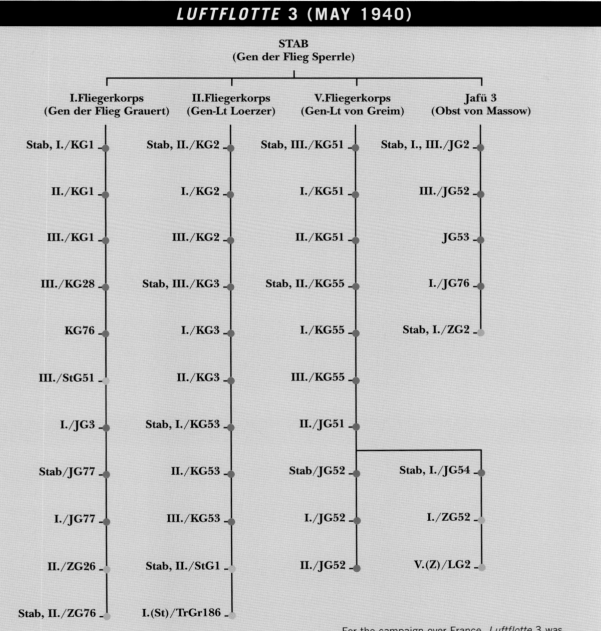

LUFTFLOTTE 3 (MAY 1940)

STAB
(Gen der Flieg Sperrle)

I.Fliegerkorps (Gen der Flieg Grauert)	II.Fliegerkorps (Gen-Lt Loerzer)	V.Fliegerkorps (Gen-Lt von Greim)	Jafü 3 (Obst von Massow)
Stab, I./KG1	Stab, II./KG2	Stab, III./KG51	Stab, I., III./JG2
II./KG1	I./KG2	I./KG51	III./JG52
III./KG1	III./KG2	II./KG51	JG53
III./KG28	Stab, III./KG3	Stab, II./KG55	I./JG76
KG76	I./KG3	I./KG55	Stab, I./ZG2
III./StG51	II./KG3	III./KG55	
I./JG3	Stab, I./KG53	II./JG51	
Stab/JG77	II./KG53	Stab/JG52	Stab, I./JG54
I./JG77	III./KG53	I./JG52	I./ZG52
II./ZG26	Stab, II./StG1	II./JG52	V.(Z)/LG2
Stab, II./ZG76	I.(St)/TrGr186		

For the campaign over France, *Luftflotte* 3 was overwhelmingly configured for its ground-attack role in support of the German Army, with 20 bomber units. Fighter support came from elements of several *Jagdgeschwader* and a handful of Bf 110 units.

transport fleet did a sterling job in supplying both the German land forces and also the *Luftwaffe* as it established bases on captured French airfields. For example, only 24 hours after the French abandoned Charleville airfield, the Ju 52s had flown in enough supplies and personnel to convert it into a fully operational fighter base. This story was repeated across France, with each capture increasing the operational radius of the *Luftwaffe*.

Another frequently overlooked element of the *Luftwaffe* was its *Flak* anti-aircraft (AA) units, which protected the advance and also established themselves around important key features, such as bridges. While heavier anti-aircraft guns, such as the renowned *Flak* 18/36/37 88mm (3.465in) gun, could engage high-flying Allied bombers at a rate of 15–20rpm (there were also heavier 105mm/4.134in guns), smaller-calibre, fast-firing cannon made life especially hazardous for low-flying Allied fighters and ground-attack aircraft.

For example, when on 14 May formations of British Fairey Battle bombers attacked German pontoon bridges over the Meuse, 28 out of 37 aircraft were shot down, principally by German anti-aircraft guns. Even if the Allied aircraft were not hit, which they often were, the storm of anti-aircraft fire streaming up at them broke up their flight patterns and disrupted bomb-aiming accuracy. Furthermore, *Luftwaffe Flak* units often applied their formidable weapons in ground-support roles against enemy armour and troop concentrations.

Question marks

In the last week of May 1940, Hitler made one of the most controversial decisions of the war, when he ordered a temporary halt to the German Panzer advance. The Allies now had the opportunity to evacuate from the beaches of Dunkirk, and *Luftflotte* 2 was given the role of destroying the remnants of British forces from the air. This it failed to do, despite pounding the beaches and town around the clock with Ju 87s and its medium bombers. Furthermore, the presence of the RAF in strength over the beaches, including the appearance of the new Spitfire, meant that the Dunkirk evacuation cost the Germans 250 aircraft.

The failure at Dunkirk educated the *Luftwaffe* about the limits of its area-bombing capability. The Dunkirk beaches did indeed present a huge area of targets, but that was the problem – in such a mass of men and boats it was hard to achieve a decisive blow. Furthermore, although the *Luftwaffe* had established several airbases in

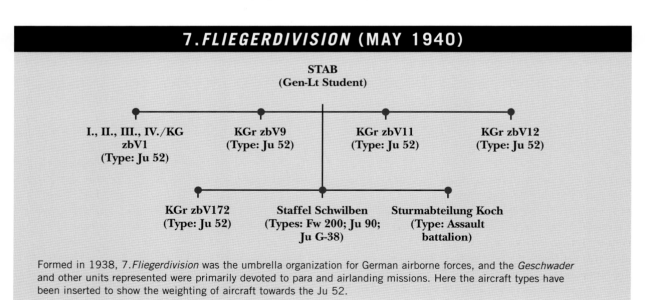

Formed in 1938, 7.*Fliegerdivision* was the umbrella organization for German airborne forces, and the *Geschwader* and other units represented were primarily devoted to para and airlanding missions. Here the aircraft types have been inserted to show the weighting of aircraft towards the Ju 52.

UNIT STRENGTH – *LUFTFLOTTE* 3 (MAY 1940)				
Luftwaffe Unit	**Base**	**Type**	**Str**	**Op**
I.FLIEGERKORPS				
Stab, I./KG1	Giesen	He 111H	39	28
II./KG1	Kirtorf	He 111H	35	23
III./KG1	Ettinghausen	He 111H	33	27
III./KG28	Bracht	He 111P	36	30
KG76	Nidda	Do 17Z	119	87
		Do 17U	1	0
III./StG51	Köln-Wahn	Ju 87B	39	31
I./JG3	Vogelsang	Bf 109E	48	38
Stab/JG77	Peppenhoven	Bf109E	4	3
I./JG77	Odendorf	Bf 109E	46	28
II./ZG26	Kaarst/Neuß	Bf 110C	35	25
Stab, II./ZG76	Köln-Wahn	Bf 110C	36	28
II.FLIEGERKORPS				
Stab, II./KG2	Ansbach	Do 17Z	43	33
		Do 17U	1	1
I./KG2	Giebelstadt	Do 17Z	36	22
III./KG2	Illesheim	Do 17Z	36	30
Stab, III./KG3	Würzburg	Do 17Z	41	34
I./KG3	Aschaffenburg	Do 17Z	35	31
II./KG3	Schweinfurt	Do 17Z	36	28
Stab, I./KG53	Roth	He 111H	43	25
II./KG53	Oedheim	He 111H	36	24
III./KG53	Schwäbisch Hall	He 111H	36	26
Stab, II./StG1	Sieburg	Ju 87B	41	36
		Do 17M	6	5
I.(St)/TrGr186	Hemweiler	Ju 87B	39	36

UNIT STRENGTH – *LUFTFLOTTE* 3 (MAY 1940)				
Luftwaffe Unit	**Base**	**Type**	**Str**	**Op**
V.FLIEGERKORPS				
Stab, III./KG51	Lansberg/Lech	He 111H	40	30
		Ju 88A-1	1	0
I./KG51	Lechfeld	He 111H	36	18
		Ju 88A-1	23	7
II./KG51	München-Reim	Ju 88A-1	38	15
Stab, II./KG55	Leipheim	He 111P	42	29
I./KG55	Neuburg-Donau	He 111P	35	25
III./KG55	Gablingen	He 111P	36	17
II./JG51	Böblingen	Bf 109E	42	30
Stab/JG52	Mannheim-Sandhofen	Bf 109E	3	3
I./JG52	Lachen/Speyerdorf	Bf 109E	46	33
II./JG52	Speyer	Bf 109E	42	28
Stab, I./JG54	Böblingen	Bf 109E	46	31
I./ZG52	Neuhausen ob Eck	Bf 110C	35	23
V.(Z)/LG2	Mannheim-Sandhofen	Bf110C	33	27
JAFÜ 3				
Stab, I., III./JG2	Frankfurt-Rebstock	Bf 109E	91	48
III./JG52	Mannheim-Sandhofen	Bf 109E	48	39
JG53	Wiesbaden-Erbenheim	Bf 109E	139	107
I./JG76	Ober-Olm	Bf 109E	46	37
Stab, I./ZG2	Darmstadt-Griesheim	Bf 110C	35	24

the immediate wake of the land advance, the fighters were still stretched in terms of range, and had limited loiter time over the beaches when compared with the RAF, flying from bases just across the Channel. The German bombers were mainly journeying from bases back in Germany, so suffered similar problems. Add the increased capability of the RAF through its Spitfires, and the *Luftwaffe* was gaining a taste of things to come.

The failure to reduce the British forces at Dunkirk was a bitter blow to Hermann Göring's easily chipped vanity.

Furthermore, some unpalatable truths were coming out of the campaign over France. France had fallen by the end of June, but by that time the *Luftwaffe* had lost some 2000 aircraft, twice as many as the RAF. The heavy cost came from a multitude of sources, including enemy fighters, ground fire and accidental damage, but it also proved the consequences of the almost reckless bravery displayed by many *Luftwaffe* fighter pilots.

Nevertheless, with the defeat of France the *Luftwaffe* now had the bases to tackle its most fearsome opponent to date – the British RAF over its home territory. This would be the true test of the *Luftwaffe*'s mettle.

Battle of Britain
and the Blitz: 1940–41

Between June and September 1940, the *Luftwaffe* attempted the effective destruction of the Royal Air Force over Britain. The attempt ultimately failed, bringing the *Luftwaffe*'s first major defeat of the war.

A Heinkel He 111 makes its bomb run over the River Thames in London during the Blitz, September 1940.

The Battle of Britain was a watershed in the history of the *Luftwaffe*. Up until this point, the *Luftwaffe* had established air superiority over every theatre, forming a devastating ground-attack service for the land forces, and a seemingly invincible fighter screen in the air. Göring's confidence was riding high. His faith in the *Luftwaffe* soared along with his ego, and he was prone to making exaggerated claims for his air force's war-winning potential.

Critical vulnerabilities

The campaigns over Poland, Denmark, Norway, Belgium, the Netherlands and France had revealed pros and cons in the *Luftwaffe*'s tactics and structure. In terms of the pros, the *Luftwaffe* had demonstrated that its greatest strength lay in its ground-support capability. Many times had German Army units stuttered to a halt in the face of a pocket of resistance, only to have that resistance shattered by the contribution of medium-bomber and dive-bomber attacks and fighter strafing runs. Furthermore, the *Luftwaffe* could provide mobile flank protection for rapidly advancing armoured units, facilitating the deep, thin penetrations on which *Blitzkrieg* so often relied. The *Luftwaffe* had also revealed a stunning new airborne-assault capability, and had fielded a potent *Flak* arm that would remain the concern of Allied pilots for the remainder of the war. In the air, its fighter pilots often evidenced superior flexibility in their tactical formations, avoiding the rigid formation flying that would characterize much of the RAF's early defence in the Battle of Britain.

And yet, the picture was not all rosy. The *Luftwaffe*'s medium bombers and dive-bombers proved to be hideously vulnerable if deprived of an escort. Regarding airborne assaults, although there had been some spectacular successes, operations over Holland had demonstrated that if surprise was not achieved, outcomes were far more uncertain. In terms of the *Luftwaffe* being a war-winning arm, furthermore, that ambition would probably always be limited by a simple factor – the weather. The periodic poor weather for which Europe, and later Russia, is renowned resulted in frequent flight groundings and curtailed operations. Add to this the thousands of aircraft lost during the first year of campaigning, and the *Luftwaffe*'s future victories were far less certain than Göring implied. The Battle of Britain would test out to destruction his theories of the *Luftwaffe*'s superiority.

Operation *Seelöwe*

On 16 July 1940, with France securely in his grasp, Adolf Hitler delivered a clear statement of intent: 'I have decided to prepare a landing operation against England, and if necessary to carry it out.'

German plans for an invasion of Britain had actually been considered and formulated as far back as November 1939, when a report was submitted to *Großadmiral* Erich Raeder, head of the German *Kriegsmarine*, giving various options as to how the operation might be conducted. Even the most cursory study, however, soon revealed that Britain would be a tough nut to crack. Its land forces were undeniably weaker than those of Germany, and following the depredations of the battle of France were in poor condition to resist *Blitzkrieg*. Even so, there were three other elements causing the German planners a headache – the English Channel, the Royal Navy and the Royal Air Force.

Channel danger

To invade Britain, German forces needed to cross the Channel, and to do that ran the risk of massacre at sea by the Royal Navy. Germany had a limited surface fleet, and its number of combat-deployable U-boats was still

III./KG4 (AUGUST 1940)

Kampfgeschwader 4 was formed in May 1939 and would be part of the *Luftwaffe*'s bomber force until 8 May 1945. During its lifespan, its principal aircraft types were the Heinkel He 111, the Dornier Do 17 and the Junkers Ju 88, operated here by III.*Gruppe*. This 30-aircraft *Gruppe* could deliver a combined maximum bombload of 69,000kg (151,800lb), if underwing bombs were also carried. III./KG4 had an impressive service record in the first years of the war, but the Battle of Britain took its toll. By 4 September 1940, it was down to 14 aircraft.

Nominal strength – 30 x Ju 88As

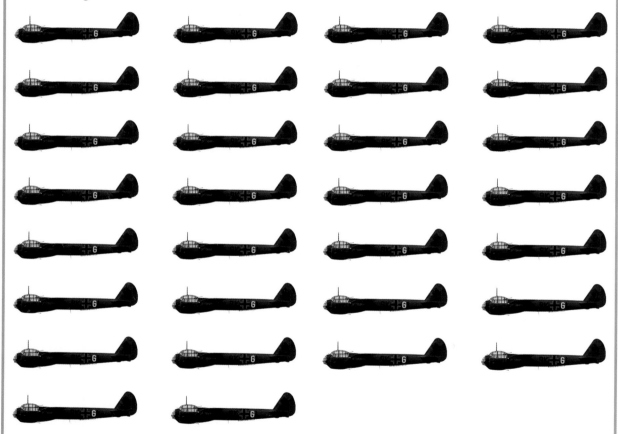

limited at this stage of the war. Therefore, the *Luftwaffe* could be used in a maritime interdiction role, but to do that it first had to achieve air superiority over the RAF. The RAF was certainly weaker than the *Luftwaffe* at this point, but its fighter arm was strengthening through production of the Spitfire and the recruitment of more pilots, plus it had all the advantages of operating time conferred on the side flying over its home territory.

The invasion plan that was eventually conceived was codenamed Operation *Seelöwe* (Sea Lion). It envisaged an initial landing of some 65,000 troops along the English south coast as the Royal Navy were kept busy in the North Sea and Mediterranean by the *Kriegsmarine* and *Luftwaffe*. The invasion was planned for September 1940, by which time it was assumed – and Göring would promise – that the RAF would have been effectively destroyed by a sustained *Luftwaffe* air campaign, known as Operation *Adler* (Eagle). Once safely ashore, German troops would push outwards into England, surround London, then drive north to complete the takeover.

Invasion doubts

Although the plan appeared robust on paper, and German forces began requisitioning barges and vessels from across the occupied territories (Germany had no specialized landing craft), doubt hung over the plan at the highest level. In July 1940, by which time the Battle of Britain had been joined, both Raeder and Hitler were questioning the viability of a Channel assault crossing. Furthermore, Hitler himself seemed to have some

reticence in principle about invading Britain. Historians have speculated over this hesitancy. Some argue that it is explained by Hitler's ill-formed desire to create an alliance between Germany and Britain, quashed when Churchill emphatically rejected any capitulation terms. More convincingly, Hitler was by mid-1940 already thinking about turning his ambitions east into Russia, and the demands of Operation *Seelöwe* would affect those plans significantly.

The final nail in Operation *Seelöwe*'s coffin was the *Luftwaffe*'s failure to crush the Royal Air Force in the summer of 1940, in a campaign that was as much about forcing Britain into compliance as it was about preparing for invasion. Göring felt that his greatest opportunity had come, that his *Luftwaffe* could spectacularly defeat an entire nation. He reckoned without the determination of the British nor the problems within his own air force.

First battles to Eagle Day

The Battle of Britain proper would not begin until August 1940, with the launch of Göring's infamous *Adlertag* (Eagle Day), but combat with the RAF over the Channel was joined well before then.

The orders for the *Luftwaffe* campaign against Britain came through on 2 July 1940, and the first objective was Britain's shipping in the Channel. Britain was acutely reliant upon its maritime traffic for the transfer of materials along its long coastline. It fell to the Ju 87s in particular to interdict this traffic, joined by Bf 109 fighters utilizing the *Kanalkampf* (Channel Battle) to explore Britain's fighter defence.

Only the Ju 87s had the relative precision to hit a single moving ship, but the tactical vulnerabilities in the aircraft that had been revealed over Dunkirk soon became more sharply apparent over the Channel. Although significant numbers of British vessels were hit and sunk, and harbour facilities damaged along the English and Welsh coastline, large numbers of Ju 87s were shot down. In one day alone, 10 July, the Germans

lost 13 aircraft over British waters, as RAF Fighter Command threw up 609 sorties from its force of Hurricanes and Spitfires.

Lessons

The outcome of the *Kanalkampf* was uncertain. On one level, the *Luftwaffe* operation had been a victory, as the Channel waters did indeed become too dangerous for British shipping and were subsequently avoided. Nevertheless, the action once again threw the spotlight on the inadequacies of the Ju 87, 62 of which were lost in August alone. In delivering its relatively slow dive attack, the Ju 87 dropped away from its fighter cover, there to be massacred in the dive or subsequent climb by far faster and more agile Hurricanes and Spitfires. Göring petulantly blamed problems in fighter

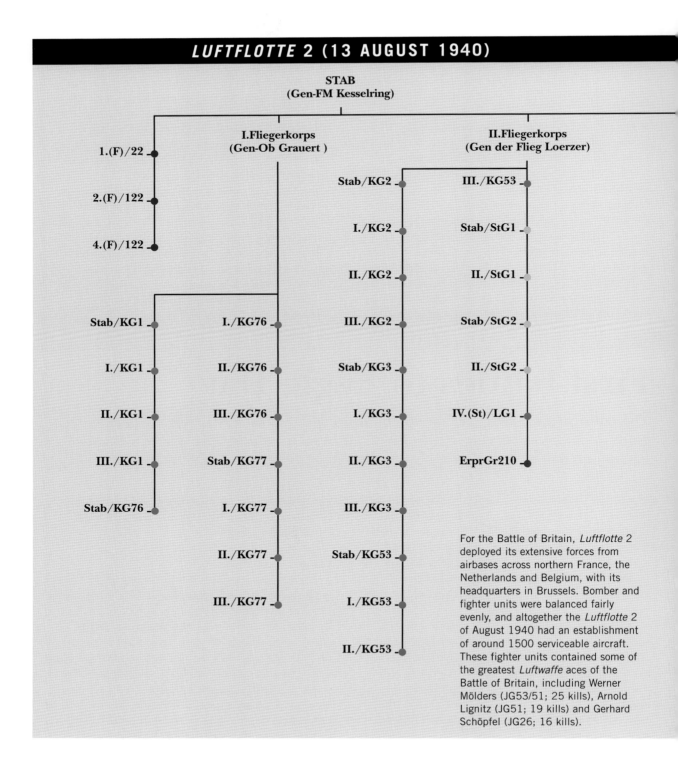

LUFTFLOTTE 2 (13 AUGUST 1940)

STAB
(Gen-FM Kesselring)

I.Fliegerkorps
(Gen-Ob Grauert)

II.Fliegerkorps
(Gen der Flieg Loerzer)

1.(F)/22

2.(F)/122

4.(F)/122

Stab/KG2

I./KG2

II./KG2

III./KG53

Stab/StG1

II./StG1

Stab/KG1   I./KG76   III./KG2   Stab/StG2

I./KG1   II./KG76   Stab/KG3   II./StG2

II./KG1   III./KG76   I./KG3   IV.(St)/LG1

III./KG1   Stab/KG77   II./KG3   ErprGr210

Stab/KG76   I./KG77   III./KG3

II./KG77   Stab/KG53

III./KG77   I./KG53

II./KG53

For the Battle of Britain, *Luftflotte* 2 deployed its extensive forces from airbases across northern France, the Netherlands and Belgium, with its headquarters in Brussels. Bomber and fighter units were balanced fairly evenly, and altogether the *Luftflotte* 2 of August 1940 had an establishment of around 1500 serviceable aircraft. These fighter units contained some of the greatest *Luftwaffe* aces of the Battle of Britain, including Werner Mölders (JG53/51; 25 kills), Arnold Lignitz (JG51; 19 kills) and Gerhard Schöpfel (JG26; 16 kills).

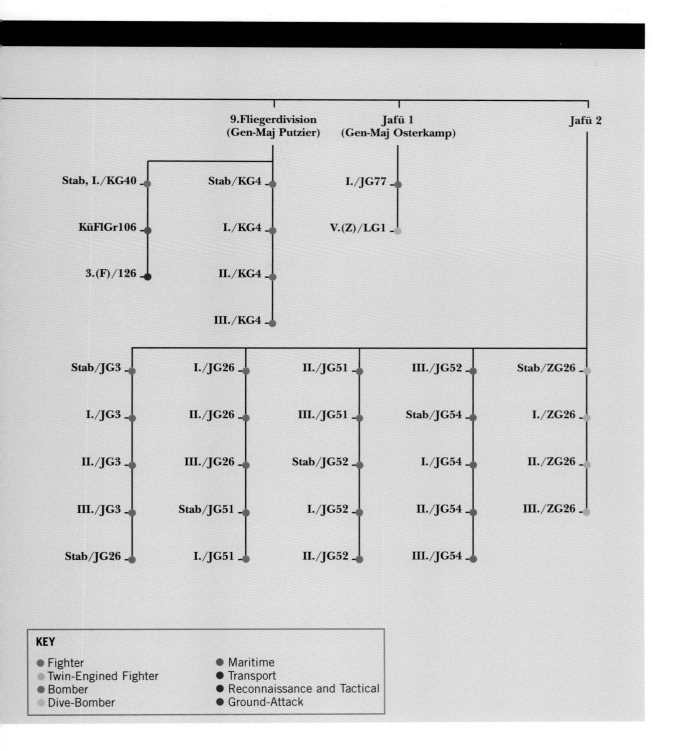

9.Fliegerdivision
(Gen-Maj Putzier)

Jafü 1
(Gen-Maj Osterkamp)

Jafü 2

Stab, I./KG40

KüFlGr106

3.(F)/126

Stab/KG4

I./KG4

II./KG4

III./KG4

I./JG77

V.(Z)/LG1

Stab/JG3

I./JG3

II./JG3

III./JG3

Stab/JG26

I./JG26

II./JG26

III./JG26

Stab/JG51

I./JG51

II./JG51

III./JG51

Stab/JG52

I./JG52

II./JG52

III./JG52

Stab/JG54

I./JG54

II./JG54

III./JG54

Stab/ZG26

I./ZG26

II./ZG26

III./ZG26

KEY

● Fighter
● Twin-Engined Fighter
● Bomber
● Dive-Bomber

● Maritime
● Transport
● Reconnaissance and Tactical
● Ground-Attack

59

WERNER MÖLDERS
(1913–1941)

Born in 1913, Werner Mölders first served in the infantry as an officer cadet during the early 1930s, before transferring to the nascent *Luftwaffe* in 1935. He showed unusual talent in flying fighters, becoming a pilot instructor by 1936. Werner stands as one of the great aces of the the *Luftwaffe*, a man who in just three years of combat flying would achieve 101 combat kills.

• He saw combat service in the Spanish Civil War in 1938, shooting down 14 enemy aircraft and helping to develop the *Schwarm* tactic that would be so critical to *Luftwaffe* fighter combat.

• He flew in combat during the German invasion of Poland and was promoted to *Gruppenkommandeur* of III./JG53 in October 1939, then *Hauptmann* on 27 May 1940.

• He served over France and then Russia with JG53 and JG51 (of which he had command) reaching an incredible final total of 101 kills by 15 July 1941.

• Ordered by Göring to stop flying combat missions, Mölders became Inspector General of Fighters, but was killed in a simple air accident on 22 November 1941.

protection for the Stuka losses, but nonetheless the Stuka's role in the forthcoming Battle of Britain would be strictly limited; it was mainly used in preparatory attacks on coastal radar stations.

Regarding the fighter combat over the Channel, there were lessons to be learnt on both sides. Just as with the Ju 87, the Channel battles also highlighted the deficiencies in fighter types. For the RAF, the Boulton Paul Defiant was the poor performer, too slow and heavy to compete against the nimble Bf 109s. It was withdrawn from daytime combat service in August 1940. For the Germans, the Bf 110, although undeniably an excellent ground-attack aircraft, proved to be unsuitable as a dogfighting aircraft – its speed was good but its manoeuvrability, when compared with a Spitfire's, was poor. Nevertheless, it would still be needed in an escort capacity during the Battle of Britain, as the Bf 109s were quickly stretched to the limit by RAF Fighter Command. Proof of that came on 8 August, when a massive dogfight over the south coast resulted in 31 Bf 109s and Ju 87s being shot down for the loss of 19 British fighters.

On 1 August 1940, Göring took receipt of Hitler's *Führer* Directive No 17, which stated that, 'The *Luftwaffe* must with all its means in their power and as quickly as possible destroy the English air force.' The directive went on to outline the priorities of the attacks, first against the RAF formations themselves, including their infrastructure and supply lines, then against the aircraft production industry.

Orders of battle

Göring and his staff had already been planning the forthcoming campaign, which they termed *Adlerangriff* (Attack of the Eagles). They had reason to be confident. The British had a front-line force of some 900 fighters, the largest percentage concentrated in the southeast, where the main engagements of the Battle of Britain would be fought. The German strength, by contrast, totalled some 2500 aircraft of all types, divided up between *Luftflotten* 2, 3 and 5 (the vast majority of the aircraft were in the first two *Luftflotten*). The words 'all types' are, however, significant. Around 1500 of the total German aircraft strength was bound up in medium bombers, dive-bombers and reconnaissance types, while the fighter strength roughly matched that of Britain – 853 operational single-seat fighters, and 189 twin-engined fighters. Furthermore, the RAF had the advantage of its Chain Home radar stations, which allowed fighter units to be scrambled in advance of German aircraft arriving over British territory.

Once over southeast England, the *Luftwaffe* fighters would typically have a shorter loiter/combat time than their foes, the British fighters having the inestimable advantage of being able to climb virtually straight from the airfield into combat. Should the German bombers want to make deeper penetrations into Britain, they would often have to do it without a single-seat fighter escort. In short, the *Luftwaffe* was not entirely in the position of strength it imagined. Future errors in

Göring's strategic thinking would turn the *Luftwaffe*'s weaknesses into fatal flaws.

Adlerangriff began on 13 August 1940. Appropriately enough, the day's onslaught was termed *Adlertag* (Eagle Day), its main focus being to destroy the RAF on the ground at its airbases throughout southern and eastern England (plus several airfields in the north), and to inflict critical attrition on its fighters in the air. Ju 87s had already hammered several British radar sites the previous day. On the 13th, the main attacks were conducted by the Do 17s of KG2, the Ju 88s of KG54 and the Ju 87s of StG77, targeting airfields and a number of additional targets, such as the Royal Aircraft Factory at Farnborough.

The bombed airfields did suffer critical damage but, predictably, the Ju 87s were shot to pieces, nine being

BF 109 UNITS – BATTLE OF BRITAIN				
Luftwaffe Unit	Base	Type	Str	Op
BF 109 UNITS				
Stab/JG2	Beaumont-le-Roger	Bf 109E	4	3
I./JG2	Beaumont-le-Roger	Bf 109E	32	27
II./JG2	Beaumont-le-Roger	Bf 109E	33	24
III./JG2	Le Havre	Bf 109E	29	20
Stab/JG3	Wiere-au-Bois	Bf 109E	2	2
I./JG3	Grandviliers	Bf 109E	30	24
II./JG3	Samer	Bf 109E	34	30
III./JG3	Desvres-le-Touquet	Bf 109E	34	25
Stab/JG26	Audembert	Bf 109E	4	2
I./JG26	Audembert	Bf 109E	34	24
II./JG26	Marquise-Ost	Bf 109E	35	29
III./JG26	Caffiers	Bf 109E	39	33
Stab/JG27	Cherbourg-Ouest	Bf 109E	5	5
I./JG27	Lumetôt	Bf 109E	39	39
II./JG27	Crépon	Bf 109E	39	27
III./JG27	Arques	Bf 109E	39	32
Stab/JG51	Wissant	Bf 109E	4	2
I./JG51	Pihen-bei-Calais	Bf 109E	29	23
II./JG51	Marquise-Ouest	Bf 109E	25	25
III./JG51	St Omer-Clairmarais	Bf 109E	39	39

BF 109 UNITS – BATTLE OF BRITAIN				
Luftwaffe Unit	Base	Type	Str	Op
BF 109 UNITS				
Stab/JG52	Coquelles	Bf 109E	2	1
I./JG52	Coquelles	Bf 109E	45	36
II./JG52	Peuplingues	Bf 109E	35	23
III./JG52	Zerbst	Bf 109E	31	16
Stab/JG53	Cherbourg	Bf 109E	4	4
I./JG53	Rennes	Bf 109E	39	37
II./JG53	Dinan	Bf 109E	30	26
III./JG53	Brest	Bf 109E	39	21
Stab/JG54	Campagne-les-Guines	Bf 109E	4	3
I./JG54	Guines-en-Calais	Bf 109E	34	24
II./JG54	Hermelingen	Bf 109E	38	36
III./JG54	Guines-en-Calais	Bf 109E	36	39
Stab/JG77	Stavanger/Trondheim	Bf 109E	-	-
I./JG77	Stavanger/Trondheim	Bf 109E	42	40
II./JG77	Stavanger/Trondheim	Bf 109E	39	35
II.(S)/LG2	Böblingen	Bf 109E-7	38	36

brought down. The next day, poor weather limited the air action, but this gave a further chance for the *Luftwaffe* to prepare for what was to come the very next day. It was an attack on an awesome scale. All three western *Luftflotten* contributed, and over 2000 aircraft sorties swarmed over Britain throughout the day. Göring planned a steadily escalating three-day campaign that would crush RAF capability.

While bomber forces attempted to punch through to their targets, the fighter escorts engaged in frantic, twisting dogfights in the blue summer skies, both sides suffering formidable losses. In August alone, as far as the figures allow an accurate reading, the *Luftwaffe* lost 229 Bf 109s, 123 Bf 110s, 75 Do 17s, 98 He 111s, 104 Ju 88s and 62 Ju 87s (the low figure for the latter masks what a high percentage of the Ju 87 force this was).

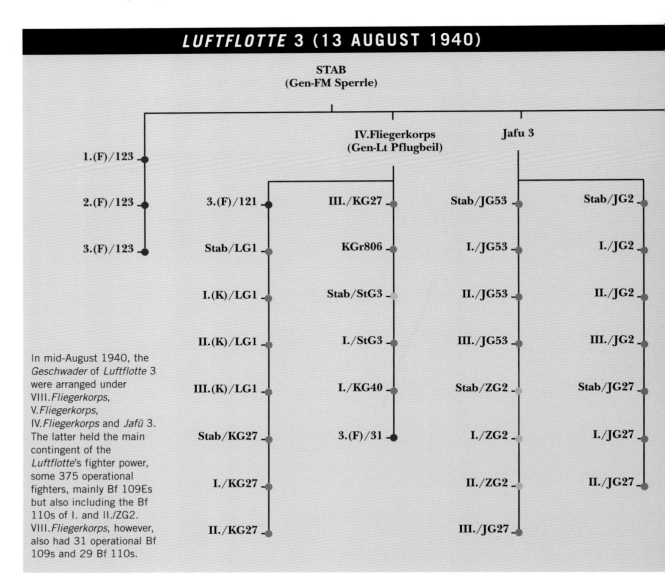

LUFTFLOTTE 3 (13 AUGUST 1940)

STAB
(Gen-FM Sperrle)

IV.Fliegerkorps
(Gen-Lt Pflugbeil)

Jafu 3

1.(F)/123				
2.(F)/123	3.(F)/121	III./KG27	Stab/JG53	Stab/JG2
3.(F)/123	Stab/LG1	KGr806	I./JG53	I./JG2
	I.(K)/LG1	Stab/StG3	II./JG53	II./JG2
	II.(K)/LG1	I./StG3	III./JG53	III./JG2
	III.(K)/LG1	I./KG40	Stab/ZG2	Stab/JG27
	Stab/KG27	3.(F)/31	I./ZG2	I./JG27
	I./KG27		II./ZG2	II./JG27
	II./KG27		III./JG27	

In mid-August 1940, the *Geschwader* of *Luftflotte* 3 were arranged under VIII.*Fliegerkorps*, V.*Fliegerkorps*, IV.*Fliegerkorps* and *Jafü* 3. The latter held the main contingent of the *Luftflotte*'s fighter power, some 375 operational fighters, mainly Bf 109Es but also including the Bf 110s of I. and II./ZG2. VIII.*Fliegerkorps*, however, also had 31 operational Bf 109s and 29 Bf 110s.

Total pilot losses numbered 229 killed or captured, 80 injured and another 263 missing.

Luftflotte 5, operating from its bases in Denmark and Norway, fared particularly badly in its initial attacks over the north of England. Because of the greater distance its aircraft had to fly, only Bf 110s were capable of providing an escort. An attack by 170 aircraft of KG26 and ZG76 against targets around

Newcastle and Sunderland met five squadrons of British fighters from Nos 12 and 13 Groups, resulting in the loss of 16 He 111s and 7 Bf 110s. In total, *Luftflotte* 5 lost 75 aircraft in one day, against 34 aircraft from 12 and 13 Groups.

Over the first five days of the campaign, the RAF had 200 aircraft destroyed, although the *Luftwaffe* staff had compiled exaggerated kill figures to suggest that the

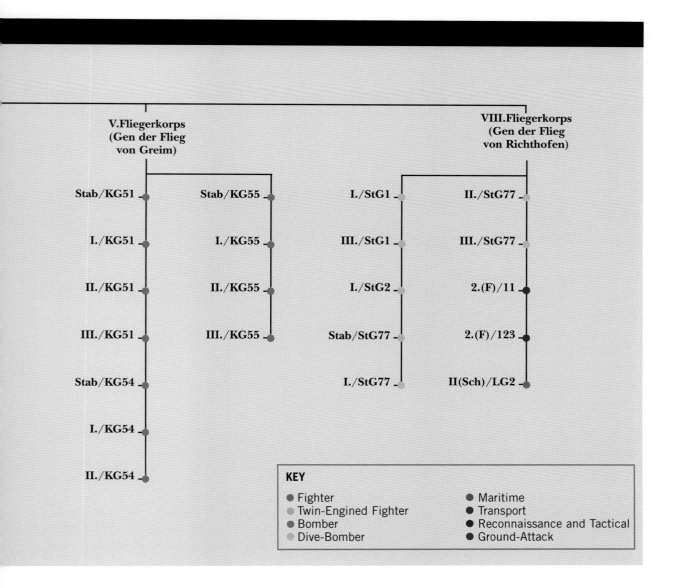

V.Fliegerkorps
(Gen der Flieg
von Greim)

VIII.Fliegerkorps
(Gen der Flieg
von Richthofen)

Stab/KG51	Stab/KG55	I./StG1	II./StG77
I./KG51	I./KG55	III./StG1	III./StG77
II./KG51	II./KG55	I./StG2	2.(F)/11
III./KG51	III./KG55	Stab/StG77	2.(F)/123
Stab/KG54		I./StG77	II(Sch)/LG2
I./KG54			
II./KG54			

KEY
- Fighter
- Twin-Engined Fighter
- Bomber
- Dive-Bomber
- Maritime
- Transport
- Reconnaissance and Tactical
- Ground-Attack

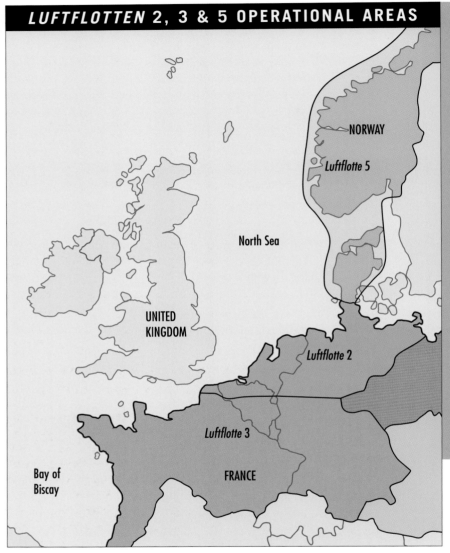

LUFTFLOTTEN 2, 3 & 5 OPERATIONAL AREAS

NORWAY

Luftflotte 5

North Sea

UNITED KINGDOM

Luftflotte 2

Luftflotte 3

FRANCE

Bay of Biscay

August 1940

A glance at the operational areas of these *Luftflotten* illustrates their relative jurisdictions during the Battle of Britain. *Luftflotten* 2 and 3, still commanded by the recently promoted field marshals Kesselring and Sperrle respectively, were both much larger than *Luftflotte* 5 to the north, and were best placed for the war over southeast England, although once the operations were extended over London in September 1940 the single-seat fighters had inadequate range to perform full-mission cover to the bombers.

Luftflotte 5, under the command of *Generaloberst* Hans-Jürgen Stumpff, who had commanded *Luftflotte* 1 until May, was hobbled by a more extreme form of this problem – such was the flying distance across the North Sea that the only escort aircraft available were Bf 110s, and missions included long periods over hostile territory.

British had only 300 aircraft left. (In fairness, British kill totals were equally prone to embellishment.) The British were able to maintain a respectable frontline strength of fighters, but only just. The RAF was also struggling to replace pilots lost in action, and to give the new recruits adequate time before putting them into combat. From 18 August, but in earnest from 24 August, matters became more critical for the British as Göring modified his tactics. The *Luftwaffe* chief reduced the number of

bombers flying on the missions, but increased the strength of the fighter escort, thereby hoping to deal a death blow to Fighter Command.

It was potentially a battle-winning strategy. On 18 August alone, the RAF lost 30 Hurricanes and 7 Spitfires, although it should be noted that on the same day the *Luftwaffe* took 61 losses, including 16 Bf 109s, completing a loss total of 228 aircraft in one week. At the end of the month, on 31 August, Fighter Command had to fly 978 sorties to combat the German incursions, having 38 aircraft shot down in the process. On 2 September, 1000 German sorties were made in a single day.

Breaking point

By 6 September, when another crucial change in *Luftwaffe* tactics occurred, RAF Fighter Command was indeed at breaking point. Should the German campaign have continued, Britain's fighter force would have been run into the ground. At the same time, however, the *Luftwaffe* was taking grievous casualties. The figures given earlier show the enormous losses in pilots suffered by the *Luftwaffe*. Britain also lost large numbers of pilots, but as the battle was over home ground, those who managed to 'bail out' could return to the fight. *Luftwaffe* pilot losses became so destabilizing that by mid-September the available fighters had only a 69 per cent

operational crew establishment. Figures for the larger aircraft were even worse: 46 per cent operational crews for Bf 110 squadrons and 59 per cent for bomber units.

Even so, the Battle of Britain was still shifting in the *Luftwaffe*'s favour. Now, however, Göring made one of his characteristic errors of judgment. (This was accompanied by his actual presence in France from 6 September, the *Reichsmarschall* having decided that the campaign would benefit from his direct command.) Believing that the RAF was effectively finished, he argued that the *Luftwaffe* could now switch its focus to the British capital, London, in the final effort to break British resistance.

Rarely in war has there been such a fateful decision. Although Göring was certainly about to unleash devastation upon British cities, he had, with this commitment, effectively lost the Battle of Britain.

From Eagle Day to defeat

Germany's decision to switch the focus of *Luftwaffe* operations to London was a strategic disaster, and it consigned the German Air Force to defeat in the Battle of Britain.

On 25 August 1940, British bombers made a relatively minor attack on the German capital, Berlin. Although the damage was comparatively insignificant, the attack incensed Hitler and embarrassed Göring, who had once very publicly pledged that no Allied bombs would ever fall on the capital of the *Reich*. In response, on 7 September the *Luftwaffe* switched the focus of its air campaign largely to bombing cities, particularly London. The first raid, on 7 September itself, saw some 300 bombers drop their payloads over London, causing huge damage; 600 fighters operated in escort.

For the next week, the *Luftwaffe* unleashed waves of daylight and night-time raids against the capital, but although the campaign was causing huge devastation below, it was fundamentally the cause of German defeat in the Battle of Britain. With German attention taken off British airfields and fighters, RAF Fighter Command was able to rebuild its strength in both aircraft and pilots. Furthermore, British fighters had increased

opportunities to harry the lumbering bombers, particularly once the German escorts turned for home, short of fuel. The effective climax of the campaign came on 15 September, when another 300-plus bomber raid made a huge assault on London in two waves, but each wave was torn apart by over 300 Spitfires and Hurricanes. Fifty-six German aircraft were shot down on that day, and ideas that the RAF was down to only a small handful of fighters were quashed.

There were many smaller engagements over the next few days, and the night-time Blitz across Britain was beginning in earnest, but on 17 September Hitler postponed Operation *Seelöwe*. By 12 October, it was essentially cancelled, although Hitler made a pledge to review the operation in 1941. Göring's pride was critically dented, and his verbal abuse of pilots had damaged relations with their commanders. In total, the *Luftwaffe* had lost 1455 aircraft in the course of its defeat between July and September 1940.

LUFTFLOTTE 2 (7 SEPT 1940)

STAB
(Gen FM Kesselring)

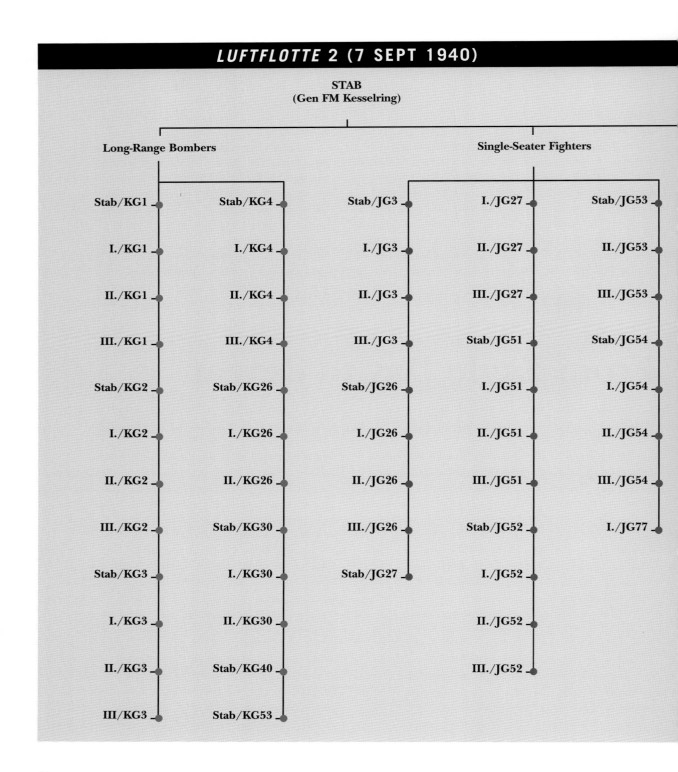

Long-Range Bombers

Stab/KG1	Stab/KG4
I./KG1	I./KG4
II./KG1	II./KG4
III./KG1	III./KG4
Stab/KG2	Stab/KG26
I./KG2	I./KG26
II./KG2	II./KG26
III./KG2	Stab/KG30
Stab/KG3	I./KG30
I./KG3	II./KG30
II./KG3	Stab/KG40
III/KG3	Stab/KG53

Single-Seater Fighters

Stab/JG3	I./JG27	Stab/JG53
I./JG3	II./JG27	II./JG53
II./JG3	III./JG27	III./JG53
III./JG3	Stab/JG51	Stab/JG54
Stab/JG26	I./JG51	I./JG54
I./JG26	II./JG51	II./JG54
II./JG26	III./JG51	III./JG54
III./JG26	Stab/JG52	I./JG77
Stab/JG27	I./JG52	
	II./JG52	
	III./JG52	

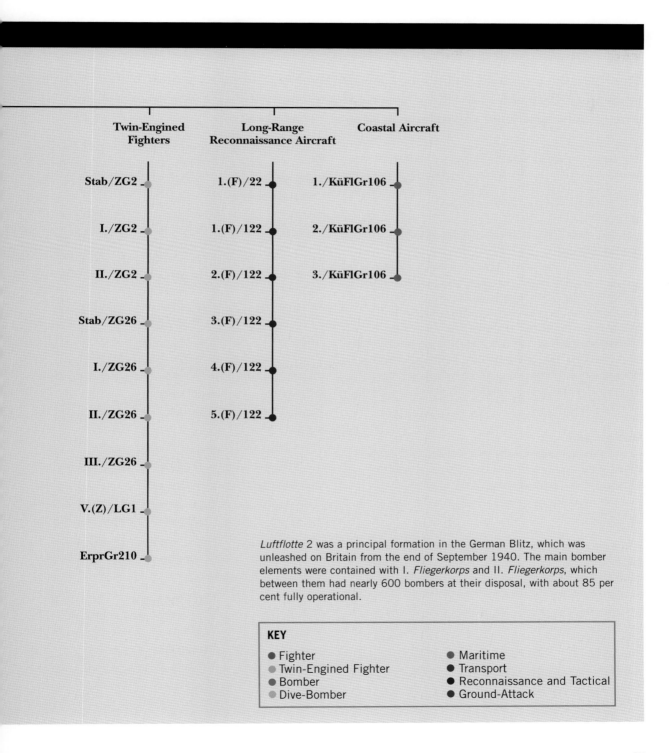

Twin-Engined Fighters

- Stab/ZG2
- I./ZG2
- II./ZG2
- Stab/ZG26
- I./ZG26
- II./ZG26
- III./ZG26
- V.(Z)/LG1
- ErprGr210

Long-Range Reconnaissance Aircraft

- 1.(F)/22
- 1.(F)/122
- 2.(F)/122
- 3.(F)/122
- 4.(F)/122
- 5.(F)/122

Coastal Aircraft

- 1./KüFlGr106
- 2./KüFlGr106
- 3./KüFlGr106

Luftflotte 2 was a principal formation in the German Blitz, which was unleashed on Britain from the end of September 1940. The main bomber elements were contained with I. *Fliegerkorps* and II. *Fliegerkorps*, which between them had nearly 600 bombers at their disposal, with about 85 per cent fully operational.

KEY

- Fighter
- Twin-Engined Fighter
- Bomber
- Dive-Bomber
- Maritime
- Transport
- Reconnaissance and Tactical
- Ground-Attack

The Blitz (1940–41)

The Blitz, the sustained night-time *Luftwaffe* bombing campaign against Britain between September 1940 and May 1941, was a clear attempt by the *Luftwaffe* to engage in strategically significant rolling attacks against urban areas.

The Battle of Britain had been a traumatic failure for Göring, one that further eroded an already crumbling reputation with Hitler and the German high command. In his petulance, he lashed out at those who had more than proven their bravery – the pilots – and appeared at a loss as to how to regain the tactical initiative.

Nevertheless, the *Luftwaffe* was still at war against Britain – by September 1940, the Axis land forces were already locking horns with the British in North Africa, and that would develop into a major front for the *Luftwaffe* in due course. Operation *Seelöwe* had been effectively cancelled, but there was no guarantee that it might not be revived in the future. In short, Britain was still a target, and while the *Luftwaffe* might not have destroyed its air force, it could now switch focus to its industrial capability.

Strategic reach

German daylight raids, some of them sizeable, against British cities continued after the climactic battle of 15 September, but by the end of the month German losses were significant enough to demand a change in tactics. For example, on 27 September mixed formations of Bf 109s, Bf 110s and Ju 88s made attacks across the southeast of England, the strategy being to distract and exhaust the RAF fighters in battle with their German counterparts, while a large force of Ju 88s slipped through to attack London, ideally when the RAF fighters were down on the ground refuelling. The strategy unwound badly, and when the final wave of bombers made their strike for London, the whole of Fighter Command's No 10 Group was waiting. That day alone cost the *Luftwaffe* 49 aircraft, including 17 Bf 109s and 18 Bf 110s.

Of course, the battle was far from one-sided. The very next day, two small groups of Ju 88s and Bf 110s flew

UNIT STRENGTH – *LUFTFLOTTE* 2 (SEPT 1940)				
Luftwaffe Unit	**Base**	**Type**	**Str**	**Op**
LONG-RANGE BOMBERS				
Stab/KG1	Rosières-en-Santerre	He 111	7	5
I./KG1	Montdidier/Clairmont	He 111	36	22
II./KG1	Montdidier/Nijmegen	He 111	36	23
III./KG1	Rosières-en-Santerre	He 111	28	19
Stab/KG2	St Lèger	Do 17Z	5	4
I./KG2	Cambrai	Do 17Z	28	21
II./KG2	St Lèger	Do 17Z	34	31
III./KG2	Cambrai-Sud	Do 17Z	29	24
Stab/KG3	Le Culot	Do 17Z	6	5
I./KG3	Le Culot	Do 17Z	34	24
II./KG3	Antwerp/Deurne	Do 17Z	27	23
III./KG3	St Trond	Do 17Z	34	29
Stab/KG4	Soesterburg	He 111	5	5
I./KG4	Soesterburg	He 111	37	16
II./KG4	Eindhoven	He 111	37	30
III./KG4	Amsterdam-Schipol	Ju 88A	35	25
Stab/KG26	Gilze-Rijen	He 111	6	3
I./KG26	Meirbeke/Courtrai	He 111	25	7
II./KG26	Gilze-Rijen	He 111	26	7
Stab/KG30	Brussels	Ju 88A	1	1
I./KG30	Brussels	Ju 88A	10	1
II./KG30	Gilze-Rijen	Ju 88A	30	24
Stab/KG40	Bordeaux	Ju 88A	2	1
Stab/KG53	Lille-Nord	Ju 88A	5	3

over England, escorted by no less than three *Jagdgeschwader* of Bf 109s – 250 fighters in total. On that day, 14 RAF fighters were shot down, for *Luftwaffe* losses of 5 aircraft.

Yet despite such corrective victories, it remained the case that the *Luftwaffe* was facing an interminable campaign of ever-mounting losses. For this reason, by the end of September it switched its operating method mainly to night-time raids by heavy bomber forces. Here was a determined effort at strategic air war, the attempt to cripple an enemy's industrial infrastructure and civilian morale throught sustained bombing.

Although we have noted the *Luftwaffe*'s limitations as a strategic air force, its bases in coastal France meant that

UNIT STRENGTH – *LUFTFLOTTE* 2 (SEPT 1940)				
Luftwaffe Unit	Base	Type	Str	Op
SINGLE-SEAT FIGHTERS				
Stab/JG3	Wierre au Bois	Bf 109E	2	2
I./JG3	Grandvilliers	Bf 109E	30	24
II./JG3	Samer	Bf 109E	34	30
III./JG3	Desvres Le Torquet	Bf 109E	34	25
Stab/JG26	Audembert	Bf 109E	4	2
I./JG26	Audembert	Bf 109E	34	24
II./JG26	Marquise-Ost	Bf 109E	35	29
III./JG26	Caffiers	Bf 109E	39	33
Stab/JG27	Cherbourg-Quest	Bf 109E	5	5
I./JG27	Plumetot	Bf 109E	39	39
II./JG27	Crépon	Bf 109E	39	27
III./JG27	Arcques	Bf 109E	39	32
Stab/JG51	Wissant	Bf 109E	4	2
I./JG51	Phihen bei Calais	Bf 109E	29	23
II./JG51	Marquise-Quest	Bf 109E	25	25
III./JG51	St Omer-Clairmarais	Bf 109E	39	39
Stab/JG52	Coque	Bf 109E	2	1
I./JG52	Coquelles	Bf 109E	45	36
II./JG52	Peuplingues	Bf 109E	35	23
III./JG52	Zerbst	Bf 109E	31	16
Stab/JG53	Cherbourg	Bf 109E	4	4
II./JG53	Dinan	Bf 109E	39	37
III./JG53	Brest	Bf 109E	30	22
Stab/JG54	Campagne-l-Guines	Bf 109E	4	2
I./JG54	Guines-en-Calaises	Bf 109E	28	23
II./JG54	Hermelingen	Bf 109E	35	27
III./JG54	Guines-en-Calaises	Bf 109E	29	23
I./JG77	StavangerTrondheim	Bf 109E	42	40

UNIT STRENGTH – *LUFTFLOTTE* 2 (SEPT 1940)				
Luftwaffe Unit	Base	Type	Str	Op
TWIN-ENGINED FIGHTERS				
Stab/ZG2	Toussous-le-Noble	Bf 110	1	–
I./ZG2	Amiens/Caen	Bf 110	20	10
II./ZG2	Guyancourt/ Caudran	Bf 110	28	10
Stab/ZG26	Lille	Bf 110	3	3
I./ZG26	Abbeville/St Omer	Bf 110	33	14
II./ZG26	Crécy	Bf 110	25	17
III./ZG26	Barly/Arques	Bf 110	25	17
V.(Z)/LG1	Ligescourt/Alençon	Bf 110	23	19
ErprGr210	Denain	Bf 109E Bf 110C/D	26	17
LONG-RANGE RECONNAISSANCE AIRCRAFT				
1.(F)/22	Lille	Do 17 Bf 110	13	9
1.(F)/122	Holland	Ju 88A	5	3
2.(F)/122	Brussels/Melsbrock	Ju 88A He 111	10	9
3.(F)/122	Eindhoven	Ju 88A He 111	11	11
4.(F)/122	Brussels	Bf 110	13	9
5.(F)/122	Haute-Fontaine	Ju 88A He 111	3	3
COASTAL AIRCRAFT				
1./KüFlGr106	Brittany	He 115	10	4
2./KüFlGr106	Brittany	Do 18	9	6
3./KüFlGr106	Borkum	He 115	9	6

the entire southern half of Britain, South Wales and the Midlands were accessible to strikes, while airbases in northern Europe brought targets in the far north of Britain within reach.

A Heinkel He 111H, for example, had an operational range of 2800km (1750 miles) with maximum fuel load, giving it the combat radius to strike at targets such as Manchester and Sheffield in the north, and ports along the Welsh coastline such as Swansea. The Ju 88 had a similar range and bombload, and together these two aircraft, with night-fighter support provided by the Bf 110, were capable of bringing sustained daily destruction to the British mainland. The strategic air war against Britain would also coincide with the horrific campaign waged by the U-boats against Britain's maritime supply lines.

UNIT STRENGTH – *LUFTFLOTTE* 5 (SEPTEMBER 1940)				
Luftwaffe Unit	Base	Type	Str	Op
SINGLE-ENGINED FIGHTERS				
II./JG77	South Norway	Bf 109E	44	35
LONG-RANGE RECONNAISSANCE AIRCRAFT				
2.(F)/22	Stavanger	Do 17	9	5
3.(F)/22	Stavanger	Do 17	9	5
1.(F)/120	Stavanger	He 111 Ju 88A	13	2
1.(F)/121	Stavanger/Aalborg	Do 17	7	2
COASTAL AIRCRAFT				
1./KüFlGr506	Stavanger	He 115	8	6
2./KüFlGr506	Trondheim/Tromso	He 115	8	5
3./KüFlGr506	Lista	He 115	8	6

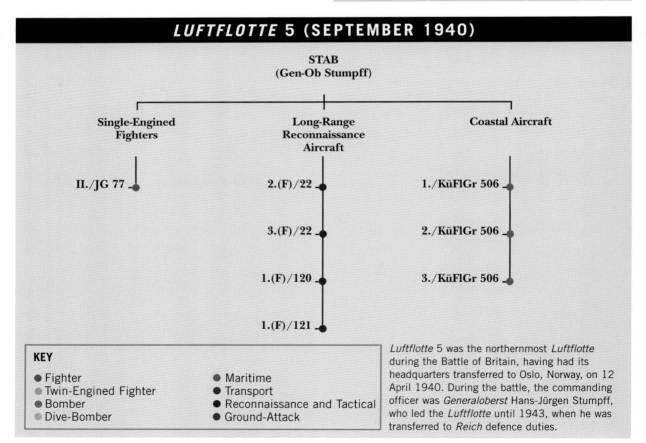

LUFTFLOTTE 5 (SEPTEMBER 1940)

STAB
(Gen-Ob Stumpff)

Single-Engined Fighters

Long-Range Reconnaissance Aircraft

Coastal Aircraft

II./JG 77

2.(F)/22

3.(F)/22

1.(F)/120

1.(F)/121

1./KüFlGr 506

2./KüFlGr 506

3./KüFlGr 506

KEY
- Fighter
- Twin-Engined Fighter
- Bomber
- Dive-Bomber
- Maritime
- Transport
- Reconnaissance and Tactical
- Ground-Attack

Luftflotte 5 was the northernmost *Luftflotte* during the Battle of Britain, having had its headquarters transferred to Oslo, Norway, on 12 April 1940. During the battle, the commanding officer was *Generaloberst* Hans-Jürgen Stumpff, who led the *Luftflotte* until 1943, when he was transferred to *Reich* defence duties.

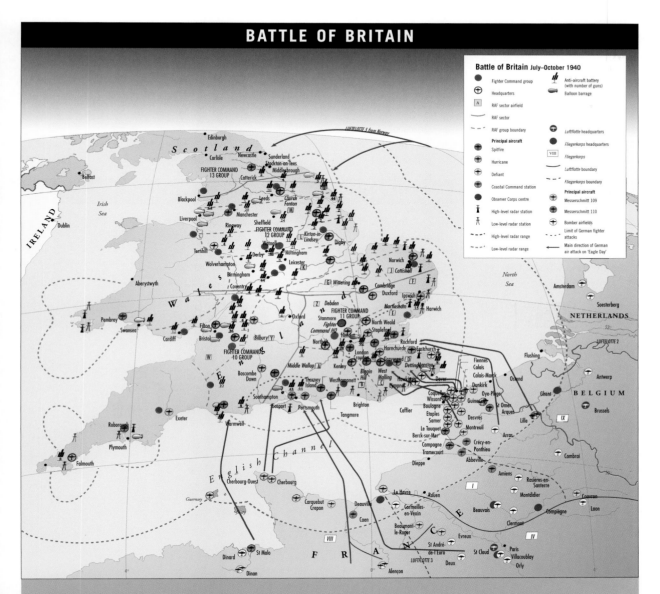

BATTLE OF BRITAIN

Battle of Britain July–October 1940

- Fighter Command group
- Headquarters
- RAF sector airfield
- RAF sector
- RAF group boundary
- **Principal aircraft**
- Spitfire
- Hurricane
- Defiant
- Coastal Command station
- Observer Corps centre
- High-level radar station
- Low-level radar station
- High-level radar range
- Low-level radar range

- Anti-aircraft battery (with number of guns)
- Balloon barrage
- Luftflotte headquarters
- Fliegerkorps headquarters
- Fliegerkorps
- Luftflotte boundary
- Fliegerkorps boundary
- **Principal aircraft**
- Messerschmitt 109
- Messerschmitt 110
- Bomber airfields
- Limit of German fighter attacks
- Main direction of German air attack on 'Eagle Day'

July–October 1940

This map of the Battle of Britain campaign illustrates some of the challenges faced by the *Luftwaffe* in executing an air war against the UK mainland. The critical importance of southeastern England as the primary battleground is illustrated by the massive concentration of German airbases on the opposite coast, this thick cluster of units straddling the dividing line between *Luftflotten* 2 and 3. Yet even flying in from these distances meant that the loiter/combat time of the German fighters was restricted compared with that of their adversaries based in southeast England, and should bombers be bound for more distant targets they might need to make do without single-seat fighter escort. This situation pales into insignificance when compared with the lot of *Luftflotte* 5, whose planes were flying in from bases in Scandinavia, the distance precluding single-seat fighter escort altogether and demanding the use of Bf 110s.

From the end of September until mid-November 1940, as many as 400 German bombers attacked British cities every night. The destruction visited upon Britain during this time, and in the subsequent bombing through to May 1941, was profound. Not only was there an enormous level of destruction, but more than 60,000 civilians were killed, one million injured, and some 250,000 children had to go through the trauma of evacuation to the countryside. Raiding at night presented major navigation problems for the *Luftwaffe* crews. To give assistance, the *Luftwaffe* communications units over on mainland Europe used three different radio 'beam riding' systems to help guide the aircraft to the target and also give the signal at the right moment for bomb release. Each of these three systems – *Knickebein*, *X-Gerät* and *Y-Gerät* – was progressively more

LUFTLOTTE 3 (7 SEPT 1940)

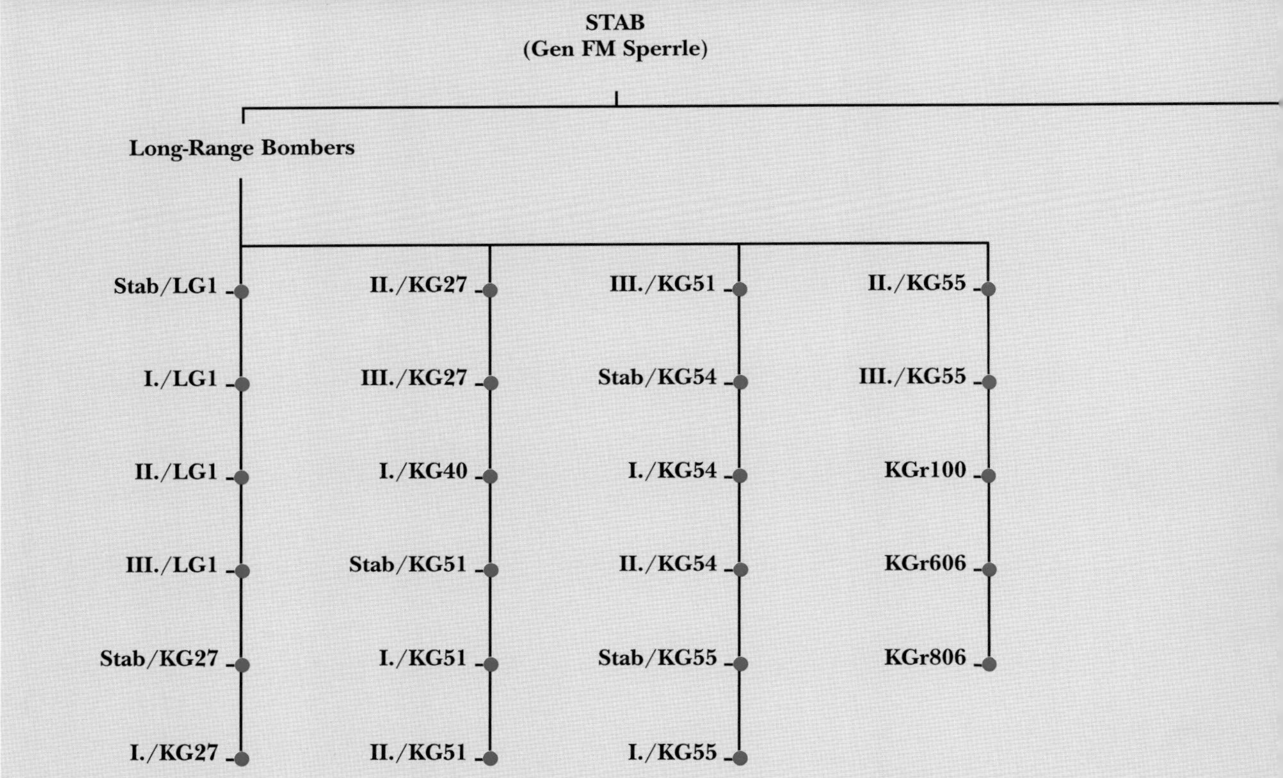

STAB
(Gen FM Sperrle)

Long-Range Bombers

Stab/LG1	II./KG27	III./KG51	II./KG55
I./LG1	III./KG27	Stab/KG54	III./KG55
II./LG1	I./KG40	I./KG54	KGr100
III./LG1	Stab/KG51	II./KG54	KGr606
Stab/KG27	I./KG51	Stab/KG55	KGr806
I./KG27	II./KG51	I./KG55	

Luftflotte 3 contained several bomber *Geschwader*, although KG55 was probably the most famous of them all. Equipped with the Heinkel He 111, the unit suffered heavily during the Battle of Britain and Blitz, losing over 70 aircraft in the period July–October 1940.

sophisticated than the former, but they never quite overcame the problems of British radio jamming, and German night-time navigation remained precarious for the duration of the Blitz.

Furthermore, as the Allies themselves would discover as the war went on, night-time bombing accuracy was also woeful. Although at this stage of the war the *Luftwaffe* would defend itself against accusations of

deliberately targeting civilians, civilian targets were inevitably hit when dropping bombs at night, in skies punctured by the further confusion of anti-aircraft fire and barrage balloons.

Night raids – First phase
The raids themselves can be divided into three relatively distinct phases, each with its own effects and

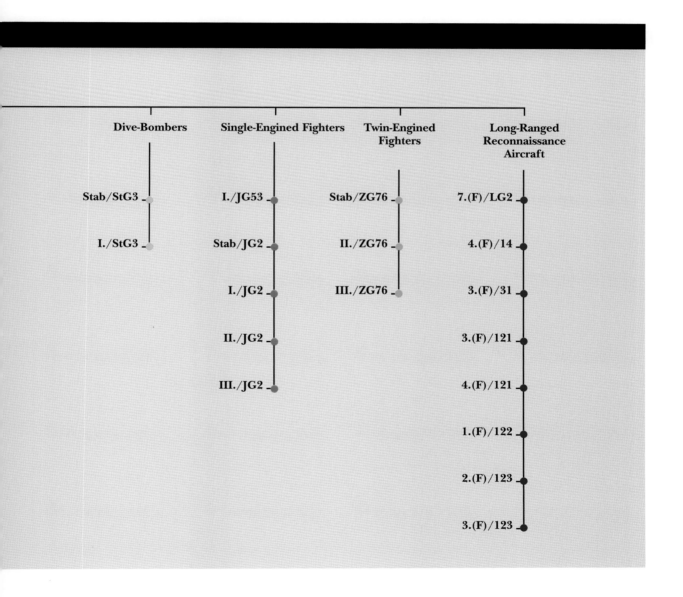

Dive-Bombers	Single-Engined Fighters	Twin-Engined Fighters	Long-Ranged Reconnaissance Aircraft
Stab/StG3	I./JG53	Stab/ZG76	7.(F)/LG2
I./StG3	Stab/JG2	II./ZG76	4.(F)/14
	I./JG2	III./ZG76	3.(F)/31
	II./JG2		3.(F)/121
	III./JG2		4.(F)/121
			1.(F)/122
			2.(F)/123
			3.(F)/123

I./KG2 (SEPTEMBER 1940)

Kampfgeschwader 2 was formed on 1 May 1939, its first commander being Oberst Johannes Fink, followed by Oberst Herbert Rieckhoff from October 1940. Throughout the war it flew primarily Dorniers, mainly the Do 17 and the Do 217, although some units also flew Ju 88s and even (in V.*Gruppe*) the Me 410. During the Battle of Britain, the commander of I./KG2 was Major Waldemar Lerche. The *Gruppe* stayed in Western Europe for the duration of the war, unlike some of other KG2 *Gruppen*, which found themselves on the Eastern Front.

Nominal strength – 28 x Do 17Zs

consequences. The first phase ran from the beginning of the daylight bombing campaign against London and other cities, roughly the end of the first week of September, until November 1940. At one point, London alone was hit by bombing raids every day except one for a whole month.

The raids switched between night and daylight attacks, and the targets included Birmingham and Bristol as well as the capital. Numbers of bombers used in the raids were heavy – in one attack on London on 15 October more than 400 bombers were sent in, and remarkably only two of them were shot down. (At this stage of the war, not only was Fighter Command in a recovery stage and adjusting to the night war, but London was also restructuring its anti-aircraft defences.)

In fact, the *Luftwaffe* was incurring perfectly sustainable losses for the delivery of major destruction on the British way of life. In October 1940, out of a total bomber force of 1420 aircraft, the *Luftwaffe* lost only

UNIT STRENGTH – *LUFTFLOTTE* 3 (SEPT 1940)				
Luftwaffe Unit	**Base**	**Type**	**Str**	**Op**
TWIN-ENGINED FIGHTERS				
Stab/ZG76	–	Bf 110	4	2
II./ZG76	Le Mans/Abbeville	Bf 110	27	11
III./ZG76	Laval	Bf 110	19	8
LONG-RANGE RECONNAISSANCE AIRCRAFT				
7.(F)/LG 2	–	Bf 110	14	9
4.(F)/14	Normandy	Bf 110 Do 17	12	9
3.(F)/31	St Brieuc	Bf 110 Do 17	9	5
3.(F)/121	Northwest France	Ju 88A He 111	10	6
4.(F)/121	Normandy	Ju 88A Do 17	13	5
1.(F)/122	near Paris	Ju 88A Do 17	10	7
2.(F)/123	near Paris	Ju 88A Do 17	10	8
3.(F)/123	Buc	Ju 88A Do 17	12	9

UNIT STRENGTH – *LUFTFLOTTE* 3 (SEPT 1940)				
Luftwaffe Unit	**Base**	**Type**	**Str**	**Op**
LONG-RANGE BOMBERS				
Stab/LG1	Orléans-Bricy	Ju 88A	2	2
I./LG1	Orléans-Bricy	Ju 88A	27	13
II./LG1	Orléans-Bricy	Ju 88A	31	19
III./LG1	Chateaudun	Ju 88A	30	9
Stab/KG27	Tours	He 111	5	4
I./KG27	Tours	He 111	35	13
II./KG27	Dinard-Bourges	He 111	32	15
III./KG27	Rennes	He 111	20	13
I./KG40	Bordeaux	Fw 200	7	4
Stab/KG51	Paris-Orly	Ju 88A	1	–
I./KG51	Melun-Villaroche	Ju 88A	33	13
II./KG51	Paris-Orly	Ju 88A	34	17
III./KG51	Etampes-Mondésir	Ju 88A	34	27
Stab/KG54	Evreux	Ju 88A	1	–
I./KG54	Evreux	Ju 88A	30	18
II./KG54	St André	Ju 88A	26	14
Stab/KG55	Villacoublay	He 111	6	6
I./KG55	Dreux	He 111	27	20
II./KG55	Chartres	He 111	30	22
III./KG55	Villacoublay	He 111	25	20
KGr100	Vannes	He 111H	28	7
KGr606	Brest/Cherbourg	Do 17	33	29
KGr806	Nantes/ Caen-Carpiquet	Ju 88A	27	18
DIVE-BOMBERS				
Stab/StG3	Brittany	Ju 87 Do 17	7	6
I./StG3	Brittany	Ju 87	37	34
SINGLE-ENGINED FIGHTERS				
I./JG53	Rennes	Bf 109E	34	27
Stab/JG2	Beaumont-le-Roger	Bf 109E	4	3
I./JG2	Beaumont-le-Roger	Bf 109E	29	24
II./JG2	Beaumont-le-Roger	Bf 109E	22	18
III./JG2	Le Havre	Bf 109E	30	19

64 planes to enemy action (plus 107 to other causes, principally accidents). The following month the figures were even better – only 14 aircraft shot down out of a total of 84 losses to all causes.

Gradually the bombing campaign shifted to night-time operations only, but that is not to say that the fighters were not playing their part. At the end of September, every *Jagdgeschwader* had converted one-third of its aircraft and pilots into a fighter-bomber role, these making hit-and-run raids across the Channel against precision targets, delivering their single 250kg (551lb) bombs. These 'Free Chase' sorties kept the RAF fighters busy, while the *Luftwaffe* fighter pilots achieved some audacious bomb strikes on key industrial targets.

Wider campaign

The strategic bombing campaign seemed to be paying off. In November, Göring decided to widen the campaign even further, to attack more cities across the United Kingdom, while maintaining the pressure on London. The targets included Coventry, Southampton, Birmingham, Bristol, Liverpool, Clydebank, Plymouth, Cardiff, Manchester, Sheffield, Swansea, Portsmouth and Avonmouth. The destruction visited on the provinces grew to a devastating level. For example, on 14/15 November, the He 111s of KG100 dropped 1000 incendiary bombs over Coventry, the resultant fires enabling some 450 other bombers to hone in on the city and drop their high-explosive cargoes. Two days later, Birmingham was attacked on a similar scale. At the end of December, a massive attack on London, once again using the thermite-charged incendiaries, turned large parts of the capital into an inferno.

This second phase of the Blitz ran until February 1941. Yet though it was apparently a success for the Germans, it was breaking neither civilian morale nor Britain's industrial capacity. The campaign was, if anything, proving that Germany's strategic bombing campaign could run on indefinitely without achieving its final goals.

Bombing the ports

In the final phase of the Blitz, from February to May 1941, the *Luftwaffe* bombers switched their main efforts to British port cities, responding to *Kriegsmarine* requests for support in the Battle of the Atlantic. During this time, only seven raids were directed at London and other inland cities.

End of the Blitz

Yet despite some intense raids around the coasts, the Blitz was drawing to a close, for several reasons. First, the *Luftwaffe*'s losses were once again mounting. The British were now putting up more effective anti-aircraft fire, frequently using radar-controlled gun laying (searchlights were also connected to radar to enhance target acquisition), and the radar-equipped night-fighters such as the Bristol Beaufighter were causing havoc. Hence while only 28 aircraft were shot down in January, 124 were shot down in May.

Even more important, however, was the fact that Germany was now preparing to invade the Soviet Union. The campaign in the East would open up an unquenchable thirst for Germany's resources, and many aircraft were soon diverted to that theatre. Although *Luftwaffe* bombers would periodically revisit Britain again throughout the war, and V-weapon attacks came in 1944, the *Luftwaffe*'s strategic campaign against Britain had essentially failed.

September 1940–May 1941

This map of the bombing campaign against Britain between September 1940 and May 1941 shows that between the three *Luftflotten* there was no corner of the United Kingdom that the *Luftwaffe* could not reach.

During the attacks on coastal cities in February–May 1941, for example, even Belfast in Northern Ireland was struck, as well as several other ports down the eastern Irish coastline. Targets in the north of England, such as Liverpool, Hull and Sheffield, were the responsibility of *Luftflotte* 2, while *Luftflotte* 5 could attack targets as far north as Glasgow, in addition to its maritime role of interdicting North Sea naval traffic.

Yet although the bombing raids were undeniably destructive, they were also incapable of delivering knock-out blows. Once *Luftwaffe* casualties began to mount again in 1941, furthermore, the raids became an unsustainable diversion from operations to the east.

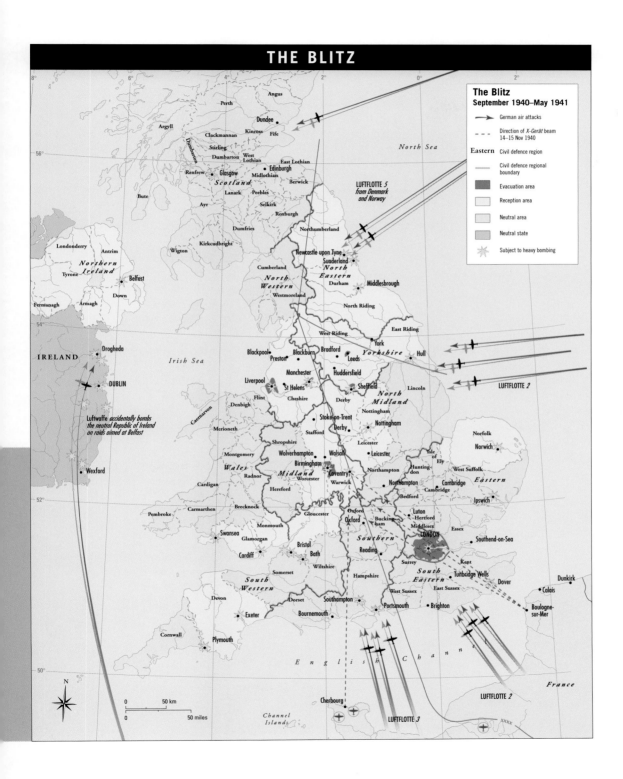

THE BLITZ

The Blitz
September 1940–May 1941

↗ German air attacks

- - - Direction of X-Gerät beam 14–15 Nov 1940

Eastern Civil defence region

Civil defence regional boundary

Evacuation area

Reception area

Neutral area

Neutral state

✳ Subject to heavy bombing

Luftwaffe accidentally bombs the neutral Republic of Ireland on raids aimed at Belfast

LUFTFLOTTE 5 from Denmark and Norway

LUFTFLOTTE 2

LUFTFLOTTE 2

LUFTFLOTTE 3

North Africa and the Mediterranean: 1941–45

The Mediterranean theatre would see the *Luftwaffe* struggling in a dramatic war of attrition and logistics in North Africa, and also witnessed the last major airborne deployment of the war.

Luftwaffe ground crew load a reconnaissance camera into a Bf 110 in North Africa.

The Mediterranean theatre (North Africa, Sicily and Italy) and the Balkans have a curious status in terms of the overall strategic drama of World War II. As the war developed, Hitler's Germany would be crushed between the hammer of the Soviet advance from the east, and the anvil of the US, British and Allied onslaught from the west. By contrast, little was strategically decided in the Mediterranean theatre, apart from the fates of individual armies. By 1945, the Allied attempt to push through to mainland Europe from the 'soft underbelly' of Italy, itself a stepping stone following victory in North Africa, had not been altogether successful, and was expending huge volumes of soldiers' blood for slow territorial gain. The war ended with both sides still locked into the rugged Italian landscape.

Nevertheless, what the Mediterranean did achieve for the Allies was the tying down of huge quantities of resources that would have served Germany better elsewhere. This included, for a time, the *Luftwaffe*. While the initial German Air Force commitments to North Africa in 1941 were the bare minimum required, as the war in the Western Desert escalated, the *Luftwaffe* was forced to pour increasing resources into the region. Not only did these take part in direct action against Allied land armies, but they also focused their attention on the island of Malta, a major RAF and Royal Navy base that came in for one of the most geographically focused and intense bombing campaigns of the entire war.

The *Luftwaffe* also came to have an integral role in the German occupation of the Balkans between March and May 1941. This campaign included one of the greatest single *Luftwaffe* operations of the entire war, the airborne invasion of Crete. The action achieved renown both for the scale of the deployment and for its eventual success in capturing Crete from the British. Nevertheless, the sheer volume of losses incurred in the operation meant that Hitler would never again launch a major parachute/airborne deployment during the entire war (see the next chapter for more detailed explanations). The Geman *Fallschirmjäger* would thereafter be almost exclusively confined to ground operations, although they would go on to distinguish themselves as regular infantry on both the Eastern and Western Fronts, and in the epic battles in central Italy around Monte Cassino.

Looking specifically at North Africa, we find the *Luftwaffe* building up general air superiority over the Western Desert and over the sea lanes across the centre of the Mediterranean Sea, but then steadily losing the advantage as Allied increases in naval and air power, plus successes on land, led to unsustainable losses in the air, a reduction in available fuel and aircraft, and the abandonment of key airbases.

Long campaign

A brief overview of the war in the Mediterranean is useful for context. In December 1940, the British in North Africa launched a lightning campaign against Italian forces in Libya. The success of this venture forced German intervention: the deployment of German units in the theatre, beginning in February 1941, commanded by the legendary *Generalmajor* Erwin Rommel. There now began a yo-yo movement of armies across North Africa, each side experiencing both long advances and long retreats, but leading to a culminating battle at El Alamein in November 1942, when the tide finally turned decisively in the Allies' favour.

The German-Italian army was subsequently pushed all the way back into Tunisia, where it was eventually squeezed out of Africa by the British advance from the east and a combined British and American offensive that began to the west with the Operation *Torch* landings in Morocco and Algeria in November 1942.

Germany's Mediterranean forces were now centred in Italy and Sicily, but the subsequent successful Allied invasion of Sicily in July 1943, then the landings in mainland Italy the following September, led to their steady retreat up through Italy's mountainous interior, although at enormous cost to the advancing Allies. The conflict ground on until the very end of the war, with the surrender of German forces in Italy coming only on 29 April 1945.

By 1945, the *Luftwaffe* in Italy was almost non-existent. From 1944, its dwindling resources were far more vital for the defence of the *Reich* against the Allied bomber campaign and the twin land advances from east and west. The Mediterranean had not been the most important of the war's theatres, but for the individual pilots who fought there the combat was as unforgiving as anywhere else on the conflict map.

The *Luftwaffe* in the Mediterranean

The *Luftwaffe* went through a steady period of expansion in its deployments to the Mediterranean, beginning with the transfer of X.*Fliegerkorps* to the theatre, which ultimately came under the control of a relocated *Luftflotte* 2.

In December 1940, at the time of General Archibald Wavell's opening campaign (Operation *Compass*) against the Italians in Egypt, the *Luftwaffe* strength in the Mediterreanean theatre was negligible. A *Luftwaffe* liaison with the Italian Air Force had been established back in June 1940, but this principally served in a minor transport role rather than performing combat duties. (German transport aircraft, for example, had been used to deploy Italian forces into Albania.) With Allied successes, however, it quickly became evident that alongside German land forces deployments under Rommel in February/March 1941, there would need to be a corresponding expansion in regional air power.

The first major *Luftwaffe* combat deployment into the region came in the form of X.*Fliegerkorps*. The units of the formation had been previously operating in

Denmark and Norway, where they gained experience in anti-shipping warfare that would be vital in the Mediterranean theatre. At the beginning of 1941,

UNIT STRENGTH – *X.FLIEGERKORPS* (12 JANUARY 1941)				
Luftwaffe Unit	**Base**	**Type**	**Str**	**Op**
X.FLIEGERKORPS				
Stab/LG1	Catania	Ju 88A-4	4	2
II./LG1	Catania	Ju 88A-4	38	38
III./LG1	Catania	Ju 88A-4	38	38
II./KG26	Comiso	He 111H-3	37	29
4./KG4	Comiso	He 111H-3	12	12
1.(F)/121	Catania	Ju 88D-1	12	2
III./ZG26	Palermo	Bf 110D-3	34	16
Stab/StG3	Trapani	Ju 87R-1	9	8
I./StG1	Trapani	Ju 87R-1	35	11
II./StG2	Trapani	Ju 87R-1	36	23

UNIT STRENGTH – *X.FLIEGERKORPS* (12 JANUARY 1941)				
Luftwaffe Unit	**Base**	**Type**	**Str**	**Op**
X.FLIEGERKORPS				
1.(F)/121	Catania	Ju 88D-1	15	9
2.(F)/123	Catania	Ju 88D-1	14	7
7./JG26	Gela	Bf 109E-7	14	11
I./JG27	Gela	Bf 109E-7	39	35
I./NJG3	Gela	Bf 110E-3	7	4
III./ZG26	North Africa	Bf 110D-3	33	25
9./ZG26	Sicily	Bf 110D-3	15	11
Stab/LG1	Catania	Ju 88A-4	1	1
II./LG1	Catania	Ju 88A-4	26	20
III./LG1	Catania	Ju 88A-4	40	11
4./KG4	Comiso	He 111H-3	12	2
II./KG26	Comiso	He 111H-3	36	19
III./KG30	Sicily	Ju88A-4/T	27	24
Stab/StG1	Sicily	Ju 87B-1	12	7
I./StG1	North Africa	Ju 87B-1	30	22
II./StG1	Sicily	Ju 87B-1	42	27
III./StG1	Sicily	Ju 87B-1	37	18
I./StG2	North Africa	Ju 87B-1	38	33
Stab/StG3	Trapani	Ju 87B-1	5	2
III./KG zbV1	Sicily	Ju 52/3m	48	32
KGr zbV9	Sicily	Ju 52/3m	29	28

X.*Fliegerkorps* had a total force of some 300 aircraft, but rapidly expanding commitments in the area drove that number up to 450 within a month. By the mid-point of 1941, the formation had approaching 550 aircraft, although not all of those were in an immediately serviceable condition.

The bulk of X.*Fliegerkorps*'s aircraft were medium bombers and transport aircraft. In June 1941, JG27 provided Bf 109 escorts and ZG26 flew Bf 110s (principally in the fighter-bomber role), but most of the other units operated Ju 88s, He 111s and Ju 52s; there was also a *Stab* and single *Gruppe* of Ju 87s. This composition indicates the priority of bombing operations against ports and shipping in Mediterranean waters, and the draw of fighter resources, for a time at least, towards the Eastern Front.

Luftflotte 2 arrives

As the scale of the fighting intensified across the Mediterranean during 1941, it became evident that a larger *Luftwaffe* presence was required to keep its commitments. In November 1941, *Luftflotte* 2 was transferred into the theatre, even though it had previously been supporting the critical push of German forces on Moscow. (*Luftflotte* 3 had been left as the principal formation guarding France.) X.*Fliegerkorps* and its associated units now came under this major umbrella organization. As we shall see in greater depth below, the shifting of *Luftflotte* 2 to the Mediterranean at such a critical time raised some eyebrows, and also shows that the North African theatre was not entirely sidelined by events much further north.

UNIT STRENGTH – *X.FLIEGERKORPS* (5 APRIL 1941)				
Luftwaffe Unit	Base	Type	Str	Op
X.FLIEGERKORPS				
1.(F)/121	Catania	Ju 88D-1	14	6
2.(F)/123	Catania	Ju 88D-1	14	4
7./JG26	Sicily	Bf 109E-7	14	10
I./NJG3	Gela	Bf 110E-3	7	4
III./ZG26	Sicily/North Africa	Bf 110D-3	48	40
II./LG1	Catania	Ju 88A-4	30	17
III./LG1	Catania	Ju 88A-4	36	19
2./KG4	Comiso	He 111H-3	12	7
II./KG26	Comiso	He 111H-3	36	20
III./KG30	Sicily	Ju88A-4/T	26	20
Stab/StG1	North Africa	Ju 87B-1	12	10
II./StG1	Sicily	Ju 87B-1	36	16
III./StG1	North Africa	Ju 87B-1	39	29
II./StG2	North Africa	Ju 87B-1	33	23
III./KG zbV1	Sicily	Ju 52/3m	47	31
KGr zbV9	Sicily	Ju 52/3m	28	28

The deployment of *Luftflotte* 2 gave Rommel enhanced anti-shipping, ground-attack and supply capabilities, the latter extremely important in a theatre where land supply lines were stretched to the extreme across a formidably barren landscape. *Luftflotte* 2 would remain in the Mediterranean for the rest of the war, its pilots, aircraft and ground crew guarding an eventually shrinking perimeter.

North Africa 1941–42

The North African theatre's greatest challenge to the armies that fought there was logistical. Unless the supplies of fuel and ammunition could be kept flowing from the North African ports, both the *Luftwaffe* and *Heer* were in danger of grinding to a halt.

On 24 March 1941, Rommel struck eastwards in his first major offensive through the Libyan desert. It proved to be enormously successful: he had reached the Halfaya

Pass by 25 April. Two major Allied offensives, *Brevity* on 15 May and *Battleaxe* on 15 June, failed to make a serious dent in the German line, but the *Crusader*

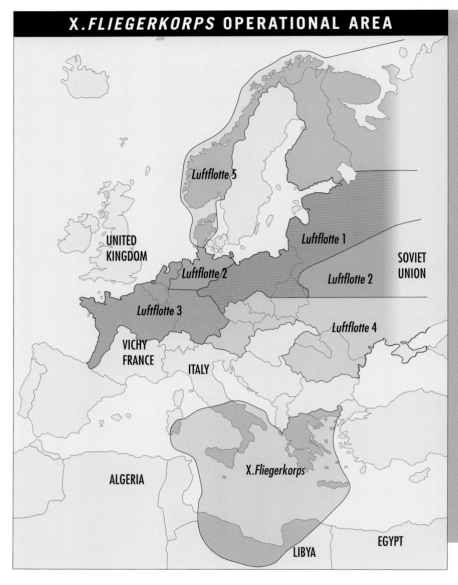

X.*FLIEGERKORPS* OPERATIONAL AREA

Luftflotte 5

Luftflotte 1

UNITED
KINGDOM

Luftflotte 2

Luftflotte 2

SOVIET
UNION

Luftflotte 3

Luftflotte 4

VICHY
FRANCE

ITALY

X.*Fliegerkorps*

ALGERIA

LIBYA

EGYPT

June 1941

X.*Fliegerkorps*, under *General der Flieger* Hans Geisler, commanding general of the formation since October 1939, was moved down from Norway and Denmark by the beginning of January 1941, being first based in Sicily. From its island headquarters, and from later bases on the North African mainland itself, its operational radius covered all of southern Italy and Sicily, the Balkans and coastal North Africa.

X.*Fliegerkorps*' jurisdiction also incorporated the area of sea between these territories, and the formation therefore was well placed to interdict Allied naval traffic fuelling the war effort in North Africa and Malta. Indeed, not long after the formation's arrival in the Mediterranean, dive-bombers of II./StG2 almost sank the carrier HMS *Illustrious*, escorting a convoy bound for Egypt. X.*Fliegerkorps*' operational area also meant that its resources would be used in the German invasion of Crete in May 1941.

By this point in the war, the main thrust of German air power was being directed towards the invasion of the Soviet Union.

onslaught of 18 November was a different matter. By 6 January 1942, Rommel was back at his start line around El Agheila.

In one of the dizzying reversals for which the Western Desert campaign is known, Rommel was once again on the advance by the end of January, and he did not stop until the end of June, by which time the Allies were pushed back into Egypt around El Alamein.

Luftwaffe support

Direct *Luftwaffe* support for the North African campaign came from X.*Fliegerkorps* for most of 1941, particularly the subsidiary unit *Fliegerführer Afrika*. This unit was stationed on Libyan airbases, and flew a mix of Bf 110s, Bf 109s, Ju 88s, Ju 87s and some Hs 126s. The mixture of aircraft types provided the complete ground-attack and fighter portfolio necessary to support Rommel's offensive and defensive actions. The importance of *Fliegerführer Afrika* was recognized in April 1941, when the unit received reinforcements of 50 Bf 109E-7/Trop fighters from I./JG27 and 7./JG26. (The 'Trop' suffix indicated that the aircraft were tropicalized.)

Fuel wars

Meanwhile, the rest of the German air assets in the region, which consisted of *Luftflotte* 2 from November 1941, waged war on the Allied shipping pouring supplies into open North African ports, and the Allies did likewise against Axis shipping from Italy. The major problem for Rommel was that the Allied interdiction of German shipping to ports such as Tripoli, Benghazi and Tobruk, plus the incredible length of travel from the ports to the front lines (land convoys were themselves prey to Allied air attacks), meant that fuel supplies for aircraft and armour often ran critically short.

By the beginning of 1941, *Luftwaffe* fuel shortages meant only 100 sorties a day could be flown in the Mediterranean. The deployment of *Luftflotte* 2 relieved this situation for a time. The *Luftflotte* contained over 650 aircraft in total, and hence was better able to protect convoys (land and maritime) while also inflicting greater punishment on Allied air power.

UNIT STRENGTH – *LUFTFLOTTE* 2 (17 JANUARY 1942)				
Luftwaffe Unit	Base	Type	Str	Op
X.FLIEGERKORPS				
2.(F)/123	Greece/Crete	Ju 88D-1	10	4
Jagd Staffel	Eleusis (Athens)	Bf 109F-2	10	4
1./JG53	Greece/Crete	Bf 109F-4	7	5
2./NJG2	Greece	Ju 88C-6	4	2
I./LG1	Greece/Crete	Ju 88A-4	27	13
II./LG1	Greece/Crete	Ju 88A-4	27	11
III./LG1	Greece/Crete	Ju 88A-4	12	3
2./SAGr125	Greece/Crete	Ar 196A-3	9	9
Stab/SAGr126	Greece/Crete	He 114	4	2
1./SAGr126	Greece/Crete	He 60C	13	3
2./SAGr126	Greece/Crete	He 60C	7	6
3./SAGr126	Greece/Crete	He 60C	10	5

UNIT STRENGTH – *LUFTFLOTTE* 2 (17 JANUARY 1942)				
Luftwaffe Unit	Base	Type	Str	Op
LUFTFLOTTE 2				
III./KG zbV1	–	Ju 52/3m	42	25
KGr zbV400	–	Ju 52/3m	40	26
TrGr111	–	Ju 52/3m	24	8
FLIEGERFÜHRER AFRIKA				
2.(H)/14	Libya	Bf 110C-4	16	3
1.(F)/121	Greece/Libya	Ju 88D-1	8	3
Stab/JG27	Libya/Egypt	Bf 109F-4	3	2
I./JG27	Libya/Egypt	Bf 109F-4	23	6
II./JG27	Libya/Egypt	Bf 109F-4	25	7
III./JG27	Libya/Egypt	Bf 109F-4	19	8
Jabo/JG53	Libya/Egypt	Bf109E-7/B	5	4
7./ZG26	Libya/Egypt	Bf 110D-3	8	4
Stab/StG3	Libya/Egypt	Ju 87D-1	4	2
I./StG3	Libya/Egypt	Ju 87D-1	24	23
II./StG3	Libya/Egypt	Ju 87D-1	29	20
Erg/StG1	Libya/Egypt	Ju 87D-1	12	8
II.FLIEGERKORPS				
1.(F)/122	Sicily	Ju 88D-1	10	7
Stab/JG53	Sicily	Bf 109F-4	6	6
I./JG53	Sicily	Bf 109F-4	34	21
II./JG53	Sicily	Bf 109F-4	37	25
I./NJG2	Sicily	Ju 88C-6	12	8
4./NJG2	Sicily	Ju 88C-6	5	3
III./ZG26	Sicily	Bf 110D-3	17	10
KüFlGr606	Sicily	Ju 88A-4	20	10
Stab/KG54	Sicily	Ju 88A-4	1	1
I./KG54	Sicily	Ju 88A-4	12	7
II./KG26	Sicily	He 111H-6	30	10
7./KG26	Sicily	He 111H-6	6	0
KüFlGr806	Sicily	Ju 88A-4	17	6
II./KG77	Sicily	Ju 88A-4	20	12
III./KG77	Sicily	Ju 88A-4	16	13
II.Korps TrSta	Sicily	Ju 52/3m	16	12

Yet by the time Rommel reached El Alamein, it was becoming apparent that the Allies were steadily clawing back air supremacy, aided by the huge aircraft production output of the United States. In short, the Allies could sustain air losses better than the *Luftwaffe*, and as they took over the skies once again, already serious German fuel shortages intensified. The *Luftwaffe* was beginning to lose the air war over North Africa.

I./JG53 (JANUARY 1942)

Fighter cover was as critical over the North African theatre as elsewhere, and JG53 was an important component of that cover. In late 1941, much of the unit was transferred to Sicily for operations against Malta, although III. *Gruppe* was deployed to North Africa in November. With a pause in the campaign against Malta in late summer 1942, the three *Gruppen* were split up, I./JG53 going to the Eastern Front. In November 1942, however, the whole *Geschwader* was reunited on Sicily for further actions against Malta and subsequent operations over Tunisia and Sicily.

Nominal strength – 34 x Bf 109F4s

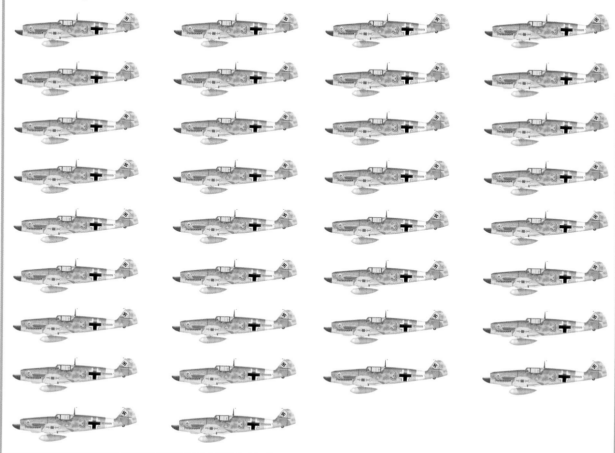

Operations against Malta

Malta was the thorn in the side of German forces in the Mediterranean theatre. Despite a pummelling *Luftwaffe* campaign against the tiny island, Malta was never entirely broken in either spirit or military capability.

Malta was critical to Allied operations in the Mediterranean. Not only did it provide a staging post for supply shipping in the region, but it also acted as a base from which RAF fighters could interdict German supply traffic heading for North Africa. For these reasons, Kesselring directed almost the full weight of *Luftflotte* 2 against the island from 2 April 1942.

The island subsequently endured one of the heaviest bombing campaigns in history. The *Luftwaffe* objectives were to destroy the tiny RAF contingent on the island; prevent Malta's resupply; and wreck the island's harbour facilities. The German high command had also

Air war in the Mediterranean, 1942

The map below clearly indicates the precarious position of Malta during the battles of 1942, sandwiched between German airbases of *Luftflotte* 2 scattered across North Africa, Sicily and the Balkans.

Once the Allies began to push German ground forces back westwards in North Africa, however, the airbases there were steadily lost, and were then used by Allied squadrons that progressively established air superiority across the Mediterranean.

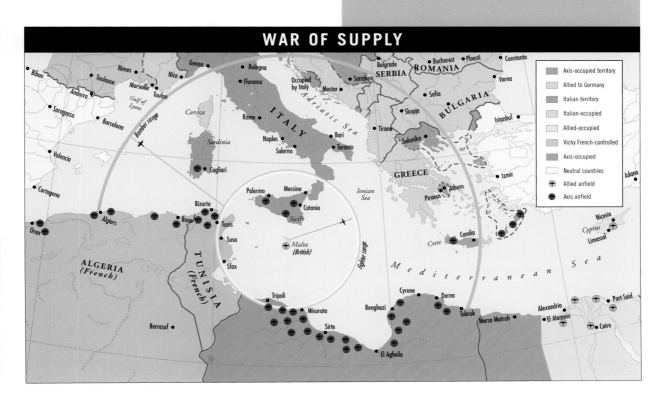

WAR OF SUPPLY

formulated Operation *Hercules*, the possible invasion of Malta using similar airborne tactics to those used in Operation *Mercury* against Crete.

Malta endured almost intolerable suffering, with less than 100 RAF fighters putting up around one dozen aircraft against each attack. Some 2000 German sorties had been delivered by 8 April, but even though the campaign ran until the end of 1942, the island was not totally incapacitated. It was a close-run matter, however. In August, for example, a major British supply convoy attempted to get through, and the massive *Luftwaffe* response resulted in the sinking of one aircraft carrier (HMS *Eagle*), two cruisers and seven merchant ships. Nonetheless, enough ships from the convoy did manage to get through to sustain the Maltese fight. The British managed to reinforce the fighter numbers by flying

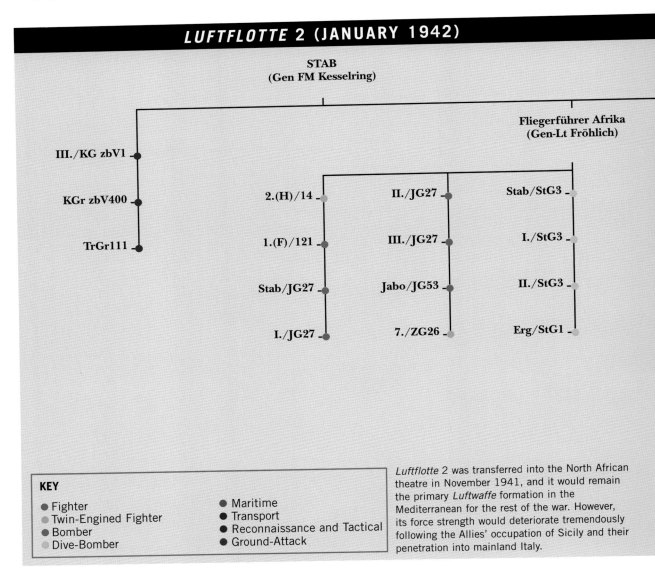

LUFTFLOTTE 2 (JANUARY 1942)

STAB
(Gen FM Kesselring)

Fliegerführer Afrika
(Gen-Lt Fröhlich)

III./KG zbV1

KGr zbV400

TrGr111

2.(H)/14

1.(F)/121

Stab/JG27

I./JG27

II./JG27

III./JG27

Jabo/JG53

7./ZG26

Stab/StG3

I./StG3

II./StG3

Erg/StG1

KEY

- Fighter
- Twin-Engined Fighter
- Bomber
- Dive-Bomber
- Maritime
- Transport
- Reconnaissance and Tactical
- Ground-Attack

Luftflotte 2 was transferred into the North African theatre in November 1941, and it would remain the primary *Luftwaffe* formation in the Mediterranean for the rest of the war. However, its force strength would deteriorate tremendously following the Allies' occupation of Sicily and their penetration into mainland Italy.

them in off nearby aircraft carriers. British anti-aircraft gunners also worked overtime, pumping up thousands of shells into the German formations.

The heroic efforts of the RAF and gunners on Malta slowly raised the number of *Luftflotte* 2 losses to unacceptable levels, these being compounded by losses suffered over North Africa. By the end of November, the offensive against Malta had effectively ceased, and the

RAF attrition on German supply convoys sailing from Italy went up commensurately. More than 30 per cent of such supply ships would end up sunk by Allied aircraft, surface vessels or submarines. The failure to subdue Malta played itself out in a similar way to the Battle of Britain, as the *Luftwaffe* found itself unable to sustain long-term losses and incapable of creating the prerequisite conditions for invasion.

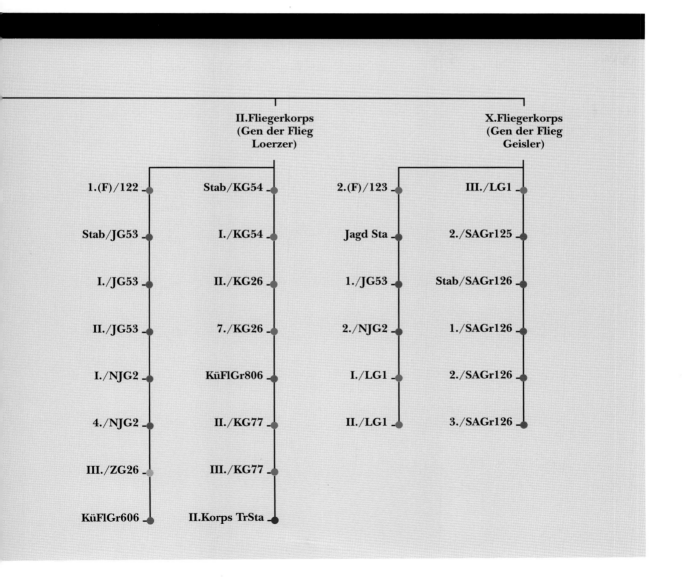

From El Alamein to Tunisia

The Allied success in the battle of El Alamein in November 1942 was the beginning of the end for German ambitions in North Africa. For the *Luftwaffe*, it also marked the start of a collapse in *Luftflotte* 2's power to influence events over the theatre, as more and more of its pilots and aircraft became victims of growing Allied air supremacy.

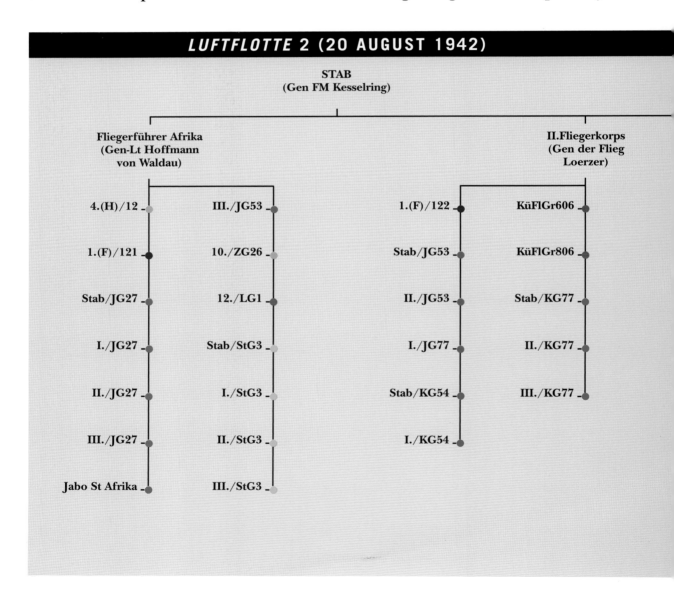

LUFTFLOTTE 2 (20 AUGUST 1942)

STAB
(Gen FM Kesselring)

Fliegerführer Afrika
(Gen-Lt Hoffmann
von Waldau)

II.Fliegerkorps
(Gen der Flieg
Loerzer)

4.(H)/12	III./JG53	1.(F)/122	KüFlGr606
1.(F)/121	10./ZG26	Stab/JG53	KüFlGr806
Stab/JG27	12./LG1	II./JG53	Stab/KG77
I./JG27	Stab/StG3	I./JG77	II./KG77
II./JG27	I./StG3	Stab/KG54	III./KG77
III./JG27	II./StG3	I./KG54	
Jabo St Afrika	III./StG3		

Prior to the defeat at El Alamein, the big gleam of light for the Germans came with the capture of Tobruk in June 1942. That success had netted the Germans 2032 tonnes (2000 tons) of fuel, enough to power both their land forces and the *Luftwaffe* into Egypt.

During the summer of 1942, furthermore, *Luftflotte* 2 had reached an impressive strength – nearly 800 aircraft of all types. A large number of these, however, were diverted for operations against the beleaguered island of Malta, where steadily the German numbers were thinned down by frenetic Allied resistance. Here was a critical factor in the subsequent fortunes of the *Luftwaffe* in the Mediterranean. The depredations of operating over Malta meant that when the storm of El Alamein broke over the Germans, there would be insufficient air resources to make a significant contribution to halting

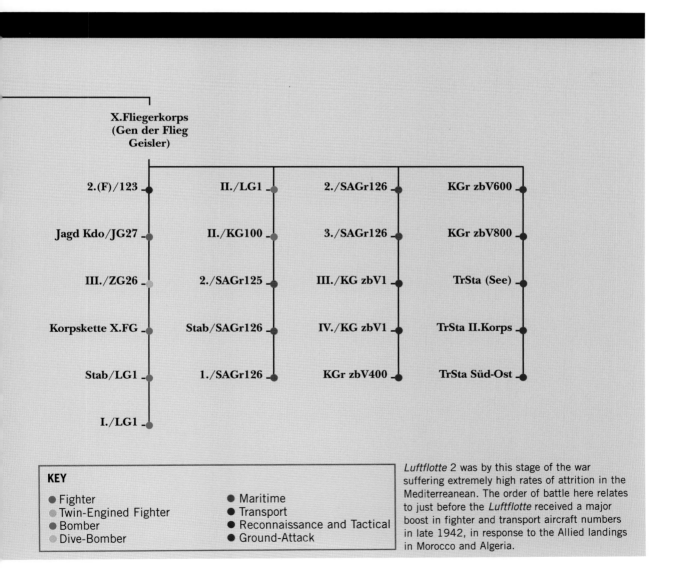

X.Fliegerkorps
(Gen der Flieg
Geisler)

2.(F)/123	II./LG1	2./SAGr126	KGr zbV600
Jagd Kdo/JG27	II./KG100	3./SAGr126	KGr zbV800
III./ZG26	2./SAGr125	III./KG zbV1	TrSta (See)
Korpskette X.FG	Stab/SAGr126	IV./KG zbV1	TrSta II.Korps
Stab/LG1	1./SAGr126	KGr zbV400	TrSta Süd-Ost
I./LG1			

KEY
- Fighter
- Twin-Engined Fighter
- Bomber
- Dive-Bomber
- Maritime
- Transport
- Reconnaissance and Tactical
- Ground-Attack

Luftflotte 2 was by this stage of the war suffering extremely high rates of attrition in the Mediterreanean. The order of battle here relates to just before the *Luftflotte* received a major boost in fighter and transport aircraft numbers in late 1942, in response to the Allied landings in Morocco and Algeria.

UNIT STRENGTH – *LUFTFLOTTE* 2 (20 AUGUST 1942)				
Luftwaffe Unit	Base	Type	Str	Op
FLIEGERFÜHRER AFRIKA				
4.(H)/12	Bie el Abd	Bf 110C-4	19	10
1.(F)/121	Fuka I./Derna	Ju 88D-1	12	4
Stab/JG27	Sanyet Quotaifiya	Bf 109F-4	2	2
I./JG27	Turbita	Bf 109F-4	23	18
II./JG27	Sanyet Quotaifiya	Bf 109F-4	24	10
III./JG27	Qasaba	Bf 109F-4	24	15
Jabo St Afrika	Haggag/Qasaba	Bf109F-4/B	12	6
III./JG53	Qasaba	Bf 109F-4	24	15
10./ZG26	Berca	Do 17Z-10	7	4
12./LG1	Berca	Ju88A-4/T	12	2
Stab/StG3	Qasaba	Ju 87D-1	7	3
I./StG3	Qasaba	Ju 87D-1	28	20
II./StG3	Qasaba	Ju 87D-1	36	21
III./StG3	Qasaba	Ju 87D-1	36	30
II.FLIEGERKORPS				
1.(F)/122	Catania	Ju 88D-1	16	7
Stab/JG53	Comiso	Bf 109F-4	3	2
II./JG53	Comiso	Bf 109F-4	34	25
I./JG77	Comiso	Bf 109F-4	23	10
Stab/KG54	Catania	Ju 88A-4	2	1
I./KG54	Gerbini	Ju 88A-4	27	8
KüFlGr606	Catania	Ju 88A-4	22	11
KüFlGr806	Catania	Ju 88A-4	24	12
Stab/KG77	Comiso	Ju 88A-4	2	1
II./KG77	Comiso	Ju 88A-4	19	13
III./KG77	Comiso	Ju 88A-4	20	7

UNIT STRENGTH – *LUFTFLOTTE* 2 (20 AUGUST 1942)				
Luftwaffe Unit	Base	Type	Str	Op
X.FLIEGERKORPS				
2.(F)/123	Skaramanga	Ju 88D-1	19	8
Jagd Kdo/JG27	Kastelli	Bf 109F-4	5	2
III./ZG26	Kastelli	Bf 110D-3	46	24
Korpskette X.FG	Kastelli	He 111H-2	5	4
Stab/LG1	Iraklion (Crete)	Ju 88A-4	2	2
I./LG1	Iraklion (Crete)	Ju 88A-4	28	11
II./LG1	Iraklion (Crete)	Ju 88A-4	36	13
II./KG100	Kalamaki	He 111H-6	28	18
2.SAGr125	Skaramanga	Ar 196A-3	11	9
Stab/SAGr126	Skaramanga	Bv 138C-1	1	1
1.SAGr126	Skaramanga	He 114	9	3
2.SAGr126	Skaramanga	He 114	9	3
3.SAGr126	Suda Bay	He 114	9	5
III./KG zbV1	–	Ju 52/3m	29	15
IV./KG zbV1	–	Ju 52/3m	39	27
KGr zbV400	–	Ju 52/3m	24	12
KGr zbV600	–	Ju 52/3m	38	29
KGr zbV800	–	Ju 52/3m	40	19
TrSta (See)	Phäleron	Bv 222	5	1
TrSta II.Korps	–	Ju 52/3m	11	7
TrSta Süd-Ost	–	Ju 52/3m	11	7

New front

The Allied air superiority, combined with a powerful land advance, had a critical effect on *Luftflotte* 2's operations. The ground forces lost almost all their close air support, particularly from Ju 87s. By mid-November, *Fliegerführer Afrika* was down to just 30 Stukas, and with only 30 serviceable Bf 109s the available escort was inadequate. Ground-support services for the aircraft were also collapsing through lack of supplies and the frequent need to abandon airbases.

Matters became worse for the ground forces but, in a sense, improved for the *Luftwaffe* on 8 November 1942. In Operation *Torch*, over 100,000 US and British soldiers landed along the coastline of Algeria and Morocco, and began an advance eastwards into Tunisia. With the

it. Yet the Allies were not having everything their own way in the air. North Africa was the making of many German fighter aces, such as Hans-Joachim Marseille, who in just three combat sorties in September 1942 shot down 17 enemy fighters. The simple equation was, however, that the Allies could find replacements more readily than the Germans. By the end of 1942, with German land forces in headlong retreat, the *Luftwaffe* had lost air supremacy.

Germans now fighting on two fronts in North Africa, Hitler finally responded to the seriousness of the situation, facing, as he was, his first major theatre defeat. Drawing aircraft off from Norway and even from the Eastern Front, Hitler boosted *Luftflotte* 2 to a peak strength of 1220 aircraft, the majority flying from bases on Sicily. A large percentage of the new aircraft were Ju 52s, over 300 in November alone, plus Me 323s and Go 242s. These flew in much-needed men (nearly 42,000 troops in November and December) and supplies to the crumbling ground forces, but the cost was punitive – 164 Ju 52s were shot down between November 1942 and January 1943.

Fliegerführer Tunisien

A new regional *Luftwaffe* formation was created in North Africa, named *Fliegerführer Tunisien* and commanded by *Generalmajor* Martin Harlinghausen. The purpose of this formation was to provide direct fighter and ground support for troops in the Tunisian theatre. A fighter unit taken from *Luftflotte* 4 helped boost fighter numbers significantly, and as the Allies struggled to develop their air facilities in western North Africa, the Germans once again enjoyed a position of power. This advantage was aided by the arrival in the theatre of a new aircraft, the Focke-Wulf Fw 190, which when it appeared was a class apart from the Allied fighters.

Yet the Allied build-up in air power was inexorable, and was just part of a combined land, sea and air campaign that by January 1943 had driven all German forces in North Africa back into a shrinking portion of Tunisia. *Luftwaffe* air losses once again began spiralling out of control. By May, when the surviving Germans were finally driven out of Africa, *Fliegerführer Tunisien* had less than 200 aircraft, and these fled to Sicily. Ju 52s were downed in horrifying numbers (177 in five weeks of April/May), often taking with them hundreds of German infantrymen.

In total, from the *Torch* landings to the moment that the last Germans left North Africa, 2422 German aircraft were lost. Just as crippling were the constant losses in pilots and other aircrew, and finding replacements (moreover, replacements who were adequately trained) was becoming a permanent anxiety. This, when combined with the failure of the *Luftwaffe* to resupply

HANS-JOACHIM MARSEILLE (1919–1942)

Born in 1919, Hans-Joachim Marseille was urbane, stylish and had an appreciation of the good life. He joined the *Luftwaffe* in 1938, and served during the Battle of Britain, although without gaining many kills.

• He arrived in Africa in April 1941, however, and developed radical dive and deflection-shooting tactics of great skill and daring. They paid off – Marseille scored 151 victories in North Africa, once shooting down 17 enemy aircraft in a single day.

• He was awarded the Knight's Cross with Oak Leaves, Swords and Diamonds. Marseille was killed on 30 September 1942 – not in combat but following an engine failure.

the German Sixth Army at Stalingrad, which fell to the Soviets in January 1943, meant that Göring's aviation force was undergoing unprecedented trauma. In the Mediterranean theatre, the focus now was on defending the island of Sicily, home to many key *Luftwaffe* airbases, and mainland Italy itself.

Italy and Sicily

By mid-1943, the war across all fronts was shifting against Germany. Squeezed out of North Africa, and in retreat after Stalingrad, the land forces were suffering horrendous casualties as the *Luftwaffe* attempted to throw up air defence with dwindling numbers.

For the operations carried out by *Luftflotte* 2 over the Mediterranean, Sicily was absolutely critical. Flying from bases at Catania, Comiso, Trapani and Gerbini, the *Luftwaffe* had used Sicily as a platform from which to project some measure of cover to land forces fighting in North Africa, and, more importantly, for striking at Malta and the Allied supply shipping that fuelled the campaign. Were Sicily to be lost, the entire balance of power in the region would shift irrevocably to the Allies, and their surge from North Africa into southern Europe would be unstoppable.

Reduced strength

As we have already seen, the fight for North Africa had resulted in a fundamental reduction in force strength for *Luftflotte* 2. Hitler, sensing the gathering storm in the Mediterranean, sought to bolster his power there with a massive transfer of fighter power, and a reorganization of the *Luftflotte*. During May and July 1943, the Mediterranean attracted a major share of new-production fighters from Germany's factories, plus fighter transfers from *Luftwaffe* units based in France – the German air campaign against Britain was all but over, apart from the launch of the notorious V-weapons later on in the war. By mid-July, there were 450 fighters in the theatre, an increase of 260 aircraft compared with just two months previously. Williamson Murray in *Strategy for Defeat* (Quantum, 2000) points out that 'Close to 40 percent of all fighter production from May 1 to July 15 went to the Mediterranean' (p. 124).

Balkan front

The war on multiple fronts stretched the German forces beyond capacity in most theatres, and the Mediterranean was no exception. Symptomatic of this was the fact that once Germany had been defeated in Tunisia, *Luftflotte* 2 was divided to accommodate new

UNIT STRENGTH – *LUFTFLOTTE* 2 (MAY 1944)				
Luftwaffe Unit	**Base**	**Type**	**Str**	**Op**
FIGHTERS				
I./JG4	Salzwedel	Bf 109	13	10
III./JG53	Arlena	Bf 109	17	13
Stab/JG77	Ferrara	Bf 109	4	3
I./JG77	Kirchhellen	Bf 109	21	10
II./JG77	Ferrara	Bf 109	52	39
TWIN-ENGINED FIGHTERS				
II./NJG6	Ghedi	Bf 110	13	11
RECONNAISSANCE AND TACTICAL AIRCRAFT				
Stab/LG1	Ghedi	Ju 88	1	1
I./LG1	Ghedi	Ju 88	20	17
II./LG1	Villafranca	Ju 88	21	17
2./AGr122	Bergamo	Me 410 Ju 88	8	4
1./AGr123	Bergamo	Ju 88	5	3
NKG11	Arlena	Bf 109	15	8
BOMBERS				
II./KG76	Aviano	Ju 88	25	13
GROUND-ATTACK AIRCRAFT				
Stab/SG4	Piacenza	Fw 190	3	2
I./SG4	Piacenza	Fw 190	14	4
II./SG4	Piacenza	Fw 190	27	9
NSG9	Tuscania	Ju 87 CR.42	37	23
MARITIME AIRCRAFT				
2./BF Gr.196	Venice	Ar 196	6	5
TRANSPORT				
II./TG1	Gallarate	SM.82	46	35

responsibilities in the Balkans. The Romanian oilfields were of central importance to German industry, while at the same time they were coming in for increased attention from Allied bombing missions. In response,

a small group of units were peeled off *Luftflotte* 2 to form *Luftwaffenkommando Süd-Ost* (Southeast), which had responsibility over all the Balkans and up into Eastern Europe, its northern border butting up against the

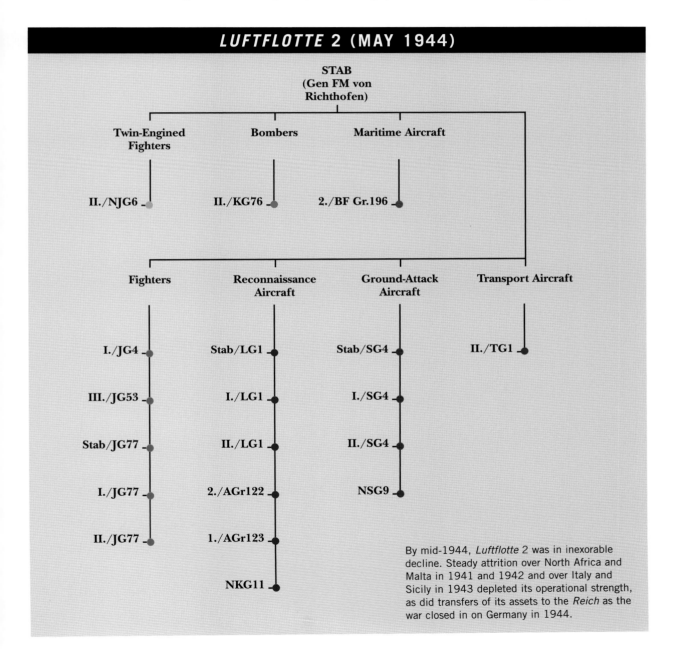

LUFTFLOTTE 2 (MAY 1944)

STAB
(Gen FM von Richthofen)

Twin-Engined Fighters — II./NJG6

Bombers — II./KG76

Maritime Aircraft — 2./BF Gr.196

Fighters: I./JG4, III./JG53, Stab/JG77, I./JG77, II./JG77

Reconnaissance Aircraft: Stab/LG1, I./LG1, II./LG1, 2./AGr122, 1./AGr123, NKG11

Ground-Attack Aircraft: Stab/SG4, I./SG4, II./SG4, NSG9

Transport Aircraft: II./TG1

By mid-1944, *Luftflotte* 2 was in inexorable decline. Steady attrition over North Africa and Malta in 1941 and 1942 and over Italy and Sicily in 1943 depleted its operational strength, as did transfers of its assets to the *Reich* as the war closed in on Germany in 1944.

Mediterranean theatre, 1943–45

Luftflotte 2 airbases in 1943–45 were concentrated throughout Sicily and mainland Italy, although many of these bases were of course lost as the Allies advanced progressively northwards. On Sicily, most of the airbases were arranged around the coastline, and at least three of these were lost in the initial landings of Operation *Husky*, the Allied invasion of the island in July 1943.

Furthermore, Allied engineers built nine airbases around Catania alone, overwhelming the German operating capability. On mainland Italy, the airbases were also scattered. There were concentrations around the Gulf of Taranto, and three airbases around Naples and Salerno caused some problems for Allied landings at the latter location on 9 September. There was a further cluster around Foggia in the east, but by the end of 1943, *Luftwaffe* strength in Italy was negligible.

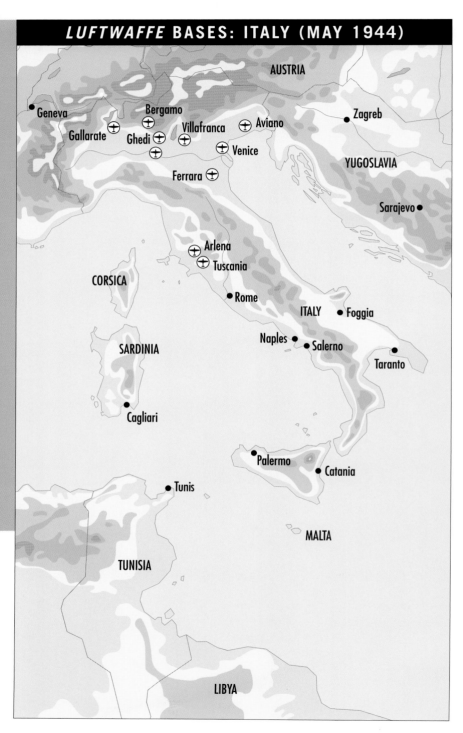

LUFTWAFFE BASES: ITALY (MAY 1944)

limits of *Luftflotte* 4's jurisdiction. *Luftwaffenkommando Süd-Ost* only had one *Gruppe* of fighters (I./JG4) in its ranks by May 1943, however, so its creation was not a serious depletion of *Luftflotte* 2's ranks.

Preparations

Once Tunisia was in Allied hands, Sicily was the next target, as agreed by the Allies at the Casablanca conference of January 1943. Although the *Luftwaffe* was now in force on the island, it was nevertheless completely dwarfed by the Allied air forces building up in the region. US aircraft output was prodigious, and in the numbers game the *Luftwaffe* would forever be the loser from now on.

The Allied invasion of Sicily, codenamed Operation *Husky*, was scheduled for 10 July 1943, and in the weeks leading up to that the *Luftwaffe* was faced with a furious air onslaught. Problems for the *Luftwaffe* were increased by the Allied capture of Pantelleria, an island 113km (70 miles) southwest of Sicily, in early June. Pantelleria provided the Allies with a advanced fighter base, meaning that its heavy bomber raids north would now benefit from a longer and deeper fighter escort. When combined with the increase in German fighter numbers, this situation resulted in a huge fighter battle over Sicily. There were grim casualties on both sides, but the Allies could afford them whereas the *Luftwaffe* could not. In June alone, 131 German fighters and 72 bombers were shot down. Under such conditions there was little that *Luftflotte* 2 could achieve as a strategic arm, and its bombers and fighter-bombers had almost no dependable escort – the fighters were struggling for their own survival.

Invasion

Operation *Husky* was launched as planned, and the scale of it was enormous – 160,000 men, 14,000 vehicles, 600 tanks and 1800 artillery guns, all put ashore by 2500 ships. The Allies also brought 4000 operational aircraft to the battle, against the 1600 aircraft remaining in *Luftflotte* 2. Allied aircraft flew combat missions around the clock to keep up pressure on the German aviators, and pounded the German airfields with relentless bombing. As an indication of the disparity in numbers, on the day of the landings, *Luftflotte* 2 managed to put up about 100 sorties, compared with the 1092 sorties flown by the Allies. In the month of July, *Luftflotte* 2 lost 711 aircraft, including 246 fighters. The Allied land campaign, although hard-contested, was equally irresistible, and by the second week of August the German land forces were evacuating to mainland Italy, with the surviving *Luftwaffe* pilots and machines soon joining them.

The soft underbelly

The defeat in Sicily set the tone for the Allied campaign in mainland Italy, which began with amphibious landings at Salerno on 9 September. On the ground, the Italian campaign was a hard, grinding slog through mountainous terrain, a battle that lasted until the end of April 1945. In the air, however, the Allies never saw their air superiority threatened by a much-depleted *Luftflotte* 2. Even in the preparatory phases to the landings, the *Luftflotte* lost 321 aircraft.

Nevertheless, in cooperation with land forces, the *Luftwaffe* was still able to make a major effort against the Salerno landings, with bombers and Fw 190 fighters attacking Allied shipping and landing craft. In one landmark attack, German bombers used Hs 293 and Fx 1400 'Fritz' guided bombs to attack Italian vessels, sinking the battleship *Roma* – this was history's first use of air-to-surface guided weapons in combat. Yet although substantial kills were inflicted upon the Allies, it was effectively the last gasp of the *Luftwaffe* in Italy. A *Luftflotte* 2 presence would remain until the end of the war, but the sheer weight of Allied air power in the theatre meant their operational relevance was negligible. B-17 and B-24 bombers delivered carpet-bombing missions against German airfields, and by the time of the later Allied landings at Anzio on 22 January 1944, there were about 270 German combat aircraft remaining in Italy, against an Allied air force of 2600 aircraft. Moreover, by this stage of the war the overwhelming priority in German air defence was in defending the *Reich* against the Allied strategic-bombing campaign. On account of this, most of the surviving *Luftflotte* 2 aircraft were withdrawn and sent back to Germany during 1943 and 1944. The Mediterranean skies, therefore, remained an Allied possession until the end of the war.

The Balkans and Greece: 1941–45

The German invasion of Yugoslavia and Greece in 1941 was a diversion from Hitler's principal focus on the Soviet Union. It was ultimately a questionable enterprise, one that some historians argue cost Hitler the war.

Men and materiel are dropped from a Ju 52 transport over Crete, May 1941.

The theory that the German invasion of Greece and Yugoslavia cost Hitler the entire war runs something as follows. The operations in the Balkans forced a delay in the German invasion of the Soviet Union. Had it not been for the Balkan 'interlude', the Germans would have been able to invade the Soviet Union during May 1941, instead of on the actual launch date of Operation *Barbarossa* – 22 June. Because of the delay, the German Army ground to a halt in a vicious Russian winter just short of Moscow in December 1941. If they had invaded in May, therefore, they could have utilized a few more weeks of good campaigning weather, advanced further, and probably taken Moscow before the end of the year. With Moscow fallen, Stalin's regime would have collapsed and Germany could have consolidated its grip over the Soviet Union, and effectively achieved all its war aims.

The theory is nice and neat, but closer consideration shows up many flaws. First, even had the Germans begun *Barbarossa* in May, there is no certainty that the earlier start date would have guaranteed the fall of Moscow – the city was powerfully defended, and even by October German supply lines were over-stretched. Second, even had the Germans grabbed Moscow, this does not equate with the fall of the Soviet Union. The vastness of the USSR would have allowed Stalin to pull his government back to the east, where there were also huge military reserves that could be used to launch a

counteroffensive. The Balkans adventure was certainly costly, but we should not ascribe Hitler's defeat to this strategic choice, which was but one amongst many poor command decisions.

Costly victories

For the *Luftwaffe*, the operations in the Balkans brought mixed results. The German Air Force undoubtedly helped secure the German victories in the region, but the use of bomber forces against cities such as Belgrade cemented a growing reputation of the *Luftwaffe* as a terror force for suppressing civilians. (In the light of later Allied bombing campaigns, such distinctions were soon meaningless.) The invasion of Crete in May 1941, however, also demonstrated that the *Luftwaffe* could almost single-handedly deliver a combined-arms operation through airborne assault troops, the *Fallschirmjäger*. Yet Crete was to be a truly Pyrrhic victory for the German paratroopers. The loss of some 7000 German soldiers during the operation shocked Hitler to the core, and led to his decision never to employ the *Fallschirmjäger* in such large-scale airborne actions ever again.

Following Crete, the principal job of the *Luftwaffe* in the Balkans was the increasingly bloody role of defending the vital Romanian oilfields against Allied air depredations, yet another theatre commitment that spread *Luftwaffe* resources ever thinner later in the war.

Yugoslavia and Greece, 1941

The *Luftwaffe* operations in Yugoslavia and Greece consisted of contrasting tactics. In Yugoslavia, the core element was a vicious punishment bombing of Belgrade, while in Greece the *Luftwaffe* performed its traditional support role.

The German involvement in the Balkans came about through Italian military failures. Mussolini, eager to stand out from under Hitler's victorious shadow, invaded Greece from Albania on 28 October 1940. After initial good progress, the Italian advance was then stalled and put into reverse by fanatical Greek

resistance, and by the end of November the Italians had actually been rolled back deep into Albania. It soon became apparent to Hitler that his hapless ally needed German intervention.

Hitler already had allies, albeit reluctant ones, in the Balkans. Both Hungary and Romania had signed pacts with Germany in the autumn of 1940, and as Germany prepared to invade Greece, Bulgaria also gave forced permission for Hitler to use the country as an invasion jumping-off point. Yet Bulgaria presented a narrow invasion front for the German land forces, so Yugoslavia's submission was also required. (The borders of northern Greece were shared almost equally by Albania, Yugoslavia and Bulgaria.) On 25 March 1941, Hitler forced Yugoslavia to sign up to the conditions of the Tripartite Pact (originally between Germany, Japan and Italy), but a coup the next day saw Prince Paul ousted by an anti-German alliance, which rejected the German authority. Hitler was incensed, and ordered Operation *Strafgericht* (Punishment) – the invasion of Yugoslavia – in retaliation. The plan included clear instructions to the *Luftwaffe*: 'Politically it is especially important that the blow against Yugoslavia is carried out with pitiless harshness ... The main task of the *Luftwaffe* is to destroy the capital city, Belgrade.'

The German air units used for the initial Balkans operations came primarily from *Luftflotte* 4. The *Luftflotte* was reinforced for the operation with substantial extra air assets from *Luftwaffe* bases as far away as France, taking its combat strength to more than 1000 aircraft. *Luftflotte* 4 was also arranged into several major *Fliegerkorps* and *Fliegerführer* subdivisions, these operating from airbases sited in Austria, Hungary and Bulgaria.

Objective Belgrade

The invasion of Yugoslavia began on 6 April 1941, as the *Wehrmacht* punched over the border with 33 divisions. *Luftwaffe* air superiority was absolute. In fact, such was the paucity of Yugoslavia's AA defence and its own air force that the previously vulnerable Ju 87 dive-bomber once again took a leading role as the spearhead of the German advance. In a matter of hours, the Yugoslav Air Force was effectively destroyed. Meanwhile, the *Luftwaffe* simultaneously devoted itself to destroying Belgrade. By

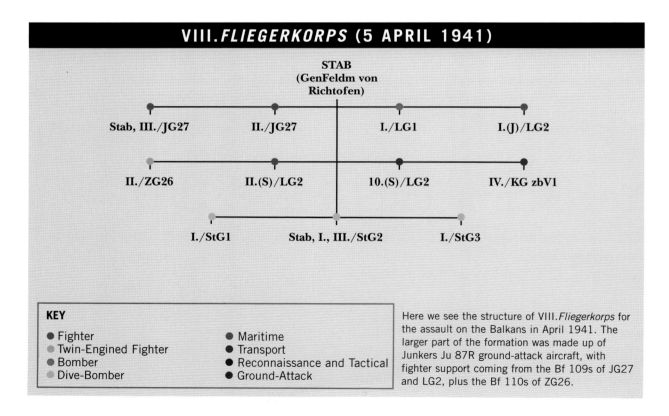

VIII.*FLIEGERKORPS* (5 APRIL 1941)

STAB
(GenFeldm von Richtofen)

Stab, III./JG27	II./JG27	I./LG1	I.(J)/LG2
II./ZG26	II.(S)/LG2	10.(S)/LG2	IV./KG zbV1
I./StG1	Stab, I., III./StG2	I./StG3	

KEY
- Fighter
- Twin-Engined Fighter
- Bomber
- Dive-Bomber
- Maritime
- Transport
- Reconnaissance and Tactical
- Ground-Attack

Here we see the structure of VIII.*Fliegerkorps* for the assault on the Balkans in April 1941. The larger part of the formation was made up of Junkers Ju 87R ground-attack aircraft, with fighter support coming from the Bf 109s of JG27 and LG2, plus the Bf 110s of ZG26.

06:00 on 6 April, the first strikes were going in, and over the next two days Belgrade would be reduced to a ruin. The attacking bombers at first concentrated on high-explosive attacks, then returned with the balance of munitions weighted towards incendiaries to get the city burning. By the end of 7 April, over 17,000 people in Belgrade had been killed.

Operation *Strafgericht* had done its work, and combined with decisive German land advances over the next week it rendered the outcome certain. Yugoslavia began peace overtures on 14 April and finally signed the surrender on 17 April.

Greece

At the same time as German forces were launching the invasion of Yugoslavia, XXX Corps was penetrating Thrace as the opening move of the German invasion of Greece. The Greek defence had been bolstered by a substantial British Army contingent numbering 62,000 men, and including some 200 British aircraft of various descriptions. However, throughout the campaign the RAF was hampered by a lack of suitable airbases. This restriction, combined with the deployment of several ageing aircraft types and the lack of a coherent Greek AA defence, led to the *Luftwaffe* quickly asserting air superiority as the German Second Army advanced southwards through Greece. The Second Army was soon joined by the the Twelfth Army once it had broken through Yugoslavia by the third week of April.

Air support

The *Luftwaffe* was central to German progress down through Greece. Because of its mountainous nature, Greece was a country ideally suited to defensive warfare. For this reason, the *Luftwaffe*'s contribution to the campaign was absolutely vital. With no serious air opposition, the *Luftwaffe* fighters and Stukas roamed over the Greek mountains, shooting up Allied supply columns snaking along narrow mountain roads, or dropping bombs in precision attacks on defensive positions. The result was that Allied positions actually became traps, and free movement was severely curtailed during daylight hours. The German armoured units on the ground were able to work their way southwards along Greece's mountain passes, while the Allies were

BALKANS (5 APRIL 1941)				
Luftwaffe Unit	**Base**	**Type**	**Str**	**Op**
LUFTFLOTTE 4				
Stab, I., III./KG2	Zwölfing	Do 17Z	65	63
III./KG3	Münchendorf	Do 17Z	28	26
		Ju 88A	3	–
II./KG4	Wien-Aspern	He 111P	28	25
KG51	Wiener Neustadt	Ju 88A	81	55
FLIEGERFÜHRER GRAZ				
I./JG27	Graz-Thalerhof	Bf 109E	33	27
Stab, V, VI/JG54	Graz-Thalerhof	Bf 109E	35	27
Stab/StG3	Graz-Thalerhof	Ju 87B	3	1
		He 111H	–	1
II./StG77	Graz-Thalerhof	Ju 87B	39	34
FLIEGERFÜHRER ARAD				
IV, III./JG54	Arad	Bf 109E	42	39
Stab, II., III./JG77	Deta	Bf 109E	92	73
I./ZG26	Szeged	Bf 110C/E	33	30
Stab, I., III./StG77	Arad	Ju 87B	82	68
		Bf 109E	5	4
		Bf 110C	1	1
VIII.FLIEGERKORPS				
Stab, III./JG27	Belica	Bf 109E	45	44
II./JG27	Sofia	Bf 109E	40	37
I.(J)/LG2	Sofia	Bf 109E	27	22
II./ZG26	Krainici	Bf 110C/E	37	25
I./LG1	Krumovo	Ju 88A	–	–
II.(S)/LG2	Sofia	Bf 109E	29	23
10.(S)/LG2	Krainici	Hs 123A	32	20
I./StG1	Krainici	Ju 87R	24	23
Stab, I., III./StG2	Belica-Nord	Ju 87B	72	69
		Ju 87R	9	9
I./StG3	Belica-Nord	Ju 87B	30	30
		Ju 87R	9	9
IV./KG zbV1	Krumovo	Ju 52	?	?
DEUTSCHE LUFTWAFFENMISSION RUMÄNIEN				
III./JG52	Bukarest-Pipera	Bf 109E	57	45

often forced to abandon their positions simply to prevent becoming outflanked or bypassed. An Allied retreat was slowly turning into an escalating rout.

Tactical operations

Not all of *Luftflotte* 4's aircraft were dedicated to the ground-support role in Greece. The main route for Allied resupply into the Balkans was through the Greek ports to the south, particularly Piraeus near Athens and harbours along the southern coast of the Peloponnese. These came in for special attention from the *Luftwaffe*, which attacked both harbour facilities and the shipping attempting to use the ports. In one incident, the British supply ship SS *Glen Fraser* was hit by a single bomb, resulting in the detonation of 254 tonnes (250 tons) of munitions within, causing the ship to disintegrate.

As the Allies fled down through Greece, the *Luftwaffe* also used airborne forces in an attempt to block the lines of retreat. On 26 April, units of FJR 2 were airlanded around the bridge crossing the Corinth Canal, the stretch of water separating mainland Greece from the Peloponnese. The intention was to capture the bridge intact, but an errant British Bofors shell detonated the pile of demolition charges removed from the bridge. The bridge was destroyed and many *Fallschirmjäger* were killed. Furthermore, the operation was actually about two days too late, as the bulk of the Allied force had already crossed the canal. Nevertheless, once reinforced, the paras took about 2000 Allied prisoners and helped harry the British all the way to the southern coast. Some 43,000 British escaped, but by 28 April Greece was in German hands.

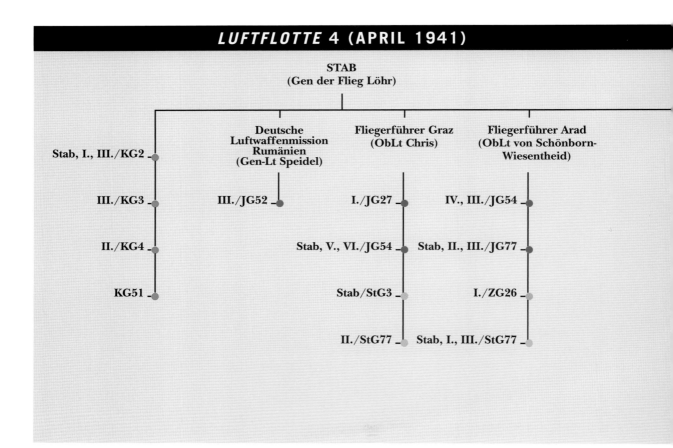

LUFTFLOTTE 4 (APRIL 1941)

STAB (Gen der Flieg Löhr)			
	Deutsche Luftwaffenmission Rumänien (Gen-Lt Speidel)	Fliegerführer Graz (ObLt Chris)	Fliegerführer Arad (ObLt von Schönborn-Wiesentheid)
Stab, I., III./KG2			
III./KG3	III./JG52	I./JG27	IV., III./JG54
II./KG4		Stab, V., VI./JG54	Stab, II., III./JG77
KG51		Stab/StG3	I./ZG26
		II./StG77	Stab, I., III./StG77

The attack on Crete

The campaigns to take Yugoslavia and mainland Greece had been relatively easy ones for the *Luftwaffe*. With the invasion of the island of Crete, however, came a far more technically and tactically demanding form of operation.

Crete looked somewhat peripheral on the map, but Hitler and his high command steadily realized that the island could not be left in Allied hands. If the Allies were to retain the island, flush with troops after the evacuation of Greece, not only could the Royal Navy flex its muscles over the Aegean and Ionian Seas, but the island could also act as an airbase for attacks against Germany's vital oilfields in Romania. By 20 April,

Fallschirmjäger commander Kurt Student had already mapped out a plan for an airborne invasion of Crete, and by early May the plan – codenamed Operation *Merkur* (Mercury) – had been given the green light.

Airborne army

The plan for *Merkur* was utterly new to the history of warfare. The overwhelming mass of the invasion would

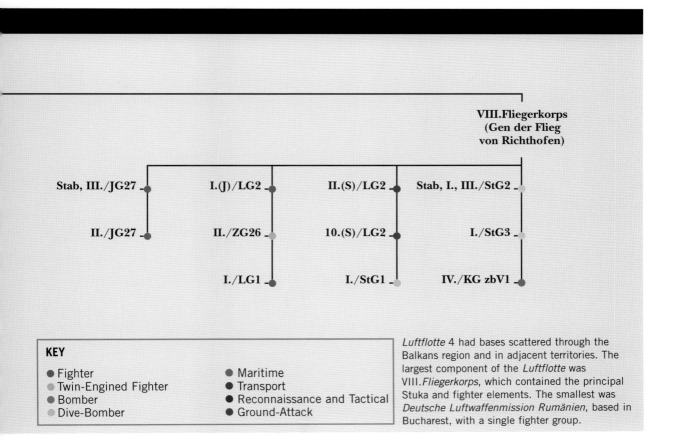

VIII.Fliegerkorps
(Gen der Flieg von Richthofen)

Stab, III./JG27	I.(J)/LG2	II.(S)/LG2	Stab, I., III./StG2
II./JG27	II./ZG26	10.(S)/LG2	I./StG3
	I./LG1	I./StG1	IV./KG zbV1

KEY

- Fighter
- Twin-Engined Fighter
- Bomber
- Dive-Bomber
- Maritime
- Transport
- Reconnaissance and Tactical
- Ground-Attack

Luftflotte 4 had bases scattered through the Balkans region and in adjacent territories. The largest component of the *Luftflotte* was VIII.*Fliegerkorps*, which contained the principal Stuka and fighter elements. The smallest was *Deutsche Luftwaffenmission Rumänien*, based in Bucharest, with a single fighter group.

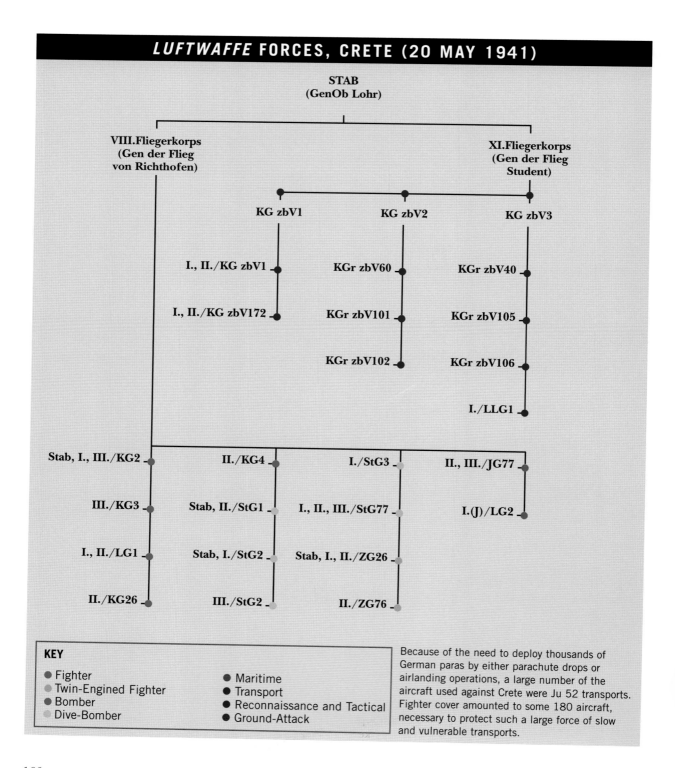

LUFTWAFFE FORCES, CRETE (20 MAY 1941)

STAB
(GenOb Lohr)

VIII.Fliegerkorps
(Gen der Flieg
von Richthofen)

XI.Fliegerkorps
(Gen der Flieg
Student)

KG zbV1

KG zbV2

KG zbV3

I., II./KG zbV1

KGr zbV60

KGr zbV40

I., II./KG zbV172

KGr zbV101

KGr zbV105

KGr zbV102

KGr zbV106

I./LLG1

Stab, I., III./KG2

II./KG4

I./StG3

II., III./JG77

III./KG3

Stab, II./StG1

I., II., III./StG77

I.(J)/LG2

I., II./LG1

Stab, I./StG2

Stab, I., II./ZG26

II./KG26

III./StG2

II./ZG76

KEY

- Fighter
- Twin-Engined Fighter
- Bomber
- Dive-Bomber
- Maritime
- Transport
- Reconnaissance and Tactical
- Ground-Attack

Because of the need to deploy thousands of German paras by either parachute drops or airlanding operations, a large number of the aircraft used against Crete were Ju 52 transports. Fighter cover amounted to some 180 aircraft, necessary to protect such a large force of slow and vulnerable transports.

VIII. *FLIEGERKORPS* (20 MAY 1941)		
Luftwaffe Unit	Base	Type
VIII.FLIEGERKORPS		
Stab, I., III./KG2	Menidi	Do 17Z
III./KG3	Menidi	Do 17Z
I., II./LG1	Eleusis	Ju 88A
II./KG26	Eleusis	He 111H
II./KG4	Rhodes-Gadurra	He 111H
Stab, II./StG1	Argos	Ju 87B
Stab, I./StG2	Molaoi/Mycene	Ju 87B
III./StG2	Scarpanto	Ju 87B
I./StG3	Argos	Ju 87B
I., II., III./StG77	Argos	Ju 87B
Stab, I., II./ZG26	Argos	Bf 110
II./ZG76	Argos	Bf 110
II., III./JG77	Molaoi	Bf 109E
I.(J)/LG2	Molaoi	Bf 109E

XI. *FLIEGERKORPS* (20 MAY 1941)		
Luftwaffe Unit	Base	Type
KAMPFGESCHWADER ZBV1		
I., II./KG zbV1	Megara/Corinth	Ju 52
I., II./KG zbV172	Megara/Corinth	Ju 52
KAMPFGESCHWADER ZBV2		
KGr zbV60	Topolia	Ju 52
KGr zbV101	Topolia	Ju 52
KGr zbV102	Topolia	Ju 52
KAMPFGESCHWADER ZBV3		
KGr zbV40	Tanagra	Ju 52
KGr zbV105	Tanagra	Ju 52
KGr zbV106	Tanagra	Ju 52
I./LLG1	Tanagra	DFS 230 Ju 52

be delivered by airborne assault – para drops and airlanding operations. Masses of Ju 52 transports, either delivering paras directly or deploying troops by assault gliders, would attempt to put down some 22,750 soldiers. The plan was for these troops to seize and hold key airfields, ports and towns dotted along Crete's northern coastline, thus allowing further reinforcements to be flown or shipped in.

The airborne assault was principally the responsibility of XI.*Fliegerkorps*, while VIII.*Fliegerkorps* operated mainly in fighter-escort and air-support roles. The tally of aircraft involved was 520 Ju 52s, 228 medium bombers, 119 Bf 109Es, 114 Bf 110s, 205 Stukas and 72 gliders (DFS 230 types). The transport element was under the command of *Generalleutnant* Gerhard Conrad.

Operation *Merkur* was divided into two initial phases, based upon two waves of attack – one in the morning, and one in the afternoon. The first phase aimed at targets on the northwest coast of Crete, and was intended to capture Maleme airbase, the nearby town of Canea and the port of Suda. The Ju 52s would then return to base for refuelling and to load up the troops and supplies for the second assault, which was to take

place against the towns and airbases of Rethymnon and Heraklion further along the coast to the east. Once an airbase was securely in German hands, further reinforcements could be flown in to build momentum for a sustained offensive.

Launching *Merkur*

The invasion of Crete began at first light on 20 May 1941, and immediately ran into some uncomfortable truths not revealed by German intelligence. First, most of the Commonwealth forces evacuated from Greece were still on Crete – German intelligence thought that many of them had been transferred on to Egypt. Also, the British commander, the New Zealand-raised Major-General Bernard Freyberg, a Victoria Cross-holder from World War I, knew the invasion was coming, although he did not know where. The consequence was that the Ju 52s and gliders flew into storms of AA and small-arms fire – the former hacking into the slow-moving aircraft targets, the latter killing hundreds of paras as they either descended to earth on parachutes or attempted to exit gliders. German casualties were absolutely enormous – one battalion alone suffered 400 men killed on the first day, out of a total complement of 600.

German bombers and fighters kept up heavy assaults on Allied ground units, and also sank Allied shipping in

II./STG77 (MAY 1941)

Sturzkampfgeschwader (or *Stukageschwader*) 77 had by the time of the Crete invasion been in combat since the opening shots of the Poland campaign back in September 1939. In May 1941, it was commanded by *Major* Graf Clemens von Schönborn-Wiesentheid, who had taken over command from *Oberstleutnant* Günther Schwartzkopff on 14 May 1940 and who would lead the *Geschwader* until 20 July 1942. After the invasion of Crete, StG77 was shipped out to the Eastern Front, where it suffered extremely heavy losses until it was wound up in late 1943. II.*Gruppe* was based at Argos, Greece, for the Crete operation.

Nominal strength – 39 x Ju 87Bs

Suda Bay. The second airborne wave in the afternoon also endured heavy casualties, but by the end of the day the Germans had at least established positions to which they were holding.

Victory/defeat

In one of the most remarkable ground actions of the war, the German troops snatched victory from looming defeat. Against an increasingly chaotic Allied defence, the *Fallschirmjäger* managed to secure first Maleme on the 21st, then all the other major objectives by the 28th. The *Luftwaffe* also kept up the pressure, shuttling in reinforcements and harassing the Allies as they were squeezed down into the south of the island. On 29 May, the surviving Allied troops began evacuation, although 18,000 were left behind as either casualties or prisoners of war. The Allies also lost three cruisers and six destroyers to Ju 87 and Ju 88 attacks.

Crete had fallen, but the operation had cost the lives of about 7000 German troops, some 44 per cent of the attacking force. Such was the cost that Hitler never used a mass airborne assault again.

INVASION OF CRETE

Crete 20–31 May 1941

The map clearly shows the principal German operational targets running along the northern coastline of Crete. What the map cannot reveal is the difficult, spiky nature of the terrain along this section of coast. A rocky, undulating landscape here made airborne landings treacherous at best – many German paratroopers became the victims of landing injuries, and German gliders were often wrenched apart by jagged surfaces. Nevertheless, over 11 days of fighting, the Germans managed to turn the situation their way. The Allied forces on Crete began evacuation on 29 May, those troops who failed to get away surrendering to the Germans on 1 June.

Defending the Balkans

By the end of May 1941, the Balkans were entirely under German subjugation. Yet the conquests in southern Europe brought with them critical responsibilities, particularly the defence of the Romanian oilfields at Ploesti.

The fall of Tunisia to the Allies in May 1943 ushered in some major changes in the way that the *Luftwaffe* was organized in the Balkans. As we have seen, *Luftflotte 2* was divided into two parts: a new *Luftflotte 2* took responsibility for operations over Italy and Sicily; the newly created *Luftwaffenkommando Süd-Ost* was to watch over German interests in the Balkans.

The war in the Balkans after the battle for Crete in May 1941 tends to be somewhat forgotten, but from the *Luftwaffe*'s point of view it was an increasingly aggressive theatre. The air operations were critical for Germany on account of the Romanian oilfields at Ploesti, a town

north of Bucharest that contained some 40 refineries which in total produced about 60 per cent of Germany's crude-oil needs. Protecting these oilfields from Allied air attacks became harrowing work for the *Luftwaffe*, particularly as the Red Army closed in on the oilfields in August 1944.

Sidelines

In September 1943, Italy surrendered to the Allies, a decision that had immediate consequences for Germany throughout the Mediterranean and the Balkans. Of vital importance was Germany's need to secure lines of communication through Balkan waters. The first action came on the island of Rhodes on 12 September, when it was occupied by a small German force and turned into a base for III./JG27 (Bf 109Gs) and StG3 (Ju 87s). These aircraft were then used to support a successful invasion of nearby Kos, and after that a landing of 800 *Fallschirmjäger* on Leros in November. This landing was achieved via para drops from 95 Ju 52 aircraft, showing that Hitler had not entirely lost faith with airborne assault, at least on a small scale.

Yugoslavia

In Yugoslavia, the Germans' most serious problem was a major partisan war, to which limited *Luftwaffe* resources were contributed. The principal *Luftwaffe* formation in the region was *Fliegerführer Kroatien*, which had a force of some 65 fighters, 120 ground-attack aircraft, 12 reconnaissance aircraft, 40 Ju 52 transports, and 45 glider tugs towing 60 gliders.

While the fighters and ground-attack aircraft were used to assault remote partisan strongholds, the glider aircraft and transports were employed in making

surprise para drops and airlanding actions. The most famous of these actions was Operation *Rösselsprung* (25 May–6 June 1944), which saw several thousand paras deployed around Drvar and Bos in Croatia as part of a mass, 20,000-troop attempt to destroy the communist partisan leadership under Tito. The raid was bitterly fought and hundreds of partisans were killed, but Tito managed to slip away from the Germans yet again.

Romanian oil

Of all the Balkan *Luftwaffe* battlegrounds, it was Romania that became the hardest-fought. As their strategic bombing campaign gathered pace through 1943, the Allies took the decision to destroy Ploesti in one decisive action – Operation *Tidal Wave*. Ploesti had suffered a minor raid from 12 B-24 Liberators back in June 1942, but the Germans were alert to the fact that more would soon come. Under the command of *Luftwaffe* officer *Oberst* Alfred Gerstenberg, Ploesti built up some of the most formidable air defences in the world. In addition to hundreds of AA guns, including 237 88mm (3.465in) and 105mm (4.134in) weapons,

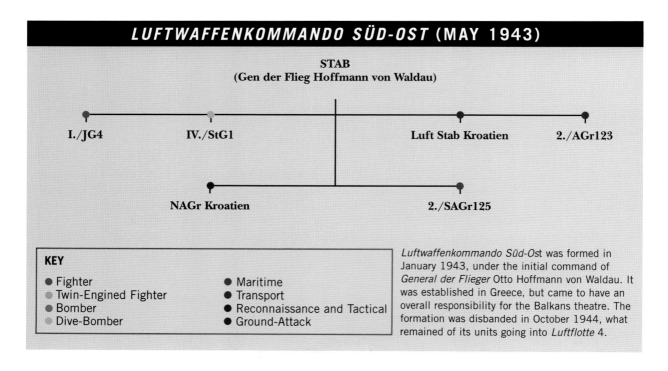

LUFTWAFFENKOMMANDO SÜD-OST (MAY 1943)

STAB
(Gen der Flieg Hoffmann von Waldau)

I./JG4   IV./StG1   Luft Stab Kroatien   2./AGr123

NAGr Kroatien   2./SAGr125

KEY

● Fighter
● Twin-Engined Fighter
● Bomber
● Dive-Bomber
● Maritime
● Transport
● Reconnaissance and Tactical
● Ground-Attack

Luftwaffenkommando Süd-Ost was formed in January 1943, under the initial command of *General der Flieger* Otto Hoffmann von Waldau. It was established in Greece, but came to have an overall responsibility for the Balkans theatre. The formation was disbanded in October 1944, what remained of its units going into *Luftflotte* 4.

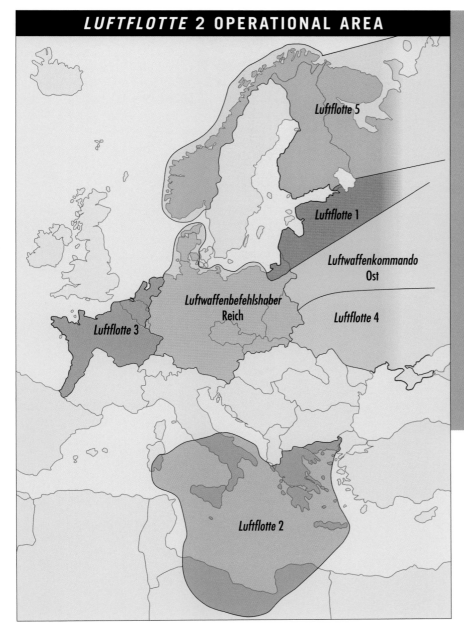

LUFTFLOTTE 2 OPERATIONAL AREA

Luftflotte 5

Luftflotte 1

Luftwaffenkommando Ost

Luftflotte 3

Luftwaffenbefehlshaber Reich

Luftflotte 4

Luftflotte 2

Luftflotte 2, July 1942

By the middle months of 1942, *Luftflotte* 2 had one of the largest areas of responsibility of any of the *Luftflotten*. It had jurisdiction over the whole Mediterranean theatre, stretching from Sardinia in the west across to Greece in the east. The big problem for *Luftflotte* 2 was indeed the length of its perimeter, for as the Allies began to make gains in North Africa it was steadily squeezed northwards into increasingly beleaguered airbases in Sicily and Italy.

Luftflotte 2 was eventually reorganized following the collapse of the Axis defence in Tunisia in mid-1943, leading to the creation of *Luftwaffenkommando Süd-Ost* and a new, more limited, *Luftflotte* 2 confined to the Italian theatre.

Gerstenberg could also call upon 52 Bf 109s and 17 Bf 110s for fighter response.

Operation *Tidal Wave* was unleashed on 1 August 1943 by 178 US B-24 Liberator bombers flying from North Africa. Unfortunately for the US crews, Gerstenberg knew that they were coming owing to German codebreaking, and the US formations were also blighted by a series of navigational and mechanical errors. The aircraft that did reach Ploesti were faced with an unbelievable storm of AA fire from *Luftwaffe Flak* crews,

LUFTWAFFENKOMMANDO SÜD-OST (MAY 1943)			
Luftwaffe Unit	Type	Str	Op
LUFTWAFFENKOMMANDO SÜD-OST			
I./JG4	Bf 109	40	40
IV./StG1	Ju 87	40	39
Luft Stab Kroatien	Ju 88	37	32
	He 46	15	11
2./AGr123	Ju 88	12	7
NAGr Kroatien	Hs 126	11	6
2./SAGr125	Ar 196	8	6

LUFTWAFFENKOMMANDO SÜD-OST (MAY 1944)			
Luftwaffe Unit	Type	Str	Op
LUFTWAFFENKOMMANDO SÜD-OST			
II./JG51	Bf 109	52	43
II./JG301	Bf 109	9	8
11./ZG26	Ju 88	16	16
6./NJG100	Do 217	15	11
13./SG151	Ju 87	7	7
NSGr7	CR.42	29	25
	Ca 314		
	Ju 87		
	He 46		
3./AGr2	Bf 110	12	10
3./AGr33	Ju 188	6	5
	Ju 88		
2./AGr123	Ju 88	8	3
	Ju 86	2	1
	Bf 109	1	0
NAGr12	Bf 109	15	5
NASt Kroatien	Hs 126	8	5
	Do 17		
	Do 215		
SAGr126	Ar 196	48	37
IV./TG1	Ju 52	45	41
II./TG4	Ju 52	39	36
II./TG5	Me 323	21	13
STS1	Ju 52	12	11
STS3	Ju 52	8	7

LUFTWAFFENKOMMANDO SÜD-OST

Luftflotte 1

Luftflotte 6

Luftflotte Reich

Luftflotte 4

Luftwaffenkommando Süd-Ost

Luftflotte 2

Luftwaffenkommando Süd-Ost, May 1944

By May 1944, *Luftwaffenkommando Süd-Ost* was fighting for its life against massive Allied air raids directed at the Romanian oilfields as well as against the advances of the Red Army from the east. Its operational remit covered all of the Balkans – Greece (and its related seas and islands), Yugoslavia, Romania, Bulgaria and Hungary – and it was bordered to the west by *Luftflotte 2*, to the northwest by *Luftflotte Reich* (the central air formation defending the German homeland) and to the north and east by *Luftflotte 4*, which was fighting for its own existence against the endless Soviet offensives.

and the German fighters added to the kills. Fifty-four bombers were lost during the raid, and although significant damage was inflicted, the Romanian oil refineries were actually exceeding their pre-raid capacity only a few weeks later.

Revisiting the site

The Germans had successfully defended Ploesti on this occasion, but US bombers began returning in April 1944 and in total flew more than 5400 sorties against the refineries, supported by 4000 fighter sorties. The sheer weight of the Allied air offensive decimated the local *Luftwaffe* units. By the beginning of June 1944, oil production from Ploesti had dropped by 50 per cent, and by another 40 per cent in the following month. Aircraft fuel production was particularly badly hit, further restricting *Luftwaffe* operations. In August 1944, Ploesti fell to the advancing Red Army.

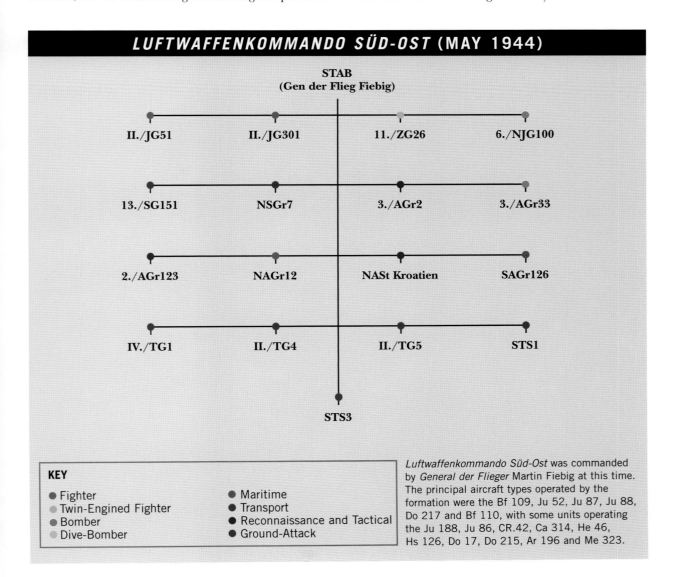

LUFTWAFFENKOMMANDO SÜD-OST (MAY 1944)

STAB
(Gen der Flieg Fiebig)

II./JG51	II./JG301	11./ZG26	6./NJG100
13./SG151	NSGr7	3./AGr2	3./AGr33
2./AGr123	NAGr12	NASt Kroatien	SAGr126
IV./TG1	II./TG4	II./TG5	STS1

STS3

KEY

- Fighter
- Twin-Engined Fighter
- Bomber
- Dive-Bomber
- Maritime
- Transport
- Reconnaissance and Tactical
- Ground-Attack

Luftwaffenkommando Süd-Ost was commanded by *General der Flieger* Martin Fiebig at this time. The principal aircraft types operated by the formation were the Bf 109, Ju 52, Ju 87, Ju 88, Do 217 and Bf 110, with some units operating the Ju 188, Ju 86, CR.42, Ca 314, He 46, Hs 126, Do 17, Do 215, Ar 196 and Me 323.

Eastern Front: 1941–45

The war on the Eastern Front was arguably the greatest conflict in human history. For the *Luftwaffe*, the experience of fighting there went from a position of almost total air supremacy to utter defeat on all fronts in the space of four bloody years.

A German fighter pilot chalks up another kill on the Eastern Front, a theatre known for its large tallies.

Alongside his declaration of war on the United States, Hitler's decision to invade the USSR in June 1941 must rank as one of the two worst possible strategic choices of the war. Despite the fact that Germany was essentially riding high on victory at this point in the conflict, several leading figures in the high command attempted to dissuade him from the enterprise. These included Hermann Göring, who was doubtless unnerved by the possibility of taking on a new, huge opponent across a landscape that was greater in size than all Germany's present conquests put together. Nonetheless, despite the reservations of many of his commanders, Hitler's mind was set. Operation *Barbarossa*, the German invasion of the Soviet Union, began on 22 June 1941.

The new war

Everything about Operation *Barbarossa* was to be on a scale never seen before. Some three million Axis troops were gathered for the onslaught, divided into three vast army groups, each with its own large-scale set of objectives. Army Group North would make a drive from East Prussia up through the Baltic states, with Leningrad as its final objective. Army Group Centre would push directly eastwards through Belorussia, its prize being the Soviet capital itself, Moscow. Army Group South was to launch itself deep into the Ukraine, heading for Kiev and beyond to the city of Stalingrad (Tsaritsyn until 1925) nestling on the Volga River.

They were facing a Red Army of formidable strategic power able to unleash, on paper, an estimated 155 divisions within operational distance of the *Barbarossa* front. Actually this number was closer to 170 divisions, but the Red Army of this time was a shadow of its former self. Stalin's purges and his centralized style of command and control meant that there was little battlefield flexibility and initiative amongst the officer class, and equipment levels were still lagging behind the needs of the enormous manpower.

Red air

For the *Luftwaffe*, the task facing them appeared even more daunting. At this point of the war, total *Luftwaffe* strength in all theatres of the conflict was 3428 aircraft, including 898 single-engined fighters and 931 twin-engined bombers, bearing in mind that not all of these aircraft would be deployed east. The Red Air Force had anywhere between 8000 and 11,000 aircraft. Soviet aircraft had also been combat-tested during the Spanish Civil War, although many of the types were found wanting against German fighters. By 1939, therefore, manufacturers such as Lavochkin, Petlyakov and Ilyushin were already producing modern types of fighter, medium bomber and ground-attack aircraft, but at the time of *Barbarossa* many units were still equipped with obsolete types, or had received scant training on the new aircraft. In short, the Red Air Force had the advantage of numbers, while the German Air Force had the advantage of experience and technology.

Battle plan

Three *Luftflotten* were devoted to the Soviet invasion – 1, 2 and 4. *Luftflotte* 1 was to act principally in support of Army Group North, although it was also permitted to take in Moscow operations. *Luftflotte* 2 was assigned squarely to Army Group Centre and the Moscow objective, while *Luftflotte* 4 took responsibility for southern operations, including commitments to Romania. Altogether the *Barbarossa* air contingents numbered around 1300 aircraft.

Reconnaissance would be a vital part of the campaign. Specially adapted Do 17 and He 111 aircraft would act as long-range surveillance aircraft, while armoured divisions benefited from Hs 126 and Fw 189 short-range reconnaissance aircraft that provided immediate insight into the obstacles ahead. The long-range aircraft had some experience over Russia already. German aircraft had for several months been making reconnaissance overflights of Soviet territory, plotting out defences and estimating unit strengths. These flights were just one of the warning signals resolutely ignored by Stalin, and there is little to suggest that the Soviet Union was in any way prepared for what hit it on 22 June 1941.

Yet looking back from our present time, there is a certain grim awareness that both the *Luftwaffe* and the *Heer* were about to embark on a conflict that would ultimately bring them nothing but disaster. In 1941, the Germans took destruction into the heart of the Soviet Union, but by 1945 the whirlwind would return and crash back into Germany itself.

Launching *Barbarossa,* 1941

Barbarossa was launched in the early hours of the morning of 22 June 1941. The initial results of the offensive completely exceeded German expectations, as all three army groups made deep penetrations into Soviet Russia.

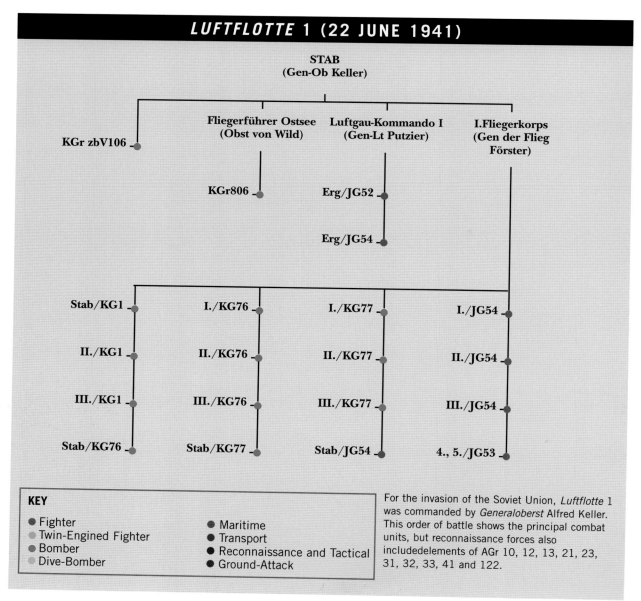

LUFTFLOTTE 1 (22 JUNE 1941)

STAB
(Gen-Ob Keller)

Fliegerführer Ostsee
(Obst von Wild)

Luftgau-Kommando I
(Gen-Lt Putzier)

I.Fliegerkorps
(Gen der Flieg Förster)

KGr zbV106

KGr806

Erg/JG52

Erg/JG54

Stab/KG1	I./KG76	I./KG77	I./JG54
II./KG1	II./KG76	II./KG77	II./JG54
III./KG1	III./KG76	III./KG77	III./JG54
Stab/KG76	Stab/KG77	Stab/JG54	4., 5./JG53

KEY

- Fighter
- Twin-Engined Fighter
- Bomber
- Dive-Bomber
- Maritime
- Transport
- Reconnaissance and Tactical
- Ground-Attack

For the invasion of the Soviet Union, *Luftflotte* 1 was commanded by *Generaloberst* Alfred Keller. This order of battle shows the principal combat units, but reconnaissance forces also includedelements of AGr 10, 12, 13, 21, 23, 31, 32, 33, 41 and 122.

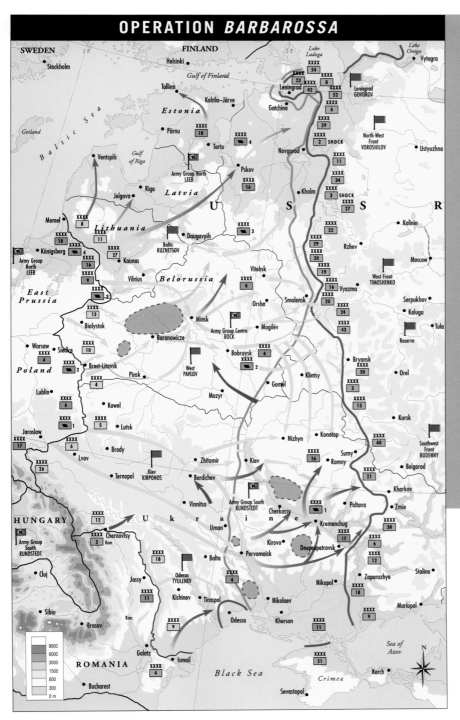

OPERATION *BARBAROSSA*

SWEDEN
Stockholm
FINLAND
Helsinki
Lake Ladoga
Lake Onega
Vytegra
Tallinn
Kohtla–Järve
Gulf of Finland
Leningrad
Leningrad GOVOROV
XXXX 54
XXXX 23
XXXX 42
XXXX 8
XXXX 52
Gatchina
Estonia
Pärnu
XXXX 18
Tartu
4
Novgorod
XXXX 4
XXXX 59
North-West Front VOROSHILOV
XXXX 2 SHOCK
Ustyuzhna
Baltic Sea
Gotland
Gulf of Riga
Ventspils
XXXX 11
Pskov
XXXX 16
Kholm
XXXX 34
XXXX 3 SHOCK
XXXX 27
Riga
Latvia
Army Group North LEEB
Daugavpils
Baltic KUZNETSOV
Jelgava
U   S   S   R
Kalinin
Memel
XXXX 8
XXXX 18
Lithuania
XXXX 11
XXXX 3
XXXX 22
Rzhev
XXXX 29
XXXX 30
Moscow
West Front TIMOSHENKO
Königsberg
XXXX 4
XXXX 27
XXXX 16
Kaunas
XXXX 9
Vilnius
Belorussia
Vitebsk
XXXX 9
XXXX 19
XXXX 16
Vyazma
XXXX 20
Serpukhov
Kaluga
Army Group North LEEB
East Prussia
XXXX 3
XXXX 13
Bialystok
Minsk
Army Group Centre BOCK
Mogilёv
Orsha
Smolensk
XXXX 24
XXXX 43
Reserve
Tula
Baranowicze
Warsaw
XXXX 10
Siedlce
XXXX 4
XXXX 2
Brest-Litovsk
Pinsk
West PAVLOV
Bobruysk
XXXX 4
XXXX 2
Klintsy
Bryansk
XXXX 50
Orel
Poland
Lublin
XXXX 6
Kowel
Mozyr
Gomel
XXXX 3
XXXX 13
Kursk
Jaroslaw
XXXX 1
XXXX 5
Lutsk
Nizhyn
Konotop
Southwest Front BUDENNY
XXXX 17
XXXX 6
Brody
XXXX 26
Lvov
Zhitomir
Kiev
XXXX 40
Sumy
Romny
XXXX 21
Belgorod
Ternopol
Kiev KIRPONOS
Berdichev
XXXX 16
Kharkov
HUNGARY
XXXX 12
Vinnitsa
Army Group South RUNDSTEDT
Cherkassy
XXXX 1
Poltava
Zmie
XXXX 38
Army Group South RUNDSTEDT
Chernovtsy
XXXX 3 Rom
Uman
Kirovo
Kremenchug
XXXX 17
XXXX 6
XXXX 12
Ukraine
XXXX 18
Balta
Pervomaisk
Dnepropetrovsk
Cluj
Jassy
Odessa TYULENEV
XXXX 4
Zaporozhye
Nikopol
Stalino
Kishinev
XXXX 11
Tiraspol
Nikolaev
XXXX 18
Mariupol
XXXX 9
Sibiu
Brasov
XXXX 9
Odessa
Kherson
XXXX 11
Galatz
Ismail
ROMANIA
XXXX 4
Black Sea
XXXX 51
Sea of Azov
Kerch
Crimea
Bucharest
Sevastopol

9000
6000
3000
1500
600
300
0 m

N

22 June–early October 1941

The German plan involved three army groups (Army Group North, Army Group South and Army Group Centre), with the bulk of the forces concentrated in Army Groups North and Centre.

Army Group North targeted Leningrad, while Army Group Centre, which contained around half the German armour, was to shatter Soviet forces in Belorussia before heading for the Soviet capital, Moscow. Army Group South, meanwhile, was to deal with Soviet forces in the Ukraine.

The great problem for this operation was the sheer length of the front and the elongation of supply lines as the Germans advanced deeper and deeper into a seemingly limitless land. For the *Luftwaffe*, these stretched supply lines led to difficulties in obtaining everything from fuel to basic engine parts, and the replenishment issues became even more extreme during the winter.

Operation *Barbarossa*
22 June–early October 1941

→ German attack

XXXX 6 Soviet positions 22 June

Soviet units encircled

Soviet counterattacks

German front line, end of August

German front line, early October

XXXX 6 Soviet positions early October

The opening forays of *Barbarossa* were led by the *Luftwaffe*. The immediate objectives of the air campaign were twofold. First, and typical of all *Luftwaffe* campaigns to date, was to gain and maintain air supremacy. To this end as many Soviet aircraft as possible had to be destroyed on the ground, to prevent the *Luftwaffe* attackers being overwhelmed by sheer numbers. Second, the German air units were to turn their attention to ground-support to assist the Panzer advances, attacking targets of opportunity in typical *Blitzkrieg* fashion.

Surprise attack

Given the scale of the German land forces deployed for *Barbarossa*, it was hard to imagine that any sort of surprise would be achieved. Yet Stalin had cursorily ignored all the warning signs from his intelligence community, and ultimately complete suprise was achieved. Partly this was owing to the result of an argument about operational launch times. The German Army high command had contended that the *Luftwaffe* had to launch its preparatory raids before ground forces crossed the border at first light. Kesselring of *Luftflotte* 2 objected that his pilots needed to attack in the light. The problem was resolved by Kesselring agreeing to launch selected units into the air in darkness, so that they were in place and ready over the battlefield for the attack hour of 03:15.

So it was that by 03:00 hundreds of *Luftwaffe* aircraft crossed the Soviet border, flying at high altitude to minimize the risk of detection. The tactic was about to pay off in spectacular fashion.

LUFTFLOTTE 1 (JUNE 1941)				
Luftwaffe Unit	Base	Type	Str	Op
LUFTFLOTTE 1				
KGr zbV106	–	Ju 52	44	8
I.FLIEGERKORPS				
Stab/KG1	Powunden	He 111H	1	1
II./KG1	Powunden	Ju 88A	29	27
III./KG1	Eichwalde bei Labiau	Ju 88A	30	29
Stab/KG76	Gerdauen	Ju 88A	1	0
I./KG76	Gerdauen	Ju 88A	30	22
II./KG76	Jürgenfelde	Ju 88A	30	25
III./KG76	Schippenbeil	Ju 88A	29	22
Stab/KG77	Heiligenbeil	Ju88A	1	1
I./KG77	Jesau	Ju 88A	30	23
II./KG77	Wormditt	Ju 88A	31	23
III./KG77	Heiligenbeil	Ju 88A	29	20
Stab/JG54	Lindental	Bf 109F	4	3
I./JG54	Rautenberg	Bf 109F	40	34
II./JG54	Trakehnen	Bf 109F	40	33
III./JG54	Blumenfeld	Bf 109F	40	35
4., 5./JG53	Neuseidel	Bf 109F	35	33
FLIEGERFÜHRER OSTSEE				
KGr806	Prowehren	Ju 88A	30	18
LUFTGAU-KOMMANDO I				
Erg/JG52	Neuhausen	Bf 109E	30	19
Erg/JG54	Neuhausen	Bf 109E	24	19

Attacking the Red Air Force

The first few weeks of Operation *Barbarossa* were a heady time for the *Luftwaffe* pilots. They inflicted seemingly crushing losses on the Red Air Force, and the future success of the German campaign appeared assured.

The opening *Luftwaffe* assault of *Barbarossa* caught the Red Air Force in a state of total exposure. Because the Soviet air arm was undergoing re-equipping and reorganization at the time, hundreds of aircraft were lined up neatly at their airbases, as one German pilot, *Hauptmann* Hans von Hahn, noted as I./JG3 roared into an attack in the Lvov sector, one of the objectives of Army Group South: 'We hardly believed our eyes.

LUFTFLOTTE 2 (JUNE 1941)				
Luftwaffe Unit	Base	Type	Str	Op
LUFTFLOTTE 2				
Stab/JG53	Krzewica	Bf 109F	6	6
I./JG53	Krzewica	Bf 109F	35	29
III./JG53	Subolewo	Bf 109F	38	36
IV./KG zbV1	–	Ju 52	40	38
II.FLIEGERKORPS				
Stab/KG3	Deblin	Do 17Z	1	0
		Ju 88A	2	2
I./KG3	Deblin	Ju 88	41	32
II./KG3	Deblin	Ju 88	38	32
		Do 17Z	1	0
Stab/KG53	Radom	He 111H	6	4
I./KG53	Grojec	He 111H	28	18
II./KG53	Radom	He 111H	21	10
III./KG53	Radzyn	He 111H	29	20
		He 111P	2	2
Stab/StG77	Biala Podlaska	Bf 110	7	6
		Ju 87B	3	1
I./StG77	Biala Podlaska	Ju 87B	38	31
II./StG77	Woskrzenice	Ju 87B	39	27
		Bf 110	1	00
III./StG77	Woskrzenice	Ju 87B	35	28
Stab/SKG210	Radzyn	Bf 110	5	4
I./SKG210	Rogoznicka	Bf 110	41	33
II./SKG210	Rogoznicka	Bf 110	37	37
Stab/JG51	Siedlce	Bf 109	4	4
I./JG51	Starawies	Bf 109	40	38
II./JG51	Siedlce	Bf 109	40	23
III./JG51	Halaszi	Bf 109	38	30
IV./JG51	Krzewica	Bf 109	38	26

LUFTFLOTTE 2 (JUNE 1941)				
Luftwaffe Unit	Base	Type	Str	Op
VIII.FLIEGERKORPS				
Stab/KG2	Arys-Rostken	Do 17Z	11	5
I./KG2	Arys-Rostken	Do 17Z	35	19
8., 9./KG2	Lyck	Do 17Z	41	23
III./KG3	Suwalki	Do 17Z	44	18
Stab/StG1	Radczki	Bf 110	3	2
		Ju 87B	3	2
II./StG1	Radczki	Ju 87B	39	28
III./StG1	Radczki	Ju 87B	39	24
Stab/StG2	Praschnitz	Bf 110	6	4
		Ju 87B	3	3
I./StG2	Praschnitz	Ju 87B	35	19
III./StG2	Praschnitz	Ju 87R	39	20
II.(Sch)/LG2	Praschnitz	Bf 109E	38	37
10.(Sch)/LG2	–	Hs 123A	22	17
Stab/ZG26	Suwalki	Bf 110C/E	4	4
I./ZG26	Suwalki	Bf 110C/E	38	17
II./ZG26	Suwalki	Bf 110C/E	36	30
Stab/JG27	Subolewo	Bf 109E	4	4
II./JG27	Berzniki	Bf 109E	40	31
III./JG27	Subolewo	Bf 109E	40	14
II./JG52	Subolewo	Bf 109E/F	39	37
KGr zbV9	–	Ju 52	–	–
KGr zbV12	–	Ju 52	43	8

Having destroyed hundreds of Soviet aircraft, the *Luftwaffe* pilots now returned to their bases to be refuelled and rearmed for the next missions.

The Soviet response

After the first wave of the German attack, and with reports of a massive German armoured force having surged across the border, the Red Air Force began to respond in earnest. Its initial efforts were on an unwieldy scale.

Every available aircraft was hastily fuelled and armed and sent up into the air, often regardless of how much experience and training the pilot possessed. The counterattack was prodigious but uncoordinated, and

Row after row of reconnaissance planes, bombers and fighters stood lined up as if on parade. We were astonished at the number of airfields and aircraft the Russians had ranged against us.'

Presented with such targets, the *Luftwaffe* fighters, dive-bombers and medium bombers savaged the enemy aircraft across the developing front, sometimes catching entire Soviet squadrons in the process of taking off.

the German Bf 109s fell upon the Soviet aircraft like wolves. Ironically, the *Luftwaffe* aviators actually experienced problems fighting the obsolete types, such as the I-153, I-15 and I-16. These machines were slow, but they had a manoeuvrability that far outclassed the faster German fighters, which struggled to bring their guns to bear on such opponents. Although the German pilots did gain the advantage, the fight was hard, and the Soviet resistance often suicidally brave.

Regarding the Soviet bombers, these were typically massacred in huge numbers before even reaching their intended targets, or were brought down by heavy and precise German *Flak* fire.

Casualties

The biggest problems for the *Luftwaffe* pilots during the opening phases of *Barbarossa* was not so much the Red Air Force, but AA fire from the Soviet ground troops and also problems with their own bombs. The 1.8kg (4lb) SD2 and 9kg (20lb) SD10 fragmentation bombs proved to have a lethal combination of unreliable fuses and equally unreliable drop mechanisms. The result was

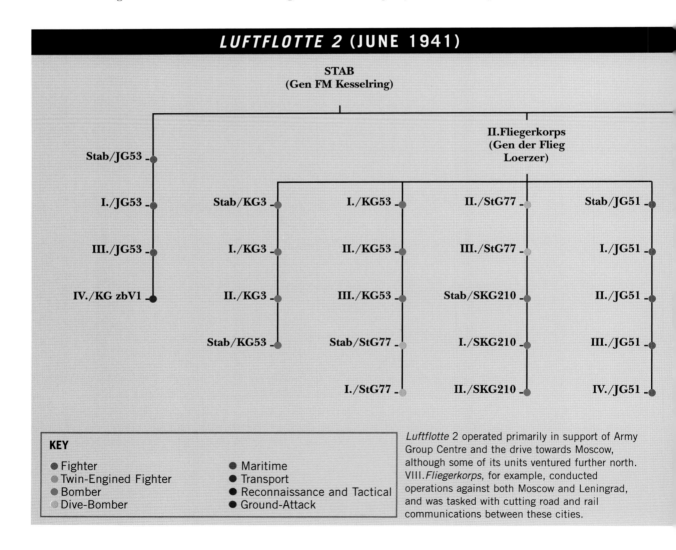

LUFTFLOTTE 2 (JUNE 1941)

STAB
(Gen FM Kesselring)

II.Fliegerkorps
(Gen der Flieg Loerzer)

Stab/JG53

I./JG53   Stab/KG3   I./KG53   II./StG77   Stab/JG51

III./JG53   I./KG3   II./KG53   III./StG77   I./JG51

IV./KG zbV1   II./KG3   III./KG53   Stab/SKG210   II./JG51

Stab/KG53   Stab/StG77   I./SKG210   III./JG51

I./StG77   II./SKG210   IV./JG51

KEY

- Fighter
- Twin-Engined Fighter
- Bomber
- Dive-Bomber
- Maritime
- Transport
- Reconnaissance and Tactical
- Ground-Attack

Luftflotte 2 operated primarily in support of Army Group Centre and the drive towards Moscow, although some of its units ventured further north. VIII.*Fliegerkorps*, for example, conducted operations against both Moscow and Leningrad, and was tasked with cutting road and rail communications between these cities.

that on several occasion such bombs armed themselves but did not drop, subsequently detonating aboard their host aircraft. Both types were quickly removed from front-line service.

Yet despite the fact that 35 German aircraft were lost to all causes on the opening day of the invasion of the Soviet Union, those figures are utterly eclipsed by Soviet devastation. Totally accurate figures are impossible to obtain, but in the region of 1800 Soviet aircraft were destroyed on that first day, mostly during German ground-attack missions. By the end of the first week, up

to 3000 aircraft may have been destroyed. Dozens of German fighter pilots became aces in a matter of days.

Yet although the Red Air Force had been horribly injured, it was far from dead. As with the ground troops, *Luftwaffe* pilots noted how seemingly irresistible the Soviet onslaught seemed. The Soviets had enormous latent industrial capacity, which they largely retained beyond the front or by moving factories east before the German land advance arrived. Once aircraft production accelerated, and the Red Air Force implemented better tactics, the *Luftwaffe* would face tougher challenges.

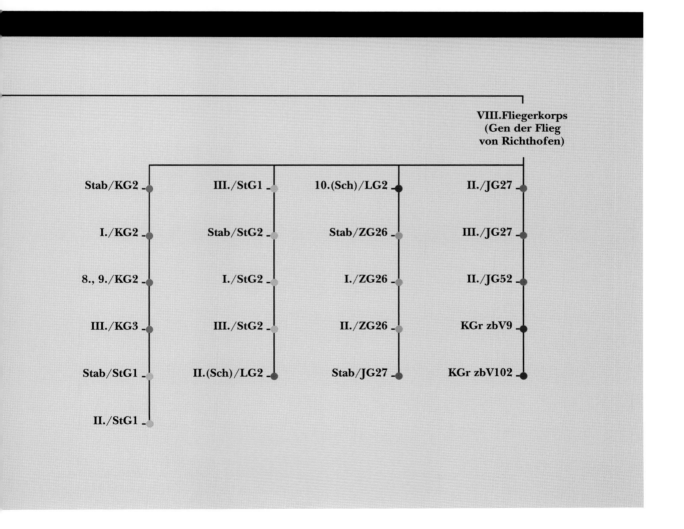

**VIII.Fliegerkorps
(Gen der Flieg
von Richthofen)**

Stab/KG2	III./StG1	10.(Sch)/LG2	II./JG27
I./KG2	Stab/StG2	Stab/ZG26	III./JG27
8., 9./KG2	I./StG2	I./ZG26	II./JG52
III./KG3	III./StG2	II./ZG26	KGr zbV9
Stab/StG1	II.(Sch)/LG2	Stab/JG27	KGr zbV102
II./StG1			

Advance to Moscow

The opening phases of *Barbarossa* were an outstanding success, but developments over subsequent weeks began to raise serious operational concerns amongst the *Luftwaffe* and the *Heer*.

On land, *Barbarossa* had the makings of a crushing German victory. On all fronts, the German Army made huge advances, and by the end of September the Soviet Army had lost over one million men dead and captured. Leningrad had been under siege since the second week of the month, Army Group Centre was only 322km (200 miles) from Moscow and Army Group South had taken cities such as Kiev and Dnepropetrovsk, and were readying themselves to encircle and snuff out an entire Soviet army group further east. The *Luftwaffe* had performed sterling service in a close-support role, keeping pace with the rapid advance. On 2 October, Operation *Taiphun* (Typhoon) was launched, the final onslaught to take Moscow. By now, however, problems were beginning to emerge.

Adverse factors

For both the *Luftwaffe* and the German Army, a number of factors now served to erode their advantage. First, the length of the advance was causing fundamental difficulties in supply, making it more and more problematic to maintain a decent tempo of operations. Second, although the Germans seemed to be winning, they were taking constant, heavy casualties. So were the Soviets, but it seemed to matter less to a side that to all appearances had almost limitless manpower and machines. Third, the constant fighting was wearing out equipment at an alarming rate. Fourth, the autumnal *rasputitsa* rains not only turned the ground into a sucking quagmire for German troops and vehicles, they also dramatically restricted flying operations for the

LUFTFLOTTE 4 (21 JUNE 1941)				
Luftwaffe Unit	Base	Type	Str	Op
LUFTFLOTTE 4				
KGr zbv 50/104	–	Ju 52	85	51
IV.FLIEGERKORPS				
Stab/KG27	Focsani-Sud	He 111H	5	5
I./KG27	Focsani-Sud	He 111H	30	22
II./KG27	Focsani-Sud	He 111H	24	21
III./KG27	Zilistea	He 111H	28	25
II./KG4	Zilistea	He 111H	24	8
Stab/JG77	Bacau	Bf 109E	2	2
II./JG77	Roman	Bf 109E	39	19
III./JG77	Roman	Bf 109F4	35	20
I.(J)/LG2	Janca	Bf 109E	40	20
V.FLIEGERKORPS				
Stab/KG51	Krosno	Ju 88A	2	2
I./KG51	Krosno	Ju 88A	22	22
II./KG51	Krosno	Ju 88A	36	29
III./KG51	Lezany	Ju 88A	32	28
Stab/KG54	Lublin-Swidnik	Ju 88A	1	1
I./KG54	Lublin-Swidnik	Ju 88A	34	31
II./KG54	Lublin-Swidnik	Ju 88A	36	33
Stab/KG55	Labunie	Bf 110	2	1
		He 111H	27	27
I./KG55	Labunie	He 111H	27	27
II./KG55	Labunie	He 111H	24	22
III./KG55	Klemensow	He 111H	25	24
Stab/JG3	Hostynne	Bf 109F	4	4
I./JG3	Dub	Bf 109F	35	28
II./JG3	Hostynne	Bf 109F	35	32
III./JG3	Modorowka	Bf 109F	35	34
DEUTSCHE LUFTWAFFEN-MISSION RUMÄNIEN				
Stab/JG52	Bucharest/Mizil	Bf 109F	4	3
III./JG52	Mizil/Pipera	Bf 109F	43	41

Luftwaffe. Finally, and critically for the German aviators, the Red Air Force steadily began to field better aircraft and better pilots. The advantage was slipping away from the Germans as they ground on towards Moscow.

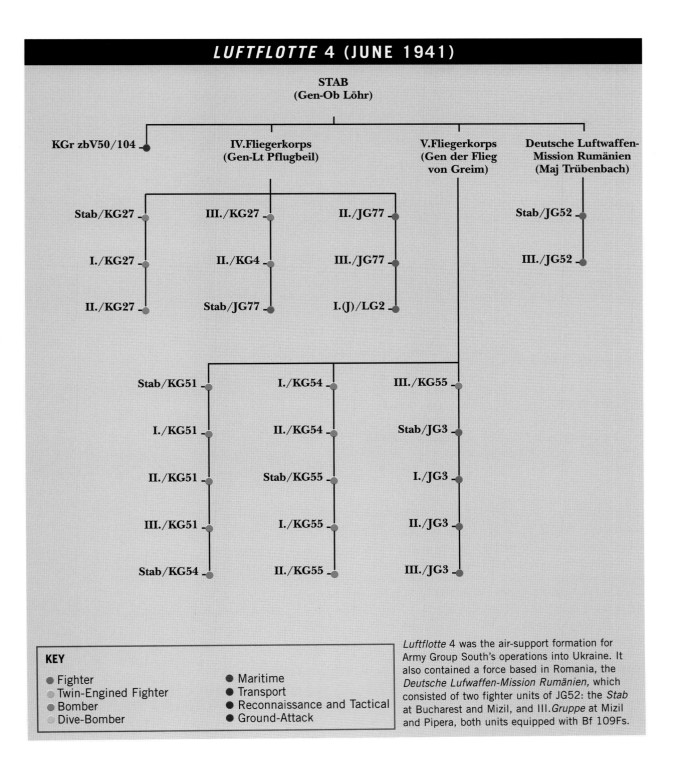

LUFTFLOTTE 4 (JUNE 1941)

STAB
(Gen-Ob Löhr)

KGr zbV50/104

IV.Fliegerkorps
(Gen-Lt Pflugbeil)

V.Fliegerkorps
(Gen der Flieg von Greim)

Deutsche Luftwaffen-
Mission Rumänien
(Maj Trübenbach)

Stab/KG27   III./KG27   II./JG77   Stab/JG52

I./KG27   II./KG4   III./JG77   III./JG52

II./KG27   Stab/JG77   I.(J)/LG2

Stab/KG51   I./KG54   III./KG55

I./KG51   II./KG54   Stab/JG3

II./KG51   Stab/KG55   I./JG3

III./KG51   I./KG55   II./JG3

Stab/KG54   II./KG55   III./JG3

KEY

● Fighter
◐ Twin-Engined Fighter
● Bomber
○ Dive-Bomber

● Maritime
● Transport
● Reconnaissance and Tactical
● Ground-Attack

Luftflotte 4 was the air-support formation for Army Group South's operations into Ukraine. It also contained a force based in Romania, the *Deutsche Lufwaffen-Mission Rumänien,* which consisted of two fighter units of JG52: the *Stab* at Bucharest and Mizil, and III.*Gruppe* at Mizil and Pipera, both units equipped with Bf 109Fs.

Stalemate

Operation *Taiphun* (Typhoon) was intended to take Moscow before Christmas 1941. The appalling Soviet winter and a massive Soviet counterattack, however, pulled the Germans to a stop within a day's journey of the Soviet capital.

By the autumn of 1941, the Red Air Force had recovered enough to mount increasingly heavy missions against the German ground forces on all fronts, but particularly around Moscow and Leningrad, on which the *Luftwaffe* had begun pounding bombing raids the previous July. Production of modern aircraft types quadrupled in Soviet factories in the second half of the year compared with the first, and included 2141 LaGG-3 fighters, 1091 Yak-1 fighters and 1293 Il-2 ground-attack aircraft. This scale of production, with over 15,000 aircraft of all types produced in the year, was way beyond anything that German industry could attempt. Furthermore, the lack of a truly strategic air component within the *Luftwaffe* meant that there was little the Germans could do to blunt this industrial output directly. Now, more than ever, Germany was paying for its pre-war decisions.

As the Soviets began to put more and more aircraft into the air, flown by pilots with an increasing amount of combat experience, *Luftwaffe* casualty figures grew exponentially, compounded by the supply and repair issues noted above. For example, von Richtofen's VIII.*Fliegerkorps* was transferred north to Leningrad from the Moscow front in August, and did heavy damage to the besieged Russian city, but while supporting ground actions against the Moscow–Leningrad railway it lost over 10 per cent of its aircraft in only 11 days. Similar loss rates were reported across the Eastern Front, and the weather conditions from October soon exacerbated the *Luftwaffe*'s situation. Whereas the *Luftwaffe* had been flying more than 1000 sorties every day in September, that figure had dropped to fewer than 300 by the end of October.

Gates of Moscow

The Russian winter had started in earnest by the beginning of December 1941, by which time lead units

of *Generalfeldmarschall* Fedor von Bock's Army Group Centre were within 32km (20 miles) of central Moscow. The sub-zero conditions had a massive impact on all operations. For the *Luftwaffe*, flights were grounded – so that the air force was unable to contribute to the ground campaign – and engines were kept running to avoid their freezing solid. Then, on 5/6 December, the Soviets began a vast counteroffensive. Although this did not succeed in forcing the Germans out of the Soviet Union, it did push them some distance back from Moscow before the front lines settled into stalemate. Now the *Luftwaffe* was locked into a long battle of attrition.

LONG-RANGE RECONNAISSANCE UNITS (JAN 1942)			
Luftwaffe Unit	Type	Strength	Serviceable
AGr OBdL 1	Do 215/Ju 88	16	4
AGr OBdL 4	Do 215/Ju 88	26	12
7(F)/JG2	Bf 110	7	6
3(F)/10 Art	Ju 88	8	4
2(F)/11	Do 17/Fw 189	7	1
3(F)/11 Art	Bf 110	6	2
4(F)/11	Ju 88	18	3
4(F)/14	Ju 88	14	4
2(F)/22	Ju 88	6	1
3(F)/22	Ju 88	6	1
1/NSt	Do 17	9	2
2/NSt	Do 17	11	4
3/NSt	Do 17	7	2
3(F)/121	Ju 88	13	2
4(F)/122	Ju 88/Bf 110	16	4
5(F)/122	Ju 88/Bf 110	12	3
Total		182	55

III./JG54 (LENINGRAD FRONT, EARLY 1942)

Jagdgeschwader 54 had incredible success during the first few months of Operation *Barbarossa*. As part of *Luftflotte* 1 operating in the northern sector of the Eastern Front, it had succeeded in destroying 1000 Soviet aircraft by 1 August, adding another 78 kills during the rest of the year; against these figures it lost only 48 aircraft in combat from June to December 1941. It added further to its tallies in the New Year, particularly once the winter weather began to clear, and became expert at hunting down Soviet night raiders, and by early April 1942 it had claimed 2000 kills. Here we see the aircraft of III.*Gruppe* – Bf 109Fs painted in their winter camouflage scheme.

Nominal strength – 40 x Bf 109Fs

Summer offensive, 1942

In June 1942, Hitler launched a powerful offensive codenamed Operation *Blau* (Blue). It was a southern operation, one aimed at capturing the vital oilfields in the Caucasus and also at taking the distant city of Stalingrad.

Operation *Blau* was to utilize two new army groups. Army Group A was to lunge directly south into the Caucasus to take the precious oilfields, while Army Group B advanced in a southwesterly direction along the River Don, taking the city of Voronezh, providing flank protection to Army Group A and also driving towards the city of Stalingrad on the River Volga, which was its ultimate objective.

New formations
By the day the operation was launched, 28 June, the *Luftwaffe* had also undergone a significant reshuffle. *Luftflotte* 2 had been shifted down into the Mediterranean, and instead the Eastern Front was now worked, from north to south, by *Luftflotte* 5 (up in Finland), *Luftflotte* 1 on the Leningrad front, *Luftwaffenkommando Ost* in the central sector and *Luftflotte* 4 in the Don–Caucasus sector. The Leningrad front was relatively static, so the bulk of the strength now lay with the more southerly formations, which would be the main air components of the summer offensive. *Luftflotte* 4 had some 1500 aircraft at its disposal, and *Luftwaffenkommando Ost* had around 600 aircraft of all types. In contrast to this, the Red Air Force received over 2000 Hurricane, P-39 Airacobra and P-40 Tomahawk fighters in 1942 from the Allies, to add to the huge inventories of indigenous aircraft that the USSR was producing.

The push to Stalingrad
Operation *Blau* played out in familiar fashion. The offensive began strongly, with Army Group A making deep progress into the Caucasus. Hitler, however, kept switching the Fourth Panzer Army between the army groups, weakening both at critical times, and the vast distances and violent opposition gradually pulled Army Group A to a halt by 18 November, short of the

intended oilfields and having to hold a front that stretched 805km (500 miles). In Army Group B, the German Sixth Army had steadily closed up to Stalingrad by mid-November, against swelling resistance from the Soviets – Stalin was determined to keep his namesake city out of German hands.

LUFTFLOTTE 4 (JULY 1942)			
Luftwaffe Unit	Type	Str	Op
BOMBERS			
Stab/KG27	He 111	2	2
I./KG27	He 111	32	20
II./KG27	He 111	31	21
III./KG27	He 111	31	8
Stab/KG51	Ju 88	2	0
I./KG51	Ju 88	30	17
II./KG51	Ju 88	33	8
III./KG51	Ju 88	28	8
Stab/KG55	He 111	4	4
I./KG55	He 111	31	19
II./KG55	He 111	30	21
III./KG55	He 111	29	20
Stab/KG76	Ju 88	3	2
I./KG76	Ju 88	27	13
II./KG76	Ju 88	33	14
III./KG76	Ju 88	38	12
Stab/KG100	He 111	1	1
I./KG100	He 111	37	13
MARITIME AIRCRAFT			
1./SAGr125	Bv 138	7	4
3./SAGr125	Bv 138	15	7

LUFTFLOTTE 4 (JULY 1942)			
Luftwaffe Unit	Type	Str	Op
FIGHTERS			
Stab/JG3	Bf 109	3	2
I./JG3	Bf 109	24	9
II./JG3	Bf 109	22	10
III./JG3	Bf 109	25	12
Stab/JG52	Bf 109	4	4
II./JG52	Bf 109	40	24
III./JG52	Bf 109	35	20
15./JG3	Bf 109	12	6
I./JG53	Bf 109	40	8
Stab/JG77	Bf 109	4	4
1./JG77	Bf 109	9	6
II./JG77	Bf 109	23	16
III./JG77	Bf 109	27	21
GROUND-ATTACK AIRCRAFT			
Stab/ZG1	Bf 110	3	2
I./ZG1	Bf 110	36	14
II./ZG1	Bf 110	31	15
III./ZG1	Bf 109	40	40
	Do 217	3	1
7./ZG2	Bf 109	12	9
II./StG1	Ju 87	39	30
Stab/StG2	Ju 87	3	3
	Bf 110	6	4
I./StG2	Ju 87	28	20
II./StG2	Ju 87	31	19
III./StG2	Ju 87	18	11
Stab/StG77	Ju 87	3	1
	Bf 110	6	4
I./StG77	Ju 87	29	20
II./StG77	Ju 87	35	28
III./StG77	Ju 87	33	13
Stab/SG1	Bf 109	2	1
I./SG1	Bf 109	31	16
II./SG1	Hs 129	28	13
	Hs 123	12	6
1.NSt	Do 17	12	8

LUFTFLOTTE 4 (1942)			
Luftwaffe Unit	Type	Str	Op
RECONNAISSANCE AIRCRAFT			
III./LG1	Ju 88	28	11
2./AGr OBdL	Ju 88	9	3
	Do 215	2	0
3./AGr121	Ju88	10	5
4./AGr121	Ju 88	10	10
4./AGr122	Ju 88	10	5
3./AGr10	Ju 88	12	4
2./AGr11	Do 17	13	2
2./AGr22	Ju 88	9	8
NAGr1	Fw 189	8	6
	Bf 110	8	4
NAGr3	Fw 189	8	5
	Bf 110	5	4
NAGr4	Fw 189	15	11
NAGr6	Hs 126	7	5
	Bf 110	7	5
NAGr7	Fw 189	15	10
NAGr8	Fw 189	21	19
NAGr9	Fw 189	15	11
NAGr10	Fw 189	15	8
	Hs 126	11	7
NAGr12	Fw 189	9	8
	Bf 110	10	4
NAGr13	Hs 126	19	15
	Bf 110	7	3
NAGr14	Fw 189	11	10
	Bf 110	8	4
NAGr16	Fw 189	12	7
TRANSPORT AIRCRAFT			
II./KG zbV1	Ju 52	35	2
KG zbV4	Ju 52	49	31
KG zbV5	Ju 52	52	22
KG zbV9	Ju 52	52	34
KGr zbV50	Ju 52	48	29
KGr zbV102	Ju 52	52	22
KGr zbV900	Ju 52	48	16

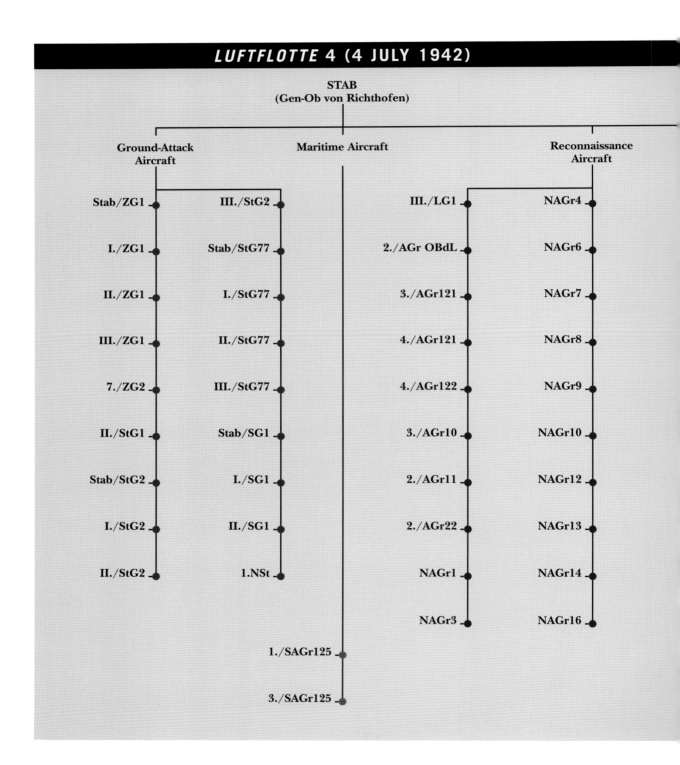

LUFTFLOTTE 4 (4 JULY 1942)

STAB
(Gen-Ob von Richthofen)

Ground-Attack
Aircraft

Maritime Aircraft

Reconnaissance
Aircraft

Ground-Attack		Maritime	Reconnaissance
Stab/ZG1	III./StG2	III./LG1	NAGr4
I./ZG1	Stab/StG77	2./AGr OBdL	NAGr6
II./ZG1	I./StG77	3./AGr121	NAGr7
III./ZG1	II./StG77	4./AGr121	NAGr8
7./ZG2	III./StG77	4./AGr122	NAGr9
II./StG1	Stab/SG1	3./AGr10	NAGr10
Stab/StG2	I./SG1	2./AGr11	NAGr12
I./StG2	II./SG1	2./AGr22	NAGr13
II./StG2	1.NSt	NAGr1	NAGr14
		NAGr3	NAGr16
	1./SAGr125		
	3./SAGr125		

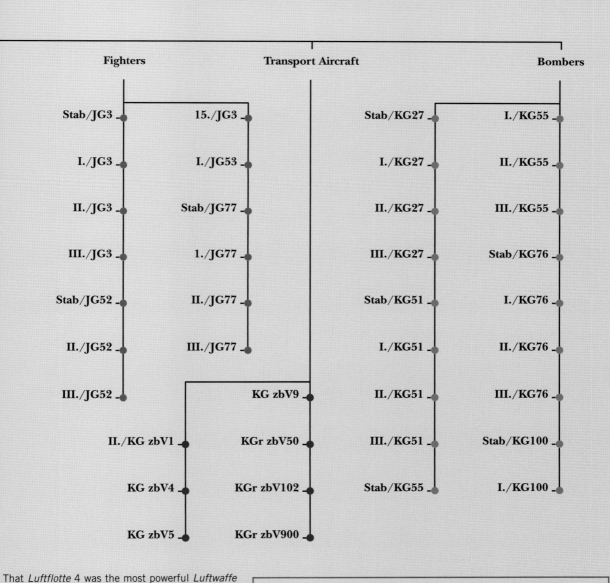

Fighters		Transport Aircraft		Bombers
Stab/JG3	15./JG3	Stab/KG27	I./KG55	
I./JG3	I./JG53	I./KG27	II./KG55	
II./JG3	Stab/JG77	II./KG27	III./KG55	
III./JG3	1./JG77	III./KG27	Stab/KG76	
Stab/JG52	II./JG77	Stab/KG51	I./KG76	
II./JG52	III./JG77	I./KG51	II./KG76	
III./JG52	KG zbV9	II./KG51	III./KG76	
II./KG zbV1	KGr zbV50	III./KG51	Stab/KG100	
KG zbV4	KGr zbV102	Stab/KG55	I./KG100	
KG zbV5	KGr zbV900			

That *Luftflotte* 4 was the most powerful *Luftwaffe* formation on the Eastern Front in mid-1942 is evident from this diagram. In total, the *Luftflotte* wielded over 1500 aircraft for Hitler's summer offensive southwards into the Caucasus and towards the city of Stalingrad.

KEY

● Fighter
● Bomber
● Maritime
● Transport
● Reconnaissance and Tactical
● Ground-Attack

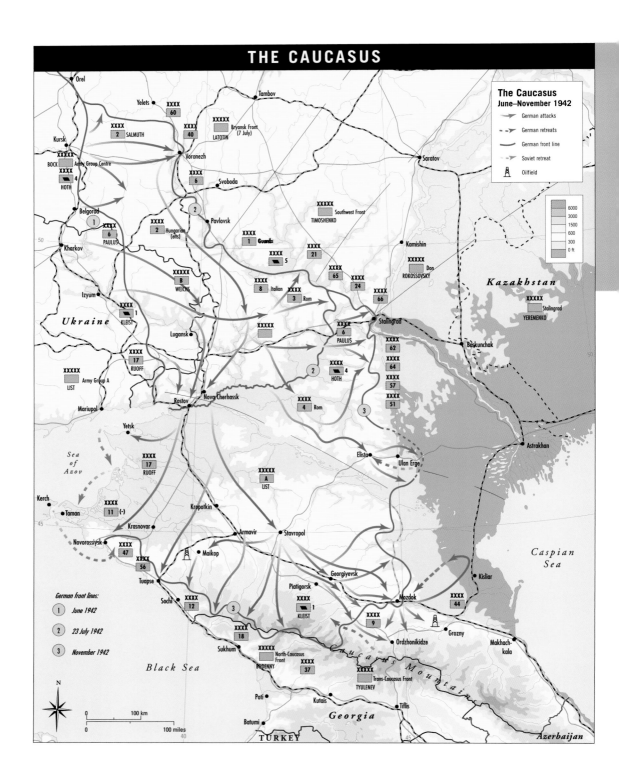

THE CAUCASUS

The Caucasus
June–November 1942

→ German attacks
⇢ German retreats
— German front line
⇢ Soviet retreat
⛏ Oilfield

6000
3000
1500
600
300
0 ft

Orel

Yelets

Tambov

XXXX 60

Kursk

XXXX 2 SALMUTH

XXXX 40

XXXXX Bryansk Front (7 July)

LATOTIN

XXXXX BOCK Army Group Centre

Voronezh

XXXX 4 HOTH

Belgorod

XXXX 6

Svoboda

Saratov

XXXX 1

XXXXX PAULUS

XXXX 2 Hungarian (elts)

Pavlovsk

XXXX 1 Guards

XXXXX Southwest Front TIMOSHENKO

Kamishin

Kharkov

XXXXX B WEICHS

XXXX 8 Italian

XXXX 5

XXXX 21

XXXX 65

XXXXX Don ROKOSSOVSKY

Kazakhstan

Izyum

XXXX 1 KLEIST

Ukraine

Lugansk

XXXX 3 Rom

XXXX 24

XXXX 66

XXXXX Stalingrad YEREMENKO

XXXX 17 RUOFF

XXXXX

XXXX 6 PAULUS

Stalingrad

Baskunchak

XXXXX Army Group A LIST

XXXX 2

XXXX 4 HOTH

XXXX 62

XXXX 64

XXXX 57

XXXX 51

Rostov

Nova Cherhassk

XXXX 4 Rom

XXXX 3

Mariupol

Yetsk

Sea of Azov

XXXX 17 RUOFF

Elista

Ulan Erge

Astrakhan

XXXXX A LIST

Kerch

Taman

XXXX 11 (-)

Krasnovar

Kropotkin

Armavir

Stavropol

XXXX 47

XXXX 56

Novorossiysk

Maikop

Georgiyevsk

Mozdok

Kisliar

Caspian Sea

Tuapse

German front lines:

1 June 1942

2 23 July 1942

3 November 1942

Sochi

XXXX 12

XXXX 3

Piatigorsk

XXXX 1 KLEIST

XXXX 9

XXXX 44

Grozny

XXXX 18

Sukhum

Ordzhonikidze

Makhach-kala

Black Sea

XXXXX North-Caucasus Front BUDENNY

XXXX 37

Caucasus Mountains

XXXXX Trans-Caucasus Front TYULENEV

Poti

Kutais

Tiflis

N

0 100 km

0 100 miles

Batumi

Georgia

TURKEY

Azerbaijan

June–October 1942

At the start of Operation *Blau*, everything seemed to be going Hitler's way. The headlong advance across open country to the Volga was spearheaded by the Sixth Army, which cut a swathe of destruction across southern Russia as it smashed its way east.

But then Hitler compounded the decision to divide his armies by making ruinous reductions in the forces available to the operations in the south. The strategic reserve was sent to the four winds: 9th and 11th Panzer Divisions were assigned to *Generalfeldmarschall* Günther von Kluge, the *Grossdeutschland* Division was also sent to Army Group Centre, *Leibstandarte*-SS *Adolf Hitler* was ordered to France to be restored to strength, and the rested Eleventh Army under *Generalfeldmarschall* Erich von Manstein was held back from taking part in the Caucasus drive.

TOP 25 *LUFTWAFFE* ACES, EASTERN FRONT			
Pilot	East	West	Total
Hptm Erich 'Bubi' Hartmann	346	6	352
Maj Gerhard Barkhorn	301	0	301
Maj Günther Rall	271	4	275
ObLt Otto Kittel	267	0	267
Maj Walter Nowotny	255	3	258
Maj Wilhelm Batz	234	3	237
Obst Hermann Graf	202	10	212
Hptm Helmut Lipfert	200	3	203
Maj Heinrich Ehrler	198	10	208
ObLt Walter Schuck	189	17	206
Hptm Joachim Brendel	189	0	189
ObLt Anton 'Toni' Hafner	184	20	204
Maj Hans Philipp	178	28	206
Hptm Walter Krupinski	177	20	197
ObLt Günther Josten	177	1	178
Maj Theodor Weissenberger	175	33	208
Hptm Günther Schack	174	0	174
ObLt Max Stotz	173	16	189
ObLt Heinz 'Johnny' Schmitt	173	0	173
Hptm Joachim Kirscher	167	21	188
Hptm Horst Ademeit	164	2	166
Maj Kurt Hans Friedrich Brändle	160	20	180
Hptm Heinrich Sturm	158	0	158
ObLt Gerhard Thyben	152	5	157
Lt Peter Düttman	152	0	152

For the *Luftwaffe*, the advance into the south was not as hotly contested as feared. Much of the Soviet air power was still wrapped smotheringly around Moscow and the central front. *Luftwaffe* units inflicted a horrifying death toll on exposed Soviet troops. Air losses were still significant, however, and numbered around 240 fighters and bombers per month from spring to autumn 1942. Furthermore, the great distances of the advances meant that the *Luftwaffe* forces had to relocate constantly to new airbases, which in turn stretched the fuel supply lines ever thinner, compressing the number of sorties flown. Yet soon the *Luftwaffe* would face a new demand – saving the German Army from the inferno raging on the streets of Stalingrad.

Stalingrad, 1942–43

The battle of Stalingrad cost over one million lives, and was arguably the true turning point in Hitler's defeat in World War II. For the *Luftwaffe*, it represented a total failure in its attempts to resupply the Sixth Army.

By mid-November 1942, German forces were in possession of around 90 per cent of the city of Stalingrad, but still the city did not fall. Stalin poured in every conceivable resource, and the city battle had descended into conditions of absolute destruction. Then, on 19/20 November, Stalin launched a vast

LUFTWAFFE LOSSES BY CAUSE, STALINGRAD	
Description	**Total**
Aircraft destroyed in action	166
Aircraft missing in action	108
Aircraft written off on take-off or landing	214
Aircrew killed in action	1100

LUFTWAFFE LOSSES BY TYPE, STALINGRAD	
Type	**Total**
Ju 52	269
He 111	169
Ju 86	42
Fw 200	9
He 177	5

STALINGRAD AIRLIFT (NOV 1942–FEB 1943)	
Requirement	**t (tons)/day**
Minimum Sixth Army needs for survival	305 (300)
Optimum Sixth Army needs for operations	610 (600)
Average *Luftwaffe* airlift	120 (118)
Maximum *Luftwaffe* airlift	368 (362)

counteroffensive to the north and south of Stalingrad, these two great pincer arms closing around the city on 23 November. Trapped inside Stalingrad were the Sixth Army and part of the German Fourth Army.

Resupply mission

Hitler was aware that there was a catastrophe in the making, and Göring committed himself to the task of keeping the trapped forces resupplied by air. Precedents gave grounds for optimism. Earlier in 1942, *Luftwaffe* airlift missions had successfully resupplied pockets of trapped German forces at Kholm and Demyansk. The latter operation had seen *Luftwaffe* transport aircraft fly in over 24,400 tonnes (24,000 tons) of supplies for a cost of 265 transport aircraft, a heavy price for success.

Yet Stalingrad was not Demyansk. The Soviet advance had seized many German airbases around the city,

meaning that the *Luftwaffe* transport aircraft had to make longer, more perilous flights. Terrible winter weather constantly reduced flying times or increased the accident rate. Reinforcement aircraft had to make journeys of over 2000km (1242 miles) from Germany, and not all survived.

Supply volumes

Yet by far the biggest problem *Luftflotte* 4 faced in resupplying the German forces at Stalingrad was that it simply was not big enough. Taking into account all the available aircraft and the restrictions upon flying time, the very best that the Germans could manage to supply was 368 tonnes (362 tons) per day. The Sixth Army alone ideally needed 610 tonnes (600 tons) of supplies to keep functioning. A relief operation by land, mounted in mid-December, nearly penetrated through the Stalingrad perimeter, but Hitler forbade *Generaloberst* Paulus, the commander of the Sixth Army, to make a breakout operation. He thereby consigned the desperate troops inside the city to certain doom.

Soviet offensive

The *Luftwaffe*'s resupply ambitions grew even more problematic during December and January. The Soviets began to push out westwards from their gains around Stalingrad, and several of the largest forward operating bases, such as those as Tatsinskaya and Morozovskaya, were lost. Göring was doing a good job of alienating front commanders such as von Richtofen; like Hitler, he made demands that airfields be held even though they were being pounded by artillery and even tank fire.

Steadily, the supply squadrons were being pushed further and further away from Stalingrad, and by mid-January they had to cover 350km (217 miles) just to reach the wrecked city. By 12 January, Stalingrad's German-held airbase was taken by the Soviets, meaning that any resupply now had to be performed by para-dropping loads, an imprecise operation that often resulted in supplies dropping directly into Soviet hands. Furthermore, the effects of the operation were whittling down the numbers of *Luftwaffe* aircraft at an alarming rate. No more than 35 per cent of transport aircraft were operational by mid-January, and for Ju 52 aircraft that number dropped down to 7 per cent. The outcome

Final battle for Stalingrad

Marshal Georgi Zhukov launched Operation *Uranus* on 19 November 1942, and within days a massive Soviet pincer movement had isolated the German Sixth Army fighting in Stalingrad. All attempts to relieve the trapped German soldiers failed, and the *Luftwaffe* was never able to make good Hermann Göring's boasts that he would sustain the city from the air. As January progressed, the noose around Stalingrad was tightened. The German forces retreated to the city, losing control of important airfields. The fighting was less fierce than it had been in September and October: the Soviets could let cold, starvation and disease do most of the work. Stalin ordered the pocket eliminated in January, and by the end of the month the surviving Germans were pressed into two small pockets on the Volga.

The Battle for Stalingrad
September 1942–February 1943

- Soviet attacks
- German counterattacks
- German retreats
- German front line
- Limit of Soviet artillery
- Soviet air support

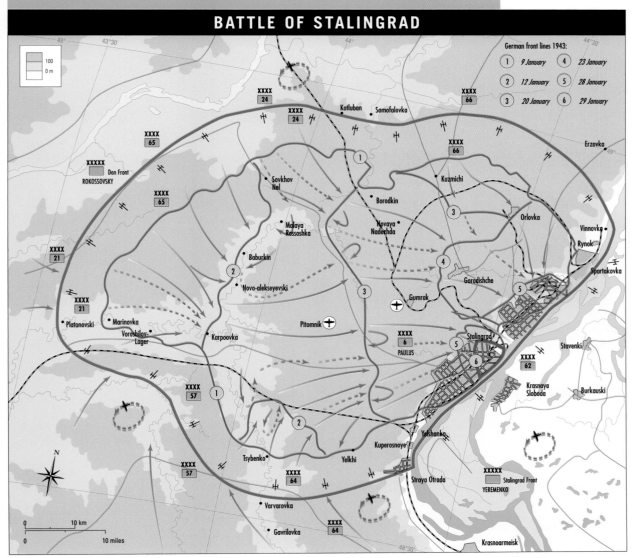

BATTLE OF STALINGRAD

was inevitable, and on 2 February Paulus surrendered his army to the Soviets, the survivors embarking on a future that involved almost certain death in a Soviet labour camp. Not only was the Stalingrad airlift a failure, and another dent in Göring's reputation, but it had also been prohibitively costly in terms of German aircraft. In total, the operation had cost almost 500 aircraft, including 269 Ju 52s and 169 He 111s. Such aircraft would have been better employed in other theatres as the tide turned against Germany.

II./KG4 (MAY 1943)

KG4 had been formed in May 1939, and by the beginning of 1943 was a veteran of campaigns in every major *Luftwaffe* theatre of engagement, including the Mediterranean and the Balkans. It was deployed to the Eastern Front for the launch of Operation *Barbarossa*, and while the *Stab* flew with Army Group North, the I. and II.*Gruppen* were part of the Army Group Centre attack towards Moscow. II.*Gruppe* then joined southern German forces for the Ukrainian offensives of 1943, and it continued in service on the Eastern Front until the end of the war.

Nominal strength – 37 aircraft

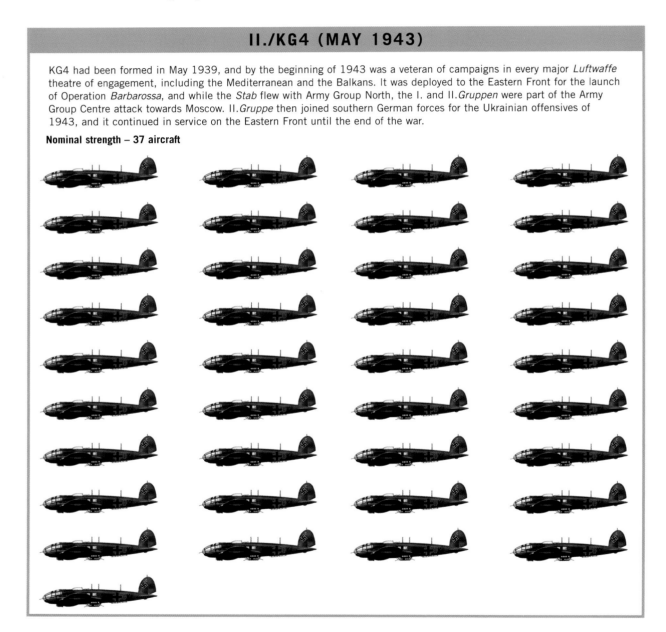

Kursk

The battle of Kursk was one of the largest military engagements in history. It is often presented as purely a tank battle, but it included a colossal air engagement from which the *Luftwaffe* never recovered.

Following its victory at Stalingrad, the Red Army maintained a strong momentum westwards, driving back the Germans along the entire trans-Caucasus front. It was a time of epic land engagements – the city of Kharkov changed hands twice during the battles – but also extremely heavy fighting in the air. By this stage of the war, the Soviet Air Force essentially enjoyed parity with the *Luftwaffe* in terms of pilot skill and the quality of aircraft, but still retained a dominant advantage over the Germans in terms of numbers. *Luftwaffe* losses were once again harrowing. Between April and June 1943, the *Luftwaffe* lost over 600 aircraft on the Eastern Front, including 256 fighters.

A brilliant counteroffensive by *Generalfeldmarschall* Erich von Manstein managed to regain some of the territory lost to the Red Army, creating in turn a swelling Soviet-held salient around the city of Kursk. Hitler now designed what he felt was an offensive to restore German fortunes on the Eastern Front. Operation *Zitadelle* (Citadel) was conceived as a massive pincer action by Army Groups Centre and South, the two arms cutting off the Kursk salient, occupied by the Soviet Central and Voronezh Fronts. Germany amassed over 1000 pieces of armour, and the *Luftwaffe* pulled in resources from every theatre. Total air assets would total 750 aircraft in *Luftflotte* 6, attached to the northern part of the operaton, and 1100 aircraft in *Luftflotte* 4 to the south. The Soviets had gathered even greater armour, infantry and air resources for the coming battle, which would involve two million personnel.

Operation *Zitadelle*

The offensive was launched on 5 July, the German armour making huge strikes into the Kursk salient, relying on the swarms of supporting aircraft to battle the

OPERATION *ZITADELLE*, KURSK (JULY 1943)		
Luftwaffe Unit	**Base**	**Type**
LUFTFLOTTE 6		
I., III., IV./JG51	Orel	Fw190A4/5
15.(S)/JG51	Seschtschinskaja	Fw 190A
I./JG54	Orel	Fw 190A2
II./KG4	Seschtschinskaja	He 111H16
III./KG4	Karatchev	He 111H16
II., III./KG51	Bryansk	Ju 88A4
I., III./KG53	Olsufjevo	He 111H16
IV./NJG5	Seschtschinskaja	Bf 110G
I., II., III./StG1	Orel	Ju 87D
10.(P)/StG2	Orel	Ju 87G
I./ZG1	Bryansk	Bf 110G
LUFTFLOTTE 4		
II./JG3	Kharkov-Roganj	Bf 109G4
III./JG3	Besonovka	Bf 109G4
I./JG52	Besonovka	Bf 109G
III./JG52	Ugrim	Bf 109G
III./KG1	Bryansk	Ju 88A4
I., II./KG3	Seschtschinskaja	Ju 88A4
I., II./KG27	Dnepropetrovsk	He 111H16
III./KG27	Kharkov-Voitschenko	He 111H16
II., III./KG55	Stalino	He 111H16
14.(E)/KG55	Poltava	He 111H Ju 88C6
I./KG100	Poltava	He 111H
1., 2., 3., 5., 6./SG1	Besonovka	Fw190A/F
7./SG1	Varvarovka	Hs 123A
PzJäSt/JG51 8.(P)/SG2	Varvarovka	Hs 129B
4.(P)/SG1 4.(P), 8.(P)/SG2	Varvarovka	Hs 129B
I., II., III./StG2	Krestowoi	Ju 87D
I., II., III./StG77	Bogodukhov	Ju 87D
2.REPÜLODANDÁR (HUNGARIAN)		
5./I.Vadászosztály	Kharkov-Voitschenko	Bf 109
3./1.Bombázó-század	Kharkov	Ju 88A4

LUFTFLOTTEN OPERATIONAL AREAS, EASTERN FRONT 1943

Luftflotte 5

Luftflotte 1

SOVIET UNION

Luftwaffenkommando Ost

Luftwaffenbefehlshaber Reich

Luftflotte 4

Eastern Front, July 1943

Luftflotte 2 was moved to take control of operations in the Mediterranean theatre and replaced in the central sector of the Eastern Front by *Luftwaffenkommando Ost*, which had a size and status similar to that of other *Luftflotten*.

The greater threat to the homeland by Allied bombing raids resulted in the creation of a stronger fighter presence in Germany in the shape of *Luftwaffenbefehlshaber Reich*.

Luftflotten 1 and *Luftflotten* 4 remained responsible for the northern and southern sectors of the Eastern Front respectively.

masses of Soviet fighters, bombers and ground-attack aircraft that responded. On the first day of action, *Luftwaffe* pilots flew over 3000 sorties, and the losses amongst Soviet aircraft were vast. In one attempted Soviet bomber attack, for example, directed at the *Luftwaffe*'s Kharkov airfields, 120 Soviet planes were shot down. German ground-attack aircraft also carved up Soviet infantry and armour formations. On 19 July, I.*Fliegerkorps* alone managed to knock out 135 Soviet tanks either temporarily or permanently, with few aircraft losses.

Failed offensive
Operation *Zitadelle* made some decent progress, particularly in the south, against fanatical resistance, but by mid-July the Germans were simply running out of steam against endless Soviet reinforcements on the

ground and in the air. *Luftwaffe* air losses meant that air supremacy was steadily passing to the Soviets, meaning that Il-2 Sturmovik ground-attack fighters could hammer the surviving German armour with greater freedom. Soviet counteroffensives between 12 and 15 July stopped, then turned back the German onslaught, and by the 23rd the Germans were in full retreat beyond their original start lines.

In June and July 1943, the *Luftwaffe* lost 1030 aircraft on the Eastern Front, major air battles having been conducted during the run-up period to Kursk as well as during *Zitadelle* itself.

The *Luftwaffe* tactics were superior to those of the Soviets, and some 1100 Soviet aircraft were downed during the battle. Yet even these losses left the Soviets with reserves of some 700 aircraft, which tipped the air battle in their favour.

LUFTWAFFE ORDER OF BATTLE, KURSK (JULY 1943)

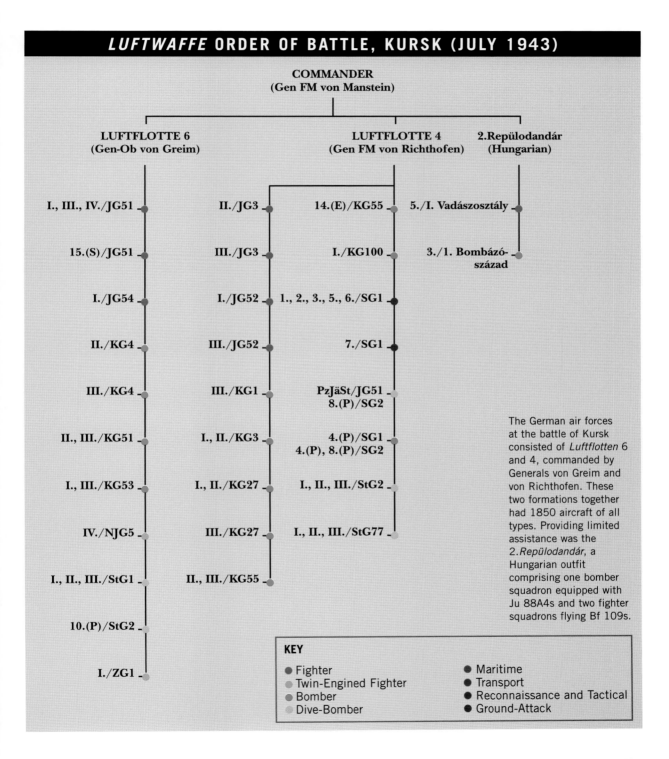

COMMANDER
(Gen FM von Manstein)

LUFTFLOTTE 6
(Gen-Ob von Greim)

LUFTFLOTTE 4
(Gen FM von Richthofen)

2.Repülodandár
(Hungarian)

LUFTFLOTTE 6	LUFTFLOTTE 4		2.Repülodandár
I., III., IV./JG51	II./JG3	14.(E)/KG55	5./I. Vadászosztály
15.(S)/JG51	III./JG3	I./KG100	3./1. Bombázó-század
I./JG54	I./JG52	1., 2., 3., 5., 6./SG1	
II./KG4	III./JG52	7./SG1	
III./KG4	III./KG1	PzJäSt/JG51 8.(P)/SG2	
II., III./KG51	I., II./KG3	4.(P)/SG1 4.(P), 8.(P)/SG2	
I., III./KG53	I., II./KG27	I., II., III./StG2	
IV./NJG5	III./KG27	I., II., III./StG77	
I., II., III./StG1	II., III./KG55		
10.(P)/StG2			
I./ZG1			

The German air forces at the battle of Kursk consisted of *Luftflotten* 6 and 4, commanded by Generals von Greim and von Richthofen. These two formations together had 1850 aircraft of all types. Providing limited assistance was the 2.*Repülodandár*, a Hungarian outfit comprising one bomber squadron equipped with Ju 88A4s and two fighter squadrons flying Bf 109s.

KEY
- Fighter
- Twin-Engined Fighter
- Bomber
- Dive-Bomber
- Maritime
- Transport
- Reconnaissance and Tactical
- Ground-Attack

Collapse in the East

The German defeat in the battle of Kursk set the scene for the remainder of the war on the Eastern Front. Apart from making temporary gains during localized offensives, the Germans would now be inexorably driven back into their homeland.

The tale of the conflict on the Eastern Front between August 1943 and May 1945 is one of steadily unfolding human disaster for Germany. Following in Kursk's wake, the Soviets maintained their momentum, driving back Army Groups Centre and South and, by the end of the year, reclaiming cities such as Kharkov, Dnepropetrovsk, Kiev and Smolensk. The eastern Ukraine was back in Soviet hands, their forces having

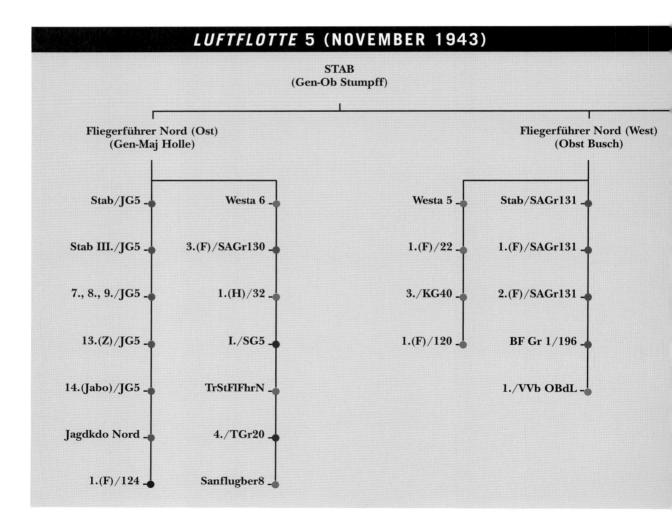

LUFTFLOTTE 5 (NOVEMBER 1943)

STAB
(Gen-Ob Stumpff)

Fliegerführer Nord (Ost)
(Gen-Maj Holle)

Fliegerführer Nord (West)
(Obst Busch)

Stab/JG5	Westa 6	Westa 5	Stab/SAGr131
Stab III./JG5	3.(F)/SAGr130	1.(F)/22	1.(F)/SAGr131
7., 8., 9./JG5	1.(H)/32	3./KG40	2.(F)/SAGr131
13.(Z)/JG5	I./SG5	1.(F)/120	BF Gr 1/196
14.(Jabo)/JG5	TrStFlFhrN		1./VVb OBdL
Jagdkdo Nord	4./TGr20		
1.(F)/124	Sanflugber8		

crossed the Dnieper River at the end of September 1943, and further north four Soviet fronts were pressing against Belorussia. For the *Luftwaffe* during this time, the retreat involved constant relocations to new airbases further back, and the usual litany of constant losses. For example, I./KG100 moved base no less than six times between July and October 1943.

Even though frontline units were receiving good machines, such as the Bf 109G-6 and improved variants of the Fw 190 series, sortie rates were collapsing in the chaos and through the constant attrition. At points during the retreat, I.*Fliegerkorps* and VIII.*Fliegerkorps*

were only able to muster some 300 sorties a day over hundreds of kilometres of front.

Production war

The fact remained that the battles of the last years of the war hung as much on equations of production and loss as they did on battlefield tactics. If we look at German aircraft production figures, we see a remarkable testament to the Third Reich's industrial resilience, despite the hammer blows of strategic bombing against its production centres. In 1943, Germany produced 10,898 fighters, 5496 ground-attack

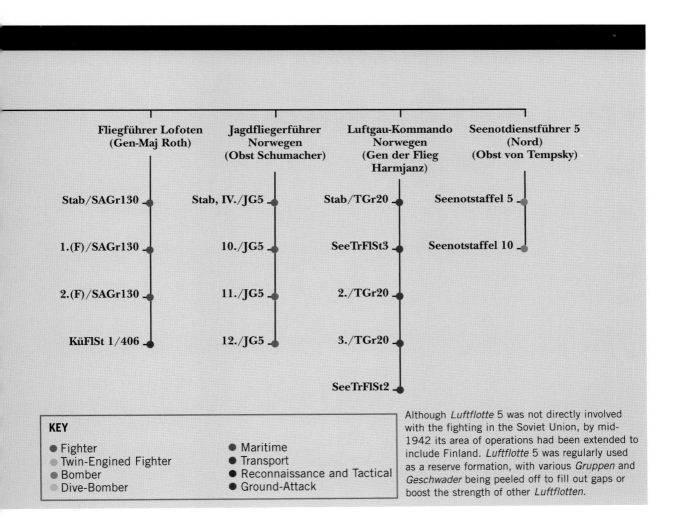

Fliegführer Lofoten (Gen-Maj Roth)	Jagdfliegerführer Norwegen (Obst Schumacher)	Luftgau-Kommando Norwegen (Gen der Flieg Harmjanz)	Seenotdienstführer 5 (Nord) (Obst von Tempsky)
Stab/SAGr130	Stab, IV./JG5	Stab/TGr20	Seenotstaffel 5
1.(F)/SAGr130	10./JG5	SeeTrFlSt3	Seenotstaffel 10
2.(F)/SAGr130	11./JG5	2./TGr20	
KüFlSt 1/406	12./JG5	3./TGr20	
		SeeTrFlSt2	

KEY
- Fighter
- Twin-Engined Fighter
- Bomber
- Dive-Bomber
- Maritime
- Transport
- Reconnaissance and Tactical
- Ground-Attack

Although *Luftflotte* 5 was not directly involved with the fighting in the Soviet Union, by mid-1942 its area of operations had been extended to include Finland. *Luftflotte* 5 was regularly used as a reserve formation, with various *Gruppen* and *Geschwader* being peeled off to fill out gaps or boost the strength of other *Luftflotten*.

aircraft, and 4789 bombers. The following year, output peaked at 26,326 fighters, 5496 ground-attack aircraft and 1982 bombers, the gross imbalance towards fighters signalling how important air defence had become for the *Reich*.

Allied fighter production
In 1944, the Soviet Union produced less than 18,000 fighters, but as the United States manufactured 38,873 fighters in this year, and flung the majority against the

Reich and diverted large numbers into Soviet hands as well, they did not actually need to match German output. Tellingly, in 1943 and 1944 the Soviets did produce over 22,000 ground-attack aircraft, signalling that ground-attack rather than air defence had become the main priority for the coming offensives.

LUFTFLOTTE 5 (30 NOVEMBER 1943)				
Luftwaffe Unit	**Base**	**Type**	**Str**	**Op**
FLIEGERFÜHRER NORD (OST)				
Stab JG5	Petsamo	Bf 109G2	2	–
Stab III./JG5	Petsamo	Bf 109G2	2	–
7., 8., 9./JG5	Petsamo	Bf 109G2	25	–
		Bf 109F4	3	–
13.(Z)/JG5	Kirkenes	Bf 110G0	1	–
		Bf 110G2	11	–
		Bf 110G4	2	–
		Bf 110F2	2	–
14.(Jabo)/JG5	Petsamo	Fw 190A	13	–
Jagdkdo Nord	Altengard	Bf 109G	1	–
1.(F)/124	Kirkenes	Ju 88D1	13	–
		Ju 88D5	1	–
		Ju 88A	4	–
		Bf 109G4	4	–
Westa 6	Banak	Ju 88D	–	–
3.(F)/SAGr130	Billefjord	Bv 138	8	–
1.(H)/32	Alakurti	Fw 189	12	–
I./SG5	Nautsi	Ju 87D	13	–
TrStFlFhrN	Rovaniemi	Ju 52/3m	5	–
4./TGr20	Kemi	Ju 52/3m	12	–
Sanflugber8	Kemi	Ju 52/3m	3	–
		Fi 156C	4	–
FLIEGERFÜHRER LOFOTEN				
Stab/SAGr130	Tromsø	Ar 196A3	1	–
1.(F)/SAGr130	Tromsø	Bv 138C1	9	–
2.(F)/SAGr130	Tromsø	Bv 138C1	10	–
KüFlSt1/406	Soerreisa	He 115B/C	11	–

LUFTFLOTTE 5 (30 NOVEMBER 1943)				
Luftwaffe Unit	**Base**	**Type**	**Str**	**Op**
FLIEGERFÜHRER NORD (WEST)				
Westa 5	Vaernes	Ju 88D	–	–
1.(F)/22	Vaernes	Ju 88D1	8	–
		Ju 88D5	1	–
3./KG40	Vaernes	Fw 200C	16	–
1.(F)/120	Sola	Ju 88D1	10	–
		Ju 88D5	1	–
		Ju 88A4	2	–
Stab/SAGr131	Sola See	Ar 196A3	1	–
1.(F)/SAGr131	Trondheim	BV138C1	8	–
2.(F)/SAGr131	Sola See	Bv 138C1	6	–
	Bergen	Ar 196A	5	–
BFS Gr 1/196	Aalborg	Ar 196A	12	–
1/VVb OBdL	Aalborg	–	1	–
JAGDFLIEGERFÜHRER NORWEGEN				
Stab, IV./JG5	Lade	Bf 109G2	12	–
10./JG5	Gossen	Bf 109G6	5	–
11./JG5	Sola	Fw 190A	21	–
12./JG5	Herdla	Fw 190A4	2	–
LUFTGAU-KOMMANDO NORWEGEN				
Stab/TGr20	Fornebu	–	–	–
SeeTrFlSt3	Hommelvik	Ju 52See	12	–
2./TGr20	Place	Ju 52	12	–
3./TGr20	Place	Ju 52	12	–
SeeTrFlSt2	Hommelvik	Ju 52See	11	–
SEENOTDIENSTFÜHRER 5 (NORD)				
Seenotstaffel 5	Stavanger	Do 24T3	7	–
		Ar 196A4	4	–
		Ar 196A0	2	–
Seenotstaffel 10	Tromsø	Do 24T3	5	–
		He 115B	2	–

The fact remained that however many aircraft Germany could output, losses were keeping pace across all the fronts. Furthermore, although aircraft could be manufactured, pilots were harder to find and train. Pilot training times were constantly trimmed, increasing the number of aircraft lost to accidents, and by January 1944 only around 60 per cent of crews were operationally ready. By May 1944, around 25 per cent of the *Luftwaffe*'s fighter pilot strength was gone, and building it back up again was a near futile struggle as the war expanded and intensified across several fronts (i.e., in Normandy and Italy) as well as on the Eastern Front.

Home defence

Throughout 1943 and into 1944, the German high command was increasingly diverting *Luftwaffe* resources from the Eastern Front to the air defence needs of the *Reich*. Often, trainee pilots would receive their instruction with Eastern Front *Gruppen*, only to be transferred back to the West once they had completed their training and gained a modicum of combat flying experience. This policy was much to the chagrin of the units facing the Red Army onslaughts, because when it was combined with combat losses, it meant that individual *Gruppen* frequently found themselves with much less than 50 per cent operational capability – and each sortie over the front lines brought fresh losses.

Tactical support

There was much debate about what the *Luftwaffe* could do on the Eastern Front to stem the Soviet tide. Most of the aviation efforts went into close air support operations for army units, which were fighting truly desperate battles of their own. From September 1943, the *Luftwaffe* had a new chief of staff, *General der Flieger* Günther Korten, following the suicide of *Generaloberst* Hans Jeschonnek on 19 August.

Korten was a long-standing command veteran of the Eastern Front campaigns, and knew that following the current policy of tactical force would simply squander away his aircraft to Soviet fighters and the increasingly effective Soviet AA systems. Korten began advocating a strategic bombing campaign directed away from the front lines and more at the centres of Soviet aircraft

and tank production, plus its infrastructural services. In fact, it was the very lack of strategic reach on the part of the *Luftwaffe* that had allowed the Soviets to maintain their massive production tallies.

Korten received approval from Hitler to implement a strategic campaign, although given the limitations in *Luftwaffe* bomber strength it would undoubtedly be constricted in its range of targets. Orders were issued

I. *GRUPPE*, JG54, BASES (MAY 1941 – MAY 1945)		
Type	**Date**	**Base**
Bf 109E/F	May 1941	Stolp-Rietz
Bf 109F	Jun 1941	Lindenthal
Bf 109F	Jul 1941	Mietau
Bf 109F	Jul 1941	Alt-Schwaneburg
Bf 109F	Jul 1941	Korovje-Selo
Bf 109F	Jul 1941	Sarudinye
Bf 109F	Sep 1941	Siverskaya
Bf 109F	Dec 1941	Krasnogvardeisk
Bf 109F/Fw 190A	Feb 1943	Heiligenbeil
Fw 190A	Mar 1943	Staraja-Russa
Fw 190A	May 1943	Nikolskoye
Fw 190A	Jun 1943	Orel
Fw 190A	Aug 1943	Poltava
Fw 190A	Oct 1943	Vitebsk
Fw 190A	Dec 1943	Orscha
Fw 190A	Jan 1944	Wesenberg
Fw 190A	Jun 1944	Reval-Laksberg
Fw 190A	Jun 1944	Polozk
Fw 190A	Jul 1944	Dünaburg
Fw 190A	Aug 1944	Riga-Skulte
Fw 190A	Sep 1944	Wenden
Fw 190A	Sep 1944	Riga-Spilve
Fw 190A	Oct 1944	Tuckum
Fw 190A/D	Oct 1944	Schrunden
Fw 190A/D	Jan 1945	Zabeln
Fw 190A/D	Mar 1945	Neuhausen
Fw 190A/D	May 1945	Flensburg

for aircraft from *Luftflotten* 4 and 6 to be withdrawn to the West for training in their new role, with a view to beginning the bombing campaign in earnest in February 1944.

Yet by this stage of the war such alterations in tactics with the resources at hand were unlikely to have theatre-changing effects. Worst still, the full force of a new series of Soviet offensives was about to engulf the whole of the Eastern Front.

Soviet apocalypse
The Red Army offensives of January–July 1944 were the true beginnings of defeat for the Germans. In the north, a major drive by the the Soviet Leningrad Front,

Volkhov Front and 2nd Baltic Front finally broke the siege of Leningrad in January, and put Army Group North into retreat through the Baltic states. In the south, five Soviet front army groups began determined drives westwards from the Dnieper. Althought the German Army Group South, Army Group A and Army Group South Ukraine resisted every kilometre of the advance, they were unable to prevent themselves being squeezed back to the eastern borderlands of Poland, Hungary and Romania by mid-April, losing appalling numbers of men in the process.

As if the problems in the south were not enough, on 22 June 1944, three years to the day since Germany had launched its own invasion of the Soviet Union,

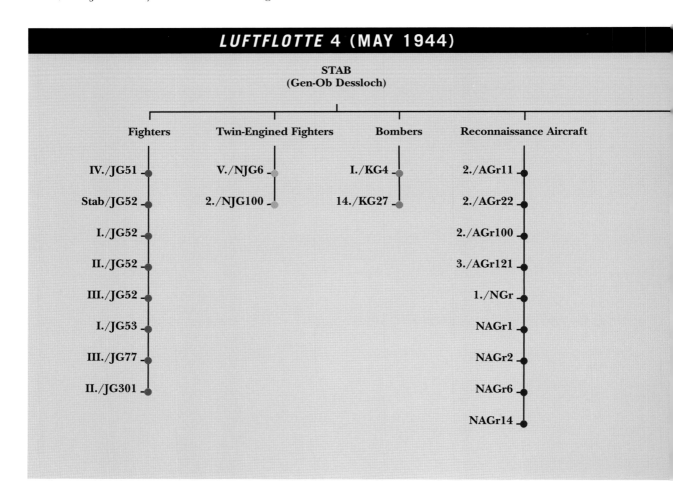

LUFTFLOTTE 4 (MAY 1944)

STAB
(Gen-Ob Dessloch)

Fighters	Twin-Engined Fighters	Bombers	Reconnaissance Aircraft
IV./JG51	V./NJG6	I./KG4	2./AGr11
Stab/JG52	2./NJG100	14./KG27	2./AGr22
I./JG52			2./AGr100
II./JG52			3./AGr121
III./JG52			1./NGr
I./JG53			NAGr1
III./JG77			NAGr2
II./JG301			NAGr6
			NAGr14

three Soviet fronts began Operation *Bagration*. The objective of this offensive was simply to crush the German Army Group Centre, drive it from Belorussia and begin the advance into eastern Poland.

Operation *Bagration* evolved into an utter massacre. An already weakened Army Group Centre was completely unable to resist the Soviet juggernaut, and entire German armies were almost wiped out. In less than a month, some 400,000 German soldiers were either killed, wounded or captured.

Powerless *Luftwaffe*

So where was the *Luftwaffe* in the midst of this catastrophe? One point that must be remembered is

that thousands of *Luftwaffe* personnel were also fighting for their lives on the ground. These personnel included several *Fallschirmjäger* units, whose tendency to be applied in 'fire brigade' roles meant that they suffered brutal casualty levels.

The 9.*Fallschirmjäger-Division* (9.FJD), for example, was formed in December 1944 out of collections of *Luftwaffe* ground personnel and drawn up into three understrength ad hoc regiments (FJR 25, 26 and 27). The division battled to prevent the Soviets crossing the Oder, but was eventually wiped out entirely during the Soviet advance on Berlin.

Fighting alongside the paratroopers were the *Luftwaffe Flak* units, the barrels of their anti-aircraft

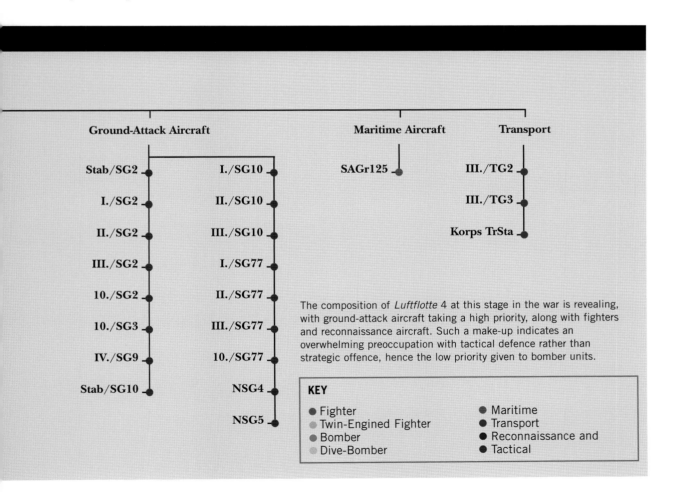

The composition of *Luftflotte* 4 at this stage in the war is revealing, with ground-attack aircraft taking a high priority, along with fighters and reconnaissance aircraft. Such a make-up indicates an overwhelming preoccupation with tactical defence rather than strategic offence, hence the low priority given to bomber units.

LUFTFLOTTE 4 (MAY 1944)			
Luftwaffe Unit	Type	Str	Op
FIGHTERS			
IV./JG51	Bf 109	30	22
Stab/JG52	Bf 109	1	1
I./JG52	Bf 109	29	10
II./JG52	Bf 109	24	18
III./JG52	Bf 109	23	20
I./JG53	Bf 109	33	31
III./JG77	Bf 109	31	28
II./JG301	Bf 109	11	10
TWIN-ENGINED FIGHTERS			
V./NJG6	Bf 110	27	22
2./NJG100	Bf 110	16	10
BOMBERS			
I./KG4	He 111	34	27
14./KG27	He 111	12	7
GROUND-ATTACK AIRCRAFT			
Stab/SG2	Ju 87	1	–
I./SG2	Ju 87	47	–
II./SG2	Fw 190	42	–
III./SG2	Ju 87	40	–
10./SG2	Ju 87	12	–
10./SG3	Ju 87	12	–
IV./SG9	Hs 129	67	–
Stab/SG10	Fw 190	5	–
I./SG10	Fw 190	32	–
II./SG10	Fw 190	31	–
III./SG10	Fw 190	40	–
I./SG77	Fw 190	34	–
II./SG77	Fw 190	33	–
III./SG77	Ju 87	39	–
10./SG77	Ju 87	12	–
NSG4	Go 145	30	–
NSG5	Go 145 / Ar 66	58 / ?	– / –
MARITIME AIRCRAFT			
SAGr125	Bv 138	15	10

guns suppressed to the horizontal to engage ground targets such as tanks.

The severity of the situation for the ground forces across the Eastern Front meant that any ambitions for delivering a strategic bombing campaign against the Soviet Union were quickly ditched. Whatever planes there were took to the skies in an attempt to at least slow the Soviet advances, or prevent the complete destruction of isolated army units.

LUFTFLOTTE 4 (MAY 1944)			
Luftwaffe Unit	Type	Str	Op
RECONNAISSANCE AIRCRAFT			
2./AGr11	Ju 88	10	7
2./AGr22	Ju 88	10	8
2./AGr100	Ju 188	11	8
3./AGr121	Ju 188	6	5
1./NGr	Do 217 / He 111	12 / ?	8 / ?
NAGr1	Fw 189	12	7
NAGr2	Bf 109	23	15
NAGr6	Fw 189	11	6
NAGr14	Bf 109	29	23
TRANSPORT AIRCRAFT			
III./TG2	Ju 52	45	43
III./TG3	Ju 52	43	42
Korps TrSta	Ju 52	24	19

June–August 1944

The Soviet summer offensive of 1944 was the most decisive single campaign of the war. Launched three years to the day after the German invasion, it involved the largest military force in history: more than 2.7 million men faced the German front lines, over one million attacking Army Group Centre alone. By the end of August, Soviet forces were in the Baltic states, over the Polish border and about to enter Romania. Of the 97 German divisions and 13 independent brigades serving with or reinforcing Army Group Centre over the operation, 17 divisions and 3 brigades were utterly destroyed, while another 50 divisions lost between 60 and 70 per cent of their manpower.

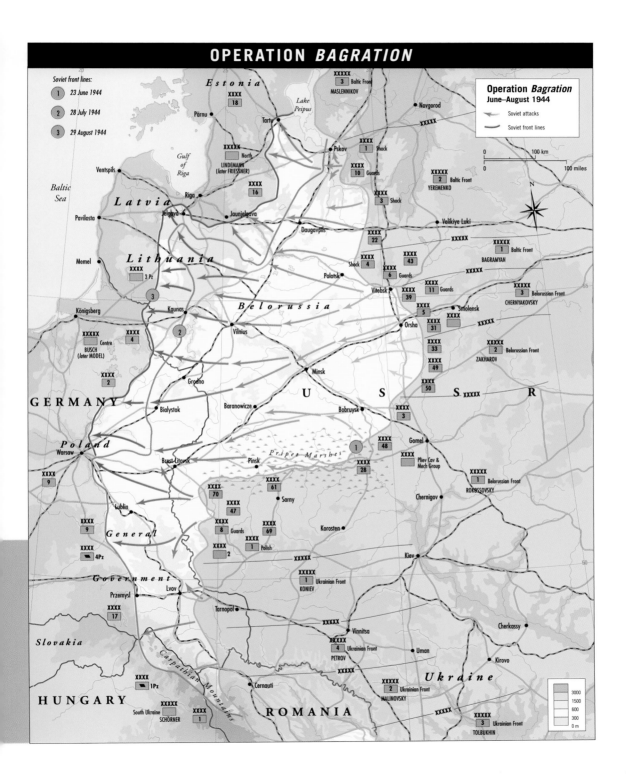

OPERATION *BAGRATION*

Soviet front lines:

1. 23 June 1944
2. 28 July 1944
3. 29 August 1944

Operation *Bagration*
June–August 1944

→ Soviet attacks

↝ Soviet front lines

0   100 km
0   100 miles

Estonia

XXXX 3 Baltic Front
MASLENNIKOV

XXXX 18

● Novgorod

Pärnu ●
Lake Peipus

Tartu ●

● Pskov

XXXX 1 Shock

XXXXX

XXXX 10 Guards

Baltic Sea

Ventspils ●

Latvia

Riga ●
XXXX 16

XXXX 3 Shock

XXXXX 2 Baltic Front
YEREMENKO

Gulf of Riga

XXXXX North
LINDEMANN
(later FRIESSNER)

Jelgavá ●
Jaunjelgava ●

● Daugavpils

● Velikiye Luki

Pavilosta ●

XXXX 22

XXXXX 1 Baltic Front
BAGRAMYAN

XXXXX

Memel ●

Lithuania

XXXX 3 Pz

Shock ● XXXX 4

XXXX 43

Polotsk ●

XXXX 6 Guards

XXXX 11 Guards

XXXXX 3 Belorussian Front
CHERNYAKOVSKY

3

Kaunas ●

Belorussia

Vitebsk ● XXXX 39

XXXX 5

● Smolensk

Königsberg ●

2

Vilnius ●

Orsha ● XXXX 31

XXXXX Centre 4
BUSCH
(later MODEL)

XXXX 33

XXXXX 2 Belorussian Front
ZAKHAROV

XXXX 49

XXXX 2

Grodno ●

Minsk ●

U   S   S   R

XXXX 50

Bialystok ●

● Bobruysk

XXXX 3

Poland

GERMANY

Warsaw ●

Baranowicze ●

XXXX 48

1

Gomel ●

XXXXX

XXXX 9

Brest-Litovsk ●

Pripet Marshes

XXXX Pliev Cav & Mech Group

XXXX 28

Pinsk ●

● Chernigov

XXXXX 1 Belorussian Front
ROKOSSOVSKY

Lublin ●

XXXX 70

XXXX 61

● Sarny

XXXX 47

XXXX 9

General

XXXX 8 Guards

XXXX 69

● Korosten

● Kiev

XXXX 4 Pz

XXXX 2

XXXX 1 Polish

Government

Lvov ●

XXXXX 1 Ukrainian Front
KONIEV

Przemysl ●

XXXX 17

Tarnopal ●

● Cherkassy

Slovakia

● Vinnitsa

XXXXX 4 Ukrainian Front
PETROV

● Uman

● Kirovo

XXXX 1 Pz

Cernauti ●

Ukraine

HUNGARY

XXXXX South Ukraine
SCHÖRNER

XXXX 1

ROMANIA

XXXXX 2 Ukrainian Front
MALINOVSKY

XXXXX 3 Ukrainian Front
TOLBUKHIN

3000
1500
600
300
0 m

Yet across the entire Eastern Front, the Red Air Force had little problem in establishing full air superiority. Taken across the whole of the front line, it had nearly 600 per cent of the aviation strength possessed by *Luftflotten* 1, 6 and 4. *Luftflotte* 6, for example, had just under 800 aircraft of all types, whereas the Soviet force facing it had just over 5000. To add insult to injury, *Luftflotte* 6 also lost 50 precious fighters to the air defence of the *Reich. Luftflotte* 4 was in no better shape. It had a total of 845 aircraft, but of these only 160 were single-seat fighter types and 390 ground-attack aircraft.

For the *Luftwaffe* aviators flying in these final missions on the Eastern Front, the contrast to the opening salvos of Operation *Barbarossa* three years previously could not have been starker. Individual German aircraft were faced with swarms of Soviet fighters, and these were not the inferior machines of the earlier years.

Not only was there the superb Yak-3, developed in 1941 but by now available in far greater numbers, but there were also thousands of Yak-9 types, which were superbly manoeuvrable, tough, heavily armed and had a top speed of 700km/h (435mph).

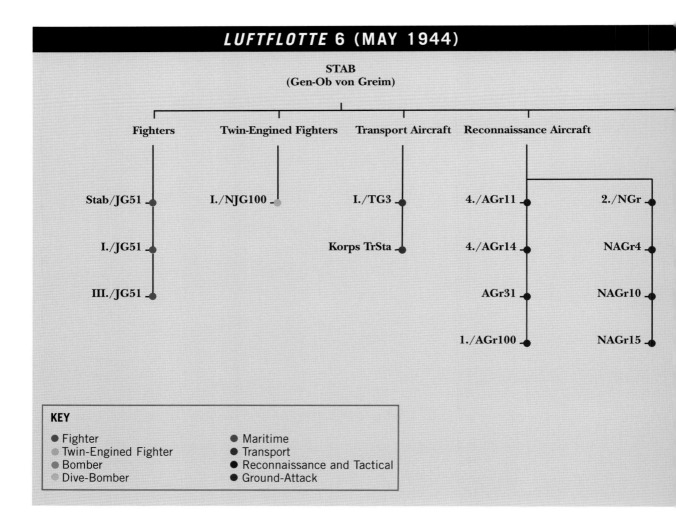

LUFTFLOTTE 6 (MAY 1944)

STAB
(Gen-Ob von Greim)

Fighters	Twin-Engined Fighters	Transport Aircraft	Reconnaissance Aircraft	
Stab/JG51	I./NJG100	I./TG3	4./AGr11	2./NGr
I./JG51		Korps TrSta	4./AGr14	NAGr4
III./JG51			AGr31	NAGr10
			1./AGr100	NAGr15

KEY
- Fighter
- Twin-Engined Fighter
- Bomber
- Dive-Bomber
- Maritime
- Transport
- Reconnaissance and Tactical
- Ground-Attack

During the final rapid Soviet advance into Germany, basing became a major headache for the *Luftwaffe*, as with every major Soviet push the ground personnel had to root up their existing base arrangements and transplant them to another location out of immediate danger. This meant they spent vital days relocating, unable to provide ground support for their aircraft. Fuel and spare parts supplies became scarce, and in the very last weeks of the war many *Luftwaffe* ground crew personnel found themselves moved from their professional work into ad hoc ground units pulled together for the final defence of the *Reich*.

Losses

Accurate figures for *Luftwaffe* losses on the Eastern Front during 1944 are extremely difficult to obtain, mainly because systems of administration were in meltdown. In June and July, however, despite reinforcement by some 150 fighters, some 325 aircraft were lost in combat, and those that could fly were rapidly running out of fuel and supplies. The *Luftwaffe* was being totally overrun by the Alied air forces on all fronts.

Total collapse was just months away, made more inevitable by the Soviet production capacities pushing

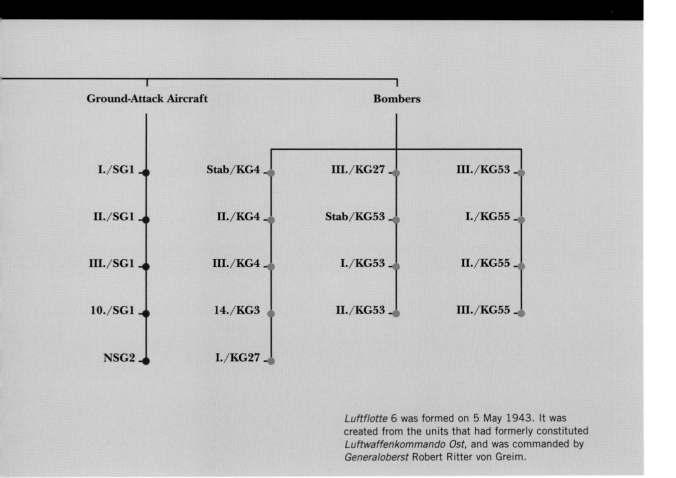

Ground-Attack Aircraft		Bombers	
I./SG1	Stab/KG4	III./KG27	III./KG53
II./SG1	II./KG4	Stab/KG53	I./KG55
III./SG1	III./KG4	I./KG53	II./KG55
10./SG1	14./KG3	II./KG53	III./KG55
NSG2	I./KG27		

Luftflotte 6 was formed on 5 May 1943. It was created from the units that had formerly constituted *Luftwaffenkommando Ost*, and was commanded by *Generaloberst* Robert Ritter von Greim.

LUFTFLOTTE 6 (MAY 1944)			
Luftwaffe Unit	Type	Str	Op
GROUND-ATTACK AIRCRAFT			
I./SG1	Ju 87	39	35
II./SG1	Ju 87	30	24
	Fw 190	12	2
III./SG1	Fw 190	42	33
10./SG1	Ju 87	12	12
NSG2	Ju 87	75	58
	Ar 66		
RECONNAISSANCE AIRCRAFT			
4./AGr11	Ju 188	11	7
	Ju 88		
4./AGr14	Ju 188	8	6
	Ju 88		
AGr31	Fw 189	5	3
1./AGr100	Ju 88	12	5
2./NGr	Do 217	12	8
NAGr4	Bf 109	38	24
	Fw 189		
	Hs 126		
NAGr10	Hs 126	27	20
	Bf 109		
	Fw 189		
NAGr15	Fw 189	19	16
TRANSPORT AIRCRAFT			
I./TG3	Ju 52	48	44
Korps TrSta	Ju 52	22	14

LUFTFLOTTE 6 (MAY 1944)			
Luftwaffe Unit	Type	Str	Op
FIGHTERS			
Stab/JG51	Bf 109	4	4
	Fw 190	16	16
I./JG51	Bf 109	44	34
III./JG51	Bf 109	40	32
TWIN-ENGINED FIGHTERS			
I./NJG100	Ju 88	32	21
	Do 217		
BOMBERS			
Stab/KG4	He 111	1	0
II./KG4	He 111	35	28
III./KG4	He 111	37	26
14./KG3	Ju 88	12	8
I./KG27	He 111	37	37
III./KG27	He 111	37	33
Stab/KG53	He 111	1	1
I./KG53	He 111	37	27
II./KG53	He 111	34	28
III./KG53	He 111	37	24
I./KG55	He 111	35	27
II./KG55	He 111	32	20
III./KG55	He 111	34	29

more and more aircraft out into action. In total during World War II, the Soviet Union built over 125,600 combat aircraft alone, and total aircraft production in 1944 rose to over 40,000 aircraft.

Building to defeat

The battle for the Eastern Front had become as impossible to sustain for the *Luftwaffe* as it had for the ground forces, and by the end of the year the Soviet frontline ran in a line that roughly tracked through (from north to south) Warsaw, Budapest and Belgrade. With the Allies also pressing in from the west, the *Luftwaffe*'s focus was now on defending the homeland.

January–May 1944

The massive Soviet advances in the Ukraine between January and May 1944 drove Germany out of Ukrainian territory and back into Romania, against the Carpathian mountains and against the eastern borders of Poland. The three principal German formations resisting the Soviets in this sector were Army Group South (Manstein), Army Group A (Kleist) and Army Group South Ukraine (Schörner). All three of these army groups had been battered in the retreats during the second half of 1943, and were critically weakened.

The Soviet offensive was launched by (from north to south): 2nd Belorussian Front (Kurochkin), 1st Ukrainian Front (Vatutin, then Zhukov), 2nd Ukrainian Front (Koniev), 3rd Ukrainian Front (Malinovsky) and 4th Ukrainian Front (Tolbukhin).

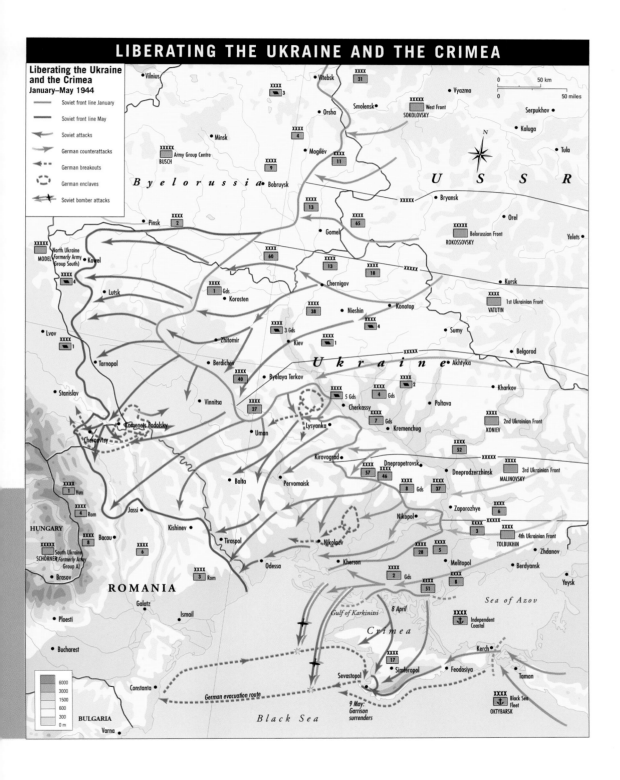

LIBERATING THE UKRAINE AND THE CRIMEA

Liberating the Ukraine and the Crimea
January–May 1944

- Soviet front line January
- Soviet front line May
- Soviet attacks
- German counterattacks
- German breakouts
- German enclaves
- Soviet bomber attacks

0   50 km
0   50 miles

Vilnius

Vitebsk

XXXX 31

XXXX 3

Orsha

Smolensk

Vyazma

Serpukhov

XXXXX West Front SOKOLOVSKY

Kaluga

Minsk

XXXX 4

Mogilёv

Tula

XXXXX Army Group Centre BUSCH

XXXX 9

XXXX 11

U   S   S   R

B y e l o r u s s i a

Bobruysk

XXXX 13

Bryansk

Orel

XXXX 2

Pinsk

XXXX 65

Gomel

XXXXX Belorussian Front ROKOSSOVSKY

Yelets

XXXXX North Ukraine (Formerly Army Group South) MODEL

Kowel

XXXX 60

XXXX 13

XXXX 18

Kursk

XXXX 4

Lutsk

XXXX 1 Gds

Korosten

Chernigov

XXXX 1st Ukrainian Front VATUTIN

Lvov

XXXX 38

Nieshin

Konotop

Sumy

Zhitomir

XXXX 3 Gds

XXXX 4

XXXX 1

Belgorod

Tarnopol

Berdichev

Kiev

U k r a i n e

Akhtyka

Stanislav

XXXX 40

Byelaya Terkov

XXXX 2

XXXX 4 Gds

Kharkov

XXXX 27

Vinnitsa

XXXX 5 Gds

Cherkassy

Poltava

Kamenets Podolsky

Uman

Lysyanka

XXXX 7 Gds

Kremenchug

XXXX 2nd Ukrainian Front KONIEV

Chernovtsy

Kirovograd

XXXX 52

Dnepropetrovsk

XXXX 57

XXXX 46

Dneprodzerzhinsk

XXXX 3rd Ukrainian Front MALINOVSKY

Balta

Pervomaisk

XXXX 8 Gds

XXXX 37

XXXX 1 Hun

Zaporozhye

XXXX 6

XXXX 4 Rom

Jassi

Kishinev

Nikopol

XXXX 3

XXXX 4th Ukrainian Front TOLBUKHIN

HUNGARY

XXXX 8 Bacau

XXXX 6

Tiraspol

Nikolaev

Melitopol

Zhdanov

XXXXX South Ukraine SCHÖRNER (Formerly Army Group A)

XXXX 28

XXXX 5

Berdyansk

Brasov

Odessa

Kherson

XXXX 8

Yeysk

ROMANIA

XXXX 3 Rom

XXXX 2 Gds

XXXX 51

Sea of Azov

Galatz

Ismail

Gulf of Karkinitsi

8 April

XXXX Independent Coastal

Ploesti

C r i m e a

Kerch

Bucharest

XXXX 17

Simferopol

Feodosiya

Taman

Constanta

German evacuation route

Sevastopol

XXXX Black Sea Fleet OKTYABRSK

BULGARIA

9 May: Garrison surrenders

Black Sea

Varna

6000
3000
1500
600
300
0 m

Northwest Europe: 1942–45

By 6 June 1944, the date of the Allied D-Day invasion, the *Luftwaffe* was mainly preoccupied with the air war on the Eastern Front and against the strategic bombing of the *Reich*. The battles in Western Europe soon added a new burden.

The Fw 190 was one of World War II's finest fighters, although it was unable to dent the Allies' numerical superiority.

From the end of the Battle of Britain to the beginning of the Normandy campaign, the *Luftwaffe* forces in the far west of Europe were essentially starved of resources. Even with the intensification of the Allied bomber war against the *Reich* in 1943 and 1944 (see the next chapter for the German war against the strategic bombing campaign), which often involved overflights of France and the Low Countries, German fighter strength in those countries was relatively low.

Force deployments
The two *Luftwaffe* formations primarily responsible for the defence of Western Europe and the approaches to Germany itself were *Luftflotte* 3 and *Luftflotte Reich*. The latter was a late addition to the order of battle, having been formed in February 1944 from the former *Luftwaffenbefehlshaber Mitte*. It was, as its name suggested, responsible for the defence of Germany itself, including territories just across its borders.

Luftflotte 3, by contrast, was an old formation dating back to February 1939, but for many years now it had played second fiddle to other theatres. In May 1944, the entire *Luftflotte* was running at a serviceable single-seat fighter strength of around 250 machines, and its resources were regularly clipped even further by demands from the Eastern Front and from the Mediterranean. The available aircraft were good, however. Most of *Luftflotte* 3's fighter strength at this time was provided by the Focke-Wulf Fw 190, undoubtedly one of the best aircraft of the entire war, although its performance could fade in high-altitude engagements. The Fw 190s stiffened the effective combat strength of *Luftflotte* 3's fighter units – JG2, JG26 and one *Staffel* of JG54. Like the British, the Germans also had a network of radar stations running along the Western European coastline, although coordination of the information provided was not as centrally structured as it was in Britain.

With the expansion of the Allied strategic bombing campaign against Germany itself, *Luftflotte* 3 was bolstered a little. There was little denying, however, that when the Allied invasion came on 6 June 1944, it was completely incapable of retaining control of the skies.

The war against the bombers

On 30 May 1942, the RAF launched a 1000-bomber raid against a German target, Cologne. Although the Allies had been bombing Germany since earlier in the war, this raid can be viewed as the beginning of the strategic bomber war over the *Reich*.

The *Luftwaffe*'s war against the Allied strategic bombing campaign is an epic story that can easily fill an entire book in its own right. Like the battle for the Atlantic, the war over the *Reich* was a conflict of both numbers and tactics. Tactically, the *Luftwaffe* held the best cards for long periods, and inflicted appalling losses upon the Allied bomber crews. Yet ultimately, vastly superior Allied numbers combined with improved defensive technologies and fighter escorts to overwhelm the *Luftwaffe* defences and turn many German cities into ashen ruins.

RAF Bomber Command primarily conducted a night campaign. Equipped from 1942 with Avro Lancaster bombers, the RAF utterly devastated several major cities,

such as Hamburg in July 1943, where up to 40,000 people were killed. In response, much of the *Luftwaffe*'s defensive air power was clawed back into Germany, with only 20 per cent of the air force left over for frontline ground-support work by the end of the year. In addition, thousands of AA guns ringed important targets, and by 1944 the personnel employed in the *Luftwaffe*'s *Flak* arm number 1.25 million.

The night war
During 1943, however, the *Luftwaffe* became increasingly expert in the tactics and technologies of night-fighting. Between Paris and Denmark stretched a chain of radar

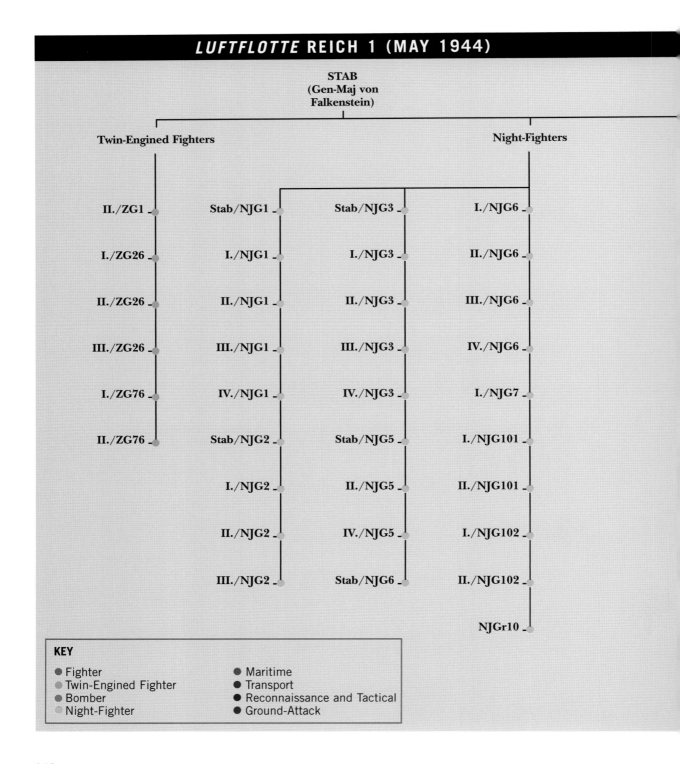

LUFTFLOTTE REICH 1 (MAY 1944)

STAB
(Gen-Maj von
Falkenstein)

Twin-Engined Fighters

Night-Fighters

Twin-Engined Fighters	NJG1	NJG3	NJG6/7
II./ZG1	Stab/NJG1	Stab/NJG3	I./NJG6
I./ZG26	I./NJG1	I./NJG3	II./NJG6
II./ZG26	II./NJG1	II./NJG3	III./NJG6
III./ZG26	III./NJG1	III./NJG3	IV./NJG6
I./ZG76	IV./NJG1	IV./NJG3	I./NJG7
II./ZG76	Stab/NJG2	Stab/NJG5	I./NJG101
	I./NJG2	II./NJG5	II./NJG101
	II./NJG2	IV./NJG5	I./NJG102
	III./NJG2	Stab/NJG6	II./NJG102
			NJGr10

KEY

- ● Fighter
- ● Twin-Engined Fighter
- ● Bomber
- ● Night-Fighter
- ● Maritime
- ● Transport
- ● Reconnaissance and Tactical
- ● Ground-Attack

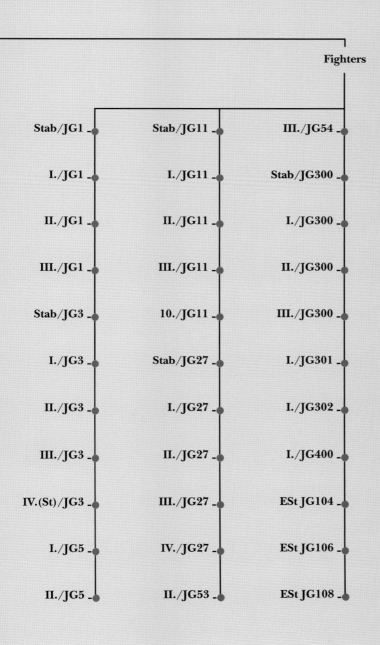

Fighters

Stab/JG1	Stab/JG11	III./JG54
I./JG1	I./JG11	Stab/JG300
II./JG1	II./JG11	I./JG300
III./JG1	III./JG11	II./JG300
Stab/JG3	10./JG11	III./JG300
I./JG3	Stab/JG27	I./JG301
II./JG3	I./JG27	I./JG302
III./JG3	II./JG27	I./JG400
IV.(St)/JG3	III./JG27	ESt JG104
I./JG5	IV./JG27	ESt JG106
II./JG5	II./JG53	ESt JG108

Luftflotte Reich was formed in February 1944 as the new organization tasked with the defence of the *Reich*. What is immediately apparent is the defensive nature of this *Luftflotte* – it consists of nothing other than fighter (single-seat and twin-engined) and night-fighter units. In total at this point, the *Luftflotte* possessed about 2500 combat aircraft, although not all of these were serviceable.

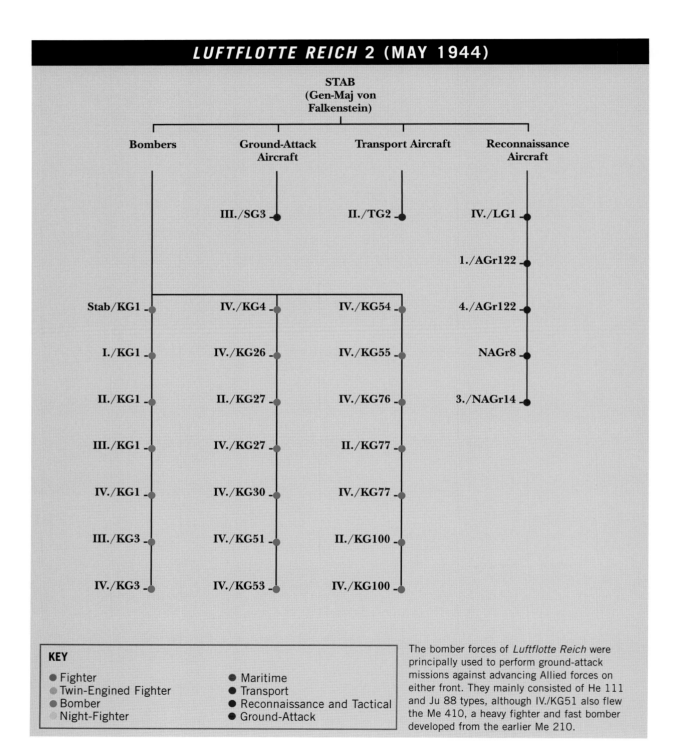

LUFTFLOTTE REICH 2 (MAY 1944)

STAB
(Gen-Maj von Falkenstein)

Bombers	Ground-Attack Aircraft	Transport Aircraft	Reconnaissance Aircraft
	III./SG3	II./TG2	IV./LG1
			1./AGr122
Stab/KG1	IV./KG4	IV./KG54	4./AGr122
I./KG1	IV./KG26	IV./KG55	NAGr8
II./KG1	II./KG27	IV./KG76	3./NAGr14
III./KG1	IV./KG27	II./KG77	
IV./KG1	IV./KG30	IV./KG77	
III./KG3	IV./KG51	II./KG100	
IV./KG3	IV./KG53	IV./KG100	

KEY
- Fighter
- Twin-Engined Fighter
- Bomber
- Night-Fighter
- Maritime
- Transport
- Reconnaissance and Tactical
- Ground-Attack

The bomber forces of *Luftflotte Reich* were principally used to perform ground-attack missions against advancing Allied forces on either front. They mainly consisted of He 111 and Ju 88 types, although IV./KG51 also flew the Me 410, a heavy fighter and fast bomber developed from the earlier Me 210.

LUFTFLOTTE REICH (MAY 1944)			
Luftwaffe Unit	Type	Str	Op
FIGHTERS			
Stab/JG1	Fw 190	2	2
I./JG1	Fw 190	43	15
II./JG1	Fw 190	42	20
III./JG1	Bf 109	48	21
Stab/JG3	Bf 109	4	2
I./JG3	Bf 109	26	9
II./JG3	Bf 109	29	23
III./JG3	Bf 109	31	9
IV.(St)/JG3	Fw 190	54	1
I./JG5	Bf 109	43	36
II./JG5	Bf 109	44	36
Stab./JG11	Bf 109	4	3
I./JG11	Fw 190	28	20
II./JG11	Bf 109	31	14
III./JG11	Fw 190	28	11
10./JG11	Fw 190	10	7
	Bf 109	?	?
Stab/JG27	Bf 109	4	4
I./JG27	Bf 109	44	34
II./JG27	Bf 109	24	12
III./JG27	Bf 109	26	20
IV./JG27	Bf 109	22	16
II./JG53	Bf 109	31	14
III./JG54	Fw 190	23	8
Stab/JG300	Fw 190	2	1
I./JG300	Bf 109	29	19
II./JG300	Fw 190	32	23
III./JG300	Bf 109	27	25
I./JG301	Bf 109	25	21
I./JG302	Bf 109	27	11
I./JG400	Me 163	10	0
ESt JG104	Bf 109	4	4
ESt JG106	Bf 109	5	3
ESt JG108	Bf 109	12	6

LUFTFLOTTE REICH (MAY 1944)			
Luftwaffe Unit	Type	Str	Op
TWIN-ENGINED FIGHTERS			
II./ZG1	Bf 110	30	15
I./ZG26	Me 410	20	6
II./ZG26	Me 410	50	24
III./ZG26	Me 262	6	1
	Bf 110	9	9
I./ZG76	Me 410	47	25
II./ZG76	Me 410	33	0
	Bf 110	3	2
NIGHT-FIGHTERS			
Stab/NJG1	He 219	2	1
	Bf 110	?	?
I./NJG1	He 219	33	26
	Me 410	?	?
II./NJG1	He 219	21	11
	Bf 110	?	?
III./NJG1	Bf 110	17	17
IV./NJG1	Bf 110	23	14
Stab/NJG2	Ju 88	4	4
I./NJG2	Ju 88	31	21
II./NJG2	Ju 88	33	19
III./NJG2	Ju 88	28	18
Stab/NJG3	Ju 88	3	3
	Bf 110	?	?
I./NJG3	Bf 110	26	22
II./NJG3	Ju 88	37	13
III./NJG3	Bf 110	29	20
IV./NJG3	Ju 88	32	21
	Bf 110	?	?
Stab/NJG5	Bf 110	3	1
II./NJG5	Bf 110	19	13
IV./NJG5	Bf 110	18	8
Stab/NGJ6	Bf 110	2	1
I./NJG6	Bf 110	24	21
	Do 217	?	?
II./NJG6	Bf 110	10	8
III./NJG6	Bf 110	18	13
IV./NJG6	Bf 110	27	22

LUFTFLOTTE REICH (MAY 1944)			
Luftwaffe Unit	Type	Str	Op
NIGHT-FIGHTERS			
I./NJG7	Ju 88	21	9
I./NJG101	Bf 110 Ju 88	39	39
II./NJG101	Do 217	38	–
I./NJG102	Bf 110	39	–
II./NJG102	Bf 110	39	–
NJGr10	Bf 109 Fw 190 He 219 Ta 154 Ju 88 Bf 110	23	–
RECONNAISSANCE AIRCRAFT			
IV./LG1	Ju 88	30	18
1./AGr122	Me 410 Bf 110	6 2	0 3
4./AGr122	Ju 188	11	–
NAGr8	Bf109	2	2
3./NAGr14	Bf109	2	0
GROUND-ATTACK AIRCRAFT			
III./SG3	Fw 190	34	31
TRANSPORT AIRCRAFT			
II./TG2	Ju 52	12	9

LUFTFLOTTE REICH (MAY 1944)			
Luftwaffe Unit	Type	Str	Op
BOMBERS			
Stab/KG1	He 177	2	1
I./KG1	He 177	30	11
II./KG1	He 177	29	0
III./KG1	He 177	30	12
IV./KG1	He 177 Ju 88	34 12	12 9
III./KG3	He 111	35	21
IV./KG3	Ju 88	23	14
IV./KG4	He 111	37	22
IV./KG26	Ju 88	34	15
II./KG27	He 111	15	12
IV./KG27	He 111	58	33
IV./KG30	Ju 88	22	12
IV./KG51	Me 410	12	5
IV./KG53	He 111	39	21
IV./KG54	Ju 88	13	9
IV./KG55	He 111	34	17
IV./KG76	Ju 88	28	10
II./KG77	Ju 88	31	21
IV./KG77	Ju 88	38	24
II./KG100	He 177	30	0
IV./KG100	He 177 Do 217	21 17	6 7

installations and control stations known as the Kammhuber Line, which provided a early-warning facility to deploy five special *Nachtjagdgeschwader* (night-fighter *Geschwader*). Radar-equipped Do 217s, He 219s, Ju 88s and Bf 110s attacked the swarms of British bombers, whose pilots subsequently modified their tactics to pass through the Kammhuber Line with greater speed and less vulnerability.

As the raids on Germany became heavier, however, the aircraft deployed with the Kammhuber Line were steadily pulled back into the *Luftwaffenbefehlshaber Mitte*, the air-defence structure covering German territory. Over Germany, the *Luftwaffe* night-fighters experimented with various different tactics, some of which gave sound results. With improved radar, the night-fighters were directed

into the enemy bomber formations, and there used their own short-range radar to destroy their targets. Improved SN2 radar sets from October 1943 detected aircraft out to 6.5km (4 miles) and could also distinguish between bombers and the 'chaff' that the Allies dispensed in huge quantities in an attempt to confuse the enemy. Night-fighters would actually enter the Allied bomber stream, dip below a target aircraft and use the new *schräge Musik* upward-firing 20mm (0.78in) cannon to fire directly into the bomber's fuel tanks and bombload.

All this essentially gave the German Air Force the upper hand in the night war, and Bomber Command losses rose to a crescendo in January–March 1944. In those three months the RAF lost 796 bombers to all

ALLIED LOSSES TO FIGHTERS AND FLAK, 1944–45		
Year	RAF Bomber Command	USAF Eighth Air Force
1944		
Jan	314	203
Feb	199	271
Mar	283	345
Apr	214	420
May	274	376
Jun	305	320
Jul	241	352
Aug	221	331
Sep	137	374
Oct	127	177
Nov	139	209
Dec	119	119
1945		
Jan	133	314
Feb	173	196
Mar	215	266
Apr	73	190

LUFTWAFFE NACHTJAGD (NIGHT-FIGHTER) ACES			
Pilot	Night	Day	Total
Maj Heinz-Wolfgang Schnaufer	121	0	121
Obst Helmut Lent	102	8	110
Maj Heinrich-Alexander zu Sayn-Wittgenstein	83	0	83
Obst Werner Streib	67	1	68
Hptm Manfred Meurer	65	0	65
Obst Günther 'Fips' Radusch	64	1	65
Maj Rudolf Schönert	64	0	64
Hptm Heinz Rökker	63	1	64
Maj Paul Zorner	59	0	59
Hptm Martin 'Tino' Becker	58	0	58
Hptm Gerhard Raht	58	0	58
Maj Wilhelm Herget	57	16	73
ObLt Kurt Welter	56	7	63
Hptm Josef Kraft	56	0	56
Hptm Heinz Strüning	56	0	56
ObLt Gustav Francsi	56	0	56
Hptm Hans-Dieter Frank	55	0	55
Ofw Heinz Vinke	54	0	54
Hptm August Geiger	53	0	53
Maj Prinz Egmont zur Lippe-Weissenfeld	51	0	51
Maj Werner Hoffmann	50	1	51
ObstLt Herbert Lütje	50	0	50
Stfw Reinhard Kollak	49	0	49
Hptm Georg-Hermann Greiner	47	4	51
Hptm Johannes Hagner	47	1	48
ObLt Paul Gildner	46	2	48
Maj Paul Semrau	46	0	46

causes. A total of 5881 bombers had been lost since January 1943, 492 against Berlin alone, and such losses forced a pause and rethink.

Day war

While the RAF's Bomber Command slugged it out over Germany at night, the US Eighth and Fifteenth Air Forces took destruction to Germany by day. In January 1943, at the Casablanca Conference, the Allies between them agreed on a Combined Bomber Offensive. The US bomber groups at first flew beyond the range of their fighter escorts, relying instead on the heavy armament provided by machine-gun-bristling planes such as the Boeing B-17 Flying Fortress.

It was a sobering experience for the US pilots. The German Fw 190s and Bf 109s carved into the formations, and during the infamous US raid on the ball-bearing works at Schweinfurt on 14 October 1943, 60 of the 291 bombers were shot down and another 100 damaged.

The Eighth Air Force was forced, for the time being, to limit its raids over Germany.

Things would change, however. The *Luftwaffe* may have appeared resurgent, but its losses were escalating on all fronts. Crew losses alone were running at a rate of around 15 per cent for January–March 1944, and the rates of night-fighter losses simply through accidents were a cause for concern.

Furthermore, by 1944 the USAAF had equipped Mustang fighters with long-range drop tanks, giving them the fuel to escort the bombers all the way to Berlin, fight for 20 minutes, and still have juice enough to return home. Now the Allies would fight on equal terms over Germany, and proved their point from 20 February 1944.

'Big Week'

On that date, both the US and British air forces launched what was later known as 'Big Week', a huge coordinated pounding of Germany fighter production facilities, with the ancillary benefit of dragging hundreds of *Luftwaffe* fighters into air for combat with the formidable North American P-51 Mustang. The operation cost the Allies 254 aircraft, mainly bombers, while the Germans lost at least 300 precious fighters. Aircraft production was set back two months. Furthermore, the mounting *Luftwaffe* losses during the day were starting to drag down the numbers of available night-fighters, and by the end of the year Bomber Command was once again pounding away at targets at night with acceptable loss rates.

Much-improved bomb-aiming systems aboard the British aircraft enabled them to hit important targets such as oil refineries with more convincing accuracy. They could still destroy area targets, however, as the unfortunte city of Dresden found out in February 1945, when raids by British and US bombers killed tens of thousands of people.

TOP *LUFTWAFFE* MUSTANG DESTROYERS		
Pilot	Kills	Total
Maj Wilhelm Steinmann	12	44
Ofw Heinrich Bartels	11	99
ObstLt Heinz Bär	10	221
Hptm Franz Schall	10	133
ObLt Wilhelm Hofmann	10	44
Hptm Emil 'Bully' Lang	9	173
Hptm Walter Krupinski	8	197
Maj Georg-Peter Eder	at least 7	78
Maj Jürgen Harder	7	65
ObLt Heinz-Gerhard Vogt	7	48
Lt Hans Fritz	7	12
Maj Erich 'Bubi' Hartmann	at least 6	352
Obst Walther Dahl	at least 6	128
Hptm Siegfried Lemke	at least 6	70

Once the Allies had begun to advance through France, and the Red Army into the German borders from the east, there was little the *Luftwaffe* could do to defeat the Allied bombing campaign. Pilots had insubstantial experience, and in January 1945 aviation fuel supplies collapsed to around 33 per cent of the necessary capacity. The *Luftwaffe* did ensure, however, that the bombing raids never had complete freedom of the skies, and at a cost to the Allies of 50,000 aircrew killed.

Normandy defence

In April 1943, Britain's Bomber Command began to shift its priorities from targets in Germany to military and infrastructural targets in western France. The signal from the Western Allies was clear – an invasion was coming.

By April 1944, the Allies were enjoying the fruits of a massive disparity in aircraft numbers when compared with the *Luftwaffe*. Looking across all theatres, at the beginning of June 1944 the United States had 19,342 combat aircraft at its disposal, and the United Kingdom

a further 8339 combat types. This total of more than 27,000 aircraft compares with only 4637 combat aircraft on the German side. Although the production totals of German aircraft would peak in 1944 (see previous chapter), the sheer scale of *Luftwaffe* losses was

voraciously gobbling up the reinforcements.
If we look at *Luftflotte* 3, the formation that would face the D-Day onslaught, it would still enter the maelstrom with only two *Geschwader* of single-seat fighters, about 170 aircraft.

Its ground-attack and bomber elements had been strengthened, but in total there would only be about 700 German machines in the air to resist the Normandy landings. On that day, the Allies would bring with them 12,000 aircraft.

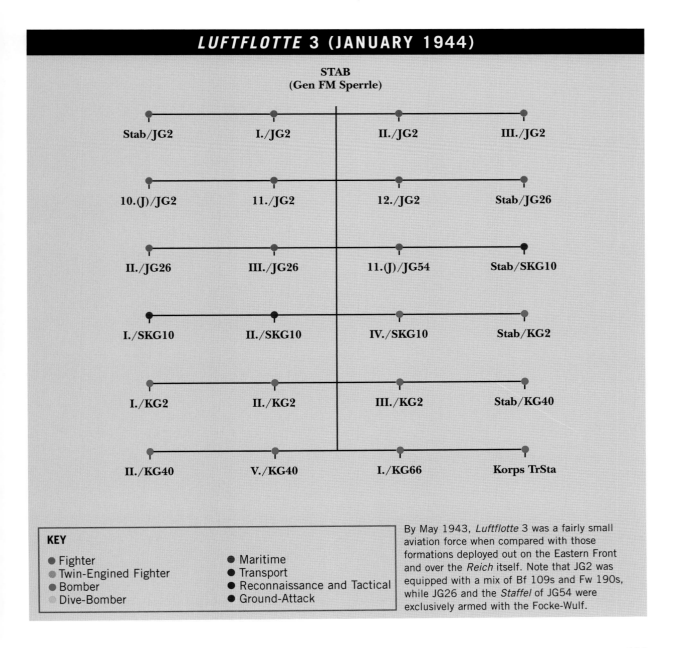

LUFTFLOTTE 3 (JANUARY 1944)

STAB
(Gen FM Sperrle)

Stab/JG2   I./JG2   II./JG2   III./JG2

10.(J)/JG2   11./JG2   12./JG2   Stab/JG26

II./JG26   III./JG26   11.(J)/JG54   Stab/SKG10

I./SKG10   II./SKG10   IV./SKG10   Stab/KG2

I./KG2   II./KG2   III./KG2   Stab/KG40

II./KG40   V./KG40   I./KG66   Korps TrSta

KEY
- Fighter
- Twin-Engined Fighter
- Bomber
- Dive-Bomber
- Maritime
- Transport
- Reconnaissance and Tactical
- Ground-Attack

By May 1943, *Luftflotte* 3 was a fairly small aviation force when compared with those formations deployed out on the Eastern Front and over the *Reich* itself. Note that JG2 was equipped with a mix of Bf 109s and Fw 190s, while JG26 and the *Staffel* of JG54 were exclusively armed with the Focke-Wulf.

LUFTFLOTTEN – AREAS OF RESPONSIBILITY

Western Europe, May 1944

This map shows the various areas over which the German *Luftflotten* had jurisdiction in the period immediately prior to the Normandy landings of June 1944.

Luftflotte 3's zone covered all of France, Belgium and the Netherlands, a huge area to which the much-thinned *Luftflotte* could do little justice. It was neighboured by *Luftflotte Reich* (previously *Luftwaffenbefehlshaber Mitte*), which was responsible for the defence of Germany against the huge Allied bombing raids against its urban areas.

Luftflotte 5 still occupied its traditional position up in Scandinavia and Finland, and would have little relevance to events following the 6 June landings. In the south *Luftflotte* 2 (or what remained of it) covered Italy in a futile attempt to restrain the Allies' air power, and *Luftwaffenkommando Süd-Ost* defended the Balkans and the critical oilfields in Romania.

LUFTFLOTTE 3 (JANUARY 1944)				
Luftwaffe Unit	Base	Type	Str	Op
IX.FLIEGERKORPS				
Stab/KG2	Soesterberg	Do 217E	4	3
I./KG2	Eindhoven	Do 217E	37	35
II./KG2	Münster-Handorf	Ju 188E	37	31
III./KG2	Gilze Rijen	Do 217E	37	36
V./KG2	Athies	Me 410A	37	25
Stab, III./KG6	Melsbroek	Ju 88A	41	40
I./KG6	Chièvres	Ju 188A	41	37
II./KG6	Le Culot	Ju 88A	39	37
Stab, I./KG30	Eindhoven	Ju 88A	41	30
II./KG30	St Trond	Ju 88A	37	31
1./KG40	Châteaudun	He 177A	9	5
Stab, I./KG54	Marx	Ju 88A	41	28
II./KG54	Wittmund	Ju 88A	37	33
I./KG66	Montdidier	Ju 88A	37	12
		He 111H	?	2
		Ju 188E	?	9
4./KG66	Vannes	Ju 188E	12	?
I./KG76	Couvron	Ju 88A	37	31
I./KG100	Châteaudun	He 177A	27	21
I./SKG100	Rosières	Fw 190G	42	20

Attrition within *Luftflotte* 3 went up commensurately with the Allied attacks over France in April. Slugging it out with escorting British Spitfires and US Mustangs, *Luftflotte* 3 lost some 24 per cent of its fighter pilot strength in that month alone. The next month, the *Luftwaffe* in its entirety lost just over half of all its single-seat fighters in combat, bringing the tally of dead fighter pilots that year to nearly 2300. Furthermore, priority targets for the Allies were *Luftflotte* 3's airbases. The assaults caused units to make frequent moves, producing chaos within a supply system that was already hampered by Allied depredations against fuel supplies, road networks and rail lines.

When the hammer blow of D-Day did finally fall, the Allies' acquisition of air superiority was completely effortless. During the daylight hours of 6 June, *Luftflotte* 3 managed fewer than 100 sorties against the 14,000 sorties flown by Allied aircraft. On this day, and throughout the remainder of the Normandy campaign, Allied fighter-bombers hunted down movements of

German armour, supplies and troops with virtual impunity, making it very difficult to move up reinforcements to the front.

Luftflotte 3 nevertheless did receive some meagre reinforcements of its own – all that could be spared from *Luftflotte Reich* and the harried formations on the Eastern Front. Between 6 and 10 June, *Luftflotte* 3 received no less than 300 additional fighters, but this was still a drop in the ocean when compared with the air resources available to the Allies.

Mounting losses

Losses were more than keeping pace with reinforcements, anyway. During the first two weeks after D-Day, the *Luftflotte* lost an astonishing 594 aircraft. The situation for the German forces on the ground over subsequent weeks was little better than that experienced by the *Luftwaffe* in the skies over France.

The Allies were certainly impressed by the fighting qualities of the German infantryman, and casualty levels amongst Allied front-line combat units approached and even exceeded those suffered by equivalent units and formations during the great battles of World War I.

IX.FLIEGERKORPS (15 JUNE 1944)				
Luftwaffe Unit	**Base**	**Type**	**Str**	**Op**
IX.FLIEGERKORPS				
Stab, I., II./KG2	Couvron	Ju 188E	75	32
III./KG2	Couvron	Do 217M	37	16
Stab/KG6	Melsbroek	Ju 88A	1	1
I./KG6	Brétigny	Ju 188A	37	11
II./KG6	Villaroche	Ju 188A	37	?
III./KG6	Ahlhorn	Ju 188A	37	11
Stab, II./KG30	Zwischenahn	Ju 88A	38	1
II./KG51	Soesterberg	Me 410A	37	10
Stab, III./KG54	Marx	Ju 88A	38	8
I./KG54	Wittmund	Ju 88A	37	9
I./KG66	Avord	Ju 88S	25	5
		Ju 188E	?	?
Stab, 5./KG76	Melsbroek	Ju 88A	13	9
Stab, I./LG1	Le Culot	Ju 88A	38	15
II./LG1	Chièvres	Ju 88A	37	19
I./SKG10	Dreux	Fw 190F	42	18

May 1944

This map of *Luftwaffe* bases around the French coastline illustrates how vulnerable German Air Force deployments in France were when faced with an Allied invasion.

Once the Allies managed to break out of Normandy, the main concentration of *Luftwaffe* fighter bases opposite the English southeast coast would be in danger of being cut off, and the Germans would also lose a cluster of bomber bases just inland.

Although the array of *Luftwaffe* airbases here may look formidable, the actual numbers of aircraft deployed at these bases was totally inadequate for resisting the Allied onslaught.

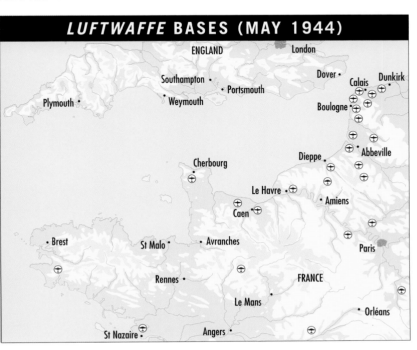

LUFTWAFFE BASES (MAY 1944)

Caen was taken at great cost by 18 July, followed by St Lô by the end of the month, the city having been reduced to rubble by Allied carpet bombing.

Breakout from Normandy

At the beginning of August, the breakout from Normandy began, and the German ground forces suffered horrifically from Allied artillery and air strikes during the escape from the Falaise gap, a pocket created by the pincerlike advance of the British and US armies. On 25 August, Paris itself had fallen, and the focus for the Allies in the West now became the drive to the Rhine River.

The *Luftwaffe* was virtually powerless to prevent this advance. Arguments broke out about the best use for the dwindling aircraft resources. For a time, the fighters switched mainly to ground-attack work, but the limited effects of strafing runs soon caused them to return to their principal duty of air defence. In this they could make no dent in regional Allied air superiority, and the total advantage in the air held by the Allies accounts for much of the Normandy victory.

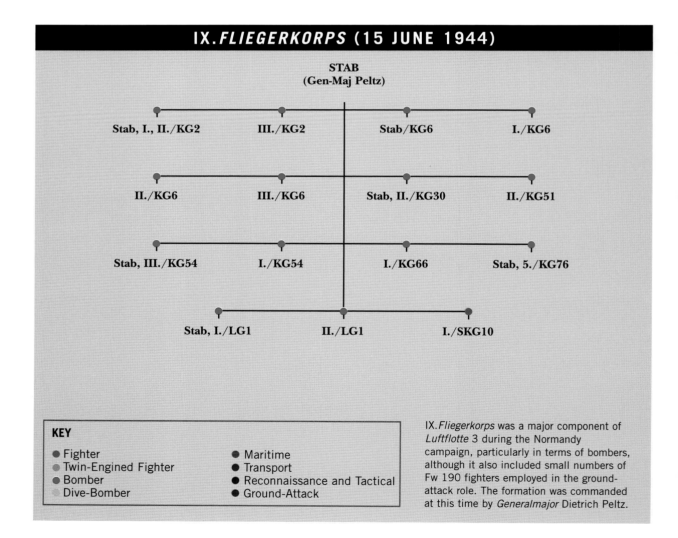

IX. *FLIEGERKORPS* (15 JUNE 1944)

STAB
(Gen-Maj Peltz)

Stab, I., II./KG2   III./KG2   Stab/KG6   I./KG6

II./KG6   III./KG6   Stab, II./KG30   II./KG51

Stab, III./KG54   I./KG54   I./KG66   Stab, 5./KG76

Stab, I./LG1   II./LG1   I./SKG10

KEY
- Fighter
- Twin-Engined Fighter
- Bomber
- Dive-Bomber
- Maritime
- Transport
- Reconnaissance and Tactical
- Ground-Attack

IX. *Fliegerkorps* was a major component of *Luftflotte* 3 during the Normandy campaign, particularly in terms of bombers, although it also included small numbers of Fw 190 fighters employed in the ground-attack role. The formation was commanded at this time by *Generalmajor* Dietrich Peltz.

The battle for Arnhem

By the middle of September, the Allies had liberated Belgium. They were now on the borders of Germany itself, and Field Marshal Montgomery planned to expedite the advance with a huge airborne operation, *Market Garden*.

On 17 September, Operation *Market Garden* was launched. The plan involved a sequence of US and British airborne landings at Veghel, Grave and Arnhem, the paras holding on to their objectives while the British XXX Corps advanced up the connecting road to relieve them and push the Allied advance to the Rhine.

Allied setback

As history now shows, the operation was a disaster, XXX Corps reaching as far as Nijmegen, well behind schedule, but being forced by German resistance to abandon the Arnhem troops to their fate. The *Luftwaffe* also contributed to the Allied defeat. Attempts to resupply the paras by airdrops were roughly handled by Bf 109 and Fw 190 fighters, the C-47s being fairly easy targets. Nonetheless, the Allies also threw up large numbers of P-51 escorts, and the *Luftwaffe* suffered consequently. On one day alone, 26 German fighters were lost over Eindhoven-Nijmegen.

JG26 (1944)				
Luftwaffe Unit	**Base**	**Type**	**Str**	**Op**
30 JUNE 1944				
Stab	Chaumont	Fw 190A8	4	1
I.Gruppe	Boissy le Bois	Fw 190A8	68	10
II.Gruppe	Guyancourt	Fw 190A8	68	6
III.Gruppe	Villacoublay	Bf 109G6	68	18
31 DECEMBER 1944				
Stab	Fürstenau	Fw 190A8	4	0
		Fw 190D9	4	1
I.Gruppe	Fürstenau	Fw 190A8	68	0
		Fw 190D9	68	32
II.Gruppe	Nordholm	Fw 190D9	68	32
III.Gruppe	Plantlünne	Bf 109G14	68	7
		Bf 109K4	68	13
		Fw 190D9	68	1
III./JG54	Varrelbusch	Fw 190D9	68	32

Ardennes offensive

The Ardennes offensive in the winter of 1944 was Hitler's last, futile gasp on the Western Front. Although it initially made good progress, and shocked the Allies, it was eventually destroyed a long way from its final objectives.

The plan for the Ardennes offensive was for a force of four German armies to cut through Allied forces in the Ardennes forest, splitting the US and British armies from one another and driving on through Belgium to capture the key port of Antwerp. It was a bold plan on Hitler's part, and rode against the advice of many of his commanders, but nevertheless it was launched on 16

December 1944. The initial advance was promising, driving back the US VIII Corps, cutting off US airborne troops in Bastogne and, by 24 December, reaching close to Dinant, some 64km (40 miles) from the start lines. Air support was initially scarcely required, as Hitler had correctly judged that the winter weather would prevent Allied flights from holding up the German advance.

OPERATION *BODENPLATTE*			
Target	Unit	Allied Forces	Effect
Antwerp-Deurne (airfield designation B.70) (Belgium)	JG77	Mostly Typhoon squadrons, 2nd TAF	Light damage
Asch (Belgium)	JG11	Four Spitfire squadrons, 2nd TAF; US 352nd Fighter Group (P-51s); US 366th Fighter Group (P-47s)	Minimal damage
Brussels-Evere (B.56)	JG26, J54	A large number of US and 2nd TAF fighters and bombers	Heavy damage
Brussels-Grimbergen (B.60)	JG26, JG54	Only six aircraft were present	Medium damage
Brussels-Melsbroek (B.58)	JG27, JG54, JG4	Three reconnaissance squadrons, 2nd TAF; three bomber squadrons, US Eighth Air Force	Heavy damage
Eindhoven (B.78) (Netherlands)	JG3	Eight Typhoon squadrons and three Spitfire squadrons, 2nd TAF	Heavy damage
Ghent/Sint-Denijs-Westrem (Belgium)	JG1	Three Polish Spitfire squadrons (Nos 302, 308 and 317), 2nd TAF	Heavy damage; intense dogfights
Gilze-Rijen (B.77) (Netherlands)	JG3, KG51	Two Boston squadrons (Nos 88 and 342), one Mitchell squadron (No 226), 137 Wing, 2nd TAF	Medium damage
Heesch (B.88) (Netherlands)	JG6	Five Spitfire squadrons, 2nd TAF	No effect
Le Culot (Belgium)	JG4	Thunderbolt squadrons, Ninth Air Force	Airfield not found; no damage
Maldegem (B.65) (Belgium)	JG1	Spitfire IXs, 485(NZ) Sqn, 2nd TAF	Heavy damage
Metz-Frescaty (France)	JG53	About 40 Thunderbolts, 365th Fighter Group, Ninth Air Force	Medium damage
Ophoven (Belgium)	JG4	Thunderbolt squadron, Ninth Air Force	Light damage
Sint-Truiden (Belgium)	JG2, JG4, SG4	Thunderbolt squadrons, Ninth Air Force	Medium damage
Volkel (B.80) (Netherlands)	JG6	56 Sqn, 486(NZ) Sqn, 122 Hawker Tempest Wing, 2nd TAF; 486(NZ) Sqn in the air	Light damage
Woensdrecht (Netherlands)	JG77	Five Spitfire squadrons, 2nd TAF; all in the air	No effect
Ursel (B.67) (Belgium)	JG1	Spitfire squadrons, 2nd TAF	Medium damage

Nevertheless, the ebullient Göring had promised Hitler some 1000 aircraft in support of the offensive. This figure amounted to around a quarter of Germany's operational air strength at the time, so many were sceptical. However, Göring did manage to gather around 800 aircraft, courtesy of Albert Speer's record aircraft production figures (Speer had taken over industrial production in 1944) and by stripping the *Reich* of much of its air defence. From 17 December, the weather improved sufficiently for the *Luftwaffe* units to fly hundreds of sorties against the Allies, but clearing

weather on 18 December allowed US bombers and escorts to conduct thunderous operations against the offensive – 63 German pilots were killed on that day alone, and by Christmas Day air superiority was firmly back in Allied hands.

Göring was not finished yet, however. On 1 January 1945, by which time the land offensive had evidently failed, Göring launched Operation *Bodenplatte* (Baseplate). This consisted of a massive 800-aircraft raid against Allied airbases in Belgium and the Netherlands, conducted principally by II.*Jadgkorps*. The operation

LUFTWAFFE CASUALTIES, OPERATION *BODENPLATTE*

Unit	KIA/MIA	POW	Wounded	Aircraft Deployed	Staff Lost
I./JG1	7	3	0		
II./JG1	10	1	1		
III./JG1	1	2	0		
Total	18	6	1	80	31%
Stab/JG2	0	1	0		
I./JG2	9	6	1		
II./JG2	3	1	1		
III./JG2	10	3	2		
Total	22	11	4	90	31%
I./JG3	3	5	0		
III./JG3	3	0	2		
IV./JG3	4	1	0		
Total	10	6	2	70	26%
I./JG4	3	0	0		
II./JG4	8	3	1		
III./JG4	1	0	0		
IV./JG4	6	2	0		
Total	18	5	1	55	42%
Stab/JG6	0	1	0		
I./JG6	4	1	1		
II./JG6	5	2	0		
III./JG6	6	3	0		
Total	15	7	1	70	33%
Stab/JG11	2	0	0		
I./JG11	4	0	0		
II./JG11	6	2	0		
III./JG11	9	2	0		
Total	21	4	0	65	38%

LUFTWAFFE CASUALTIES, OPERATION *BODENPLATTE*

Unit	KIA/MIA	POW	Wounded	Aircraft Deployed	Staff Lost
I./JG26	5	3	2		
II./JG26	4	4	1		
III./JG26	3	1	1		
Total	12	8	4	160	38%
I./JG27	6	1	0		
II./JG27	1	1	0		
III./JG27	2	0	1		
IV./JG27	2	1	0		
Total	11	3	1	85	18%
II./JG53	5	2	1		
III./JG53	0	0	2		
IV./JG53	5	2	1		
Total	10	4	4	50	36%
III./JG54	5	4	1	17	60%
IV./JG54	2	1	0	25	12%
Total	7	5	1	42	32%
I./JG77	2	1	0		
II./JG77	1	1	0		
III./JG77	3	3	0		
Total	6	5	0	105	10%
ESt/JG104	0	1	0	3	
Total (day)	150	65	19	875	
Stab/SG4	1	0	0		
III./SG4	2	1	0		
Total	3	1	0		
FlüG1	1	0	0		
NJG1	9	2	0		
NJG3	3	1	0		
NJG101	1	0	0		
Total	13	3	0		
KG(J)51	2	0	0		
Total (other)	19	4	0		
Grand Total	169	69	19		

resulted in enormous damage to some Allied airfields, and the loss of over 200 Allied aircraft. Yet in a now-familiar tale, German losses were greater – 300 aircraft destroyed. The German fighter ace Adolf Galland wrote after the Ardennes offensive that 'The *Luftwaffe* received its death blow in the Ardennes.' Certainly such losses were devastating as Germany teetered on the brink.

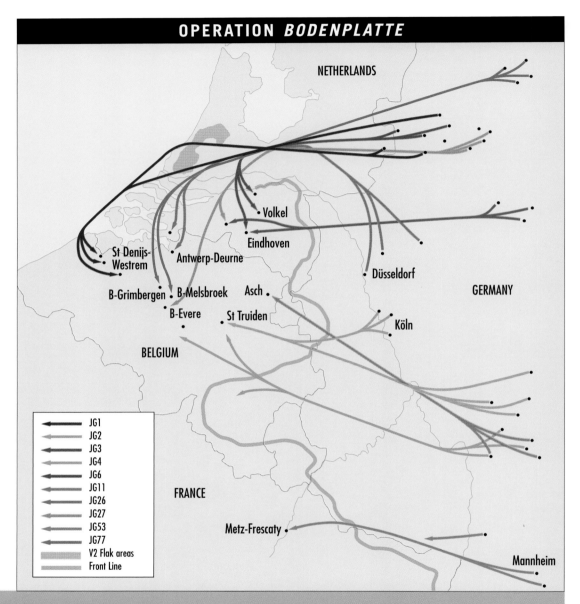

OPERATION *BODENPLATTE*

NETHERLANDS

GERMANY

Volkel

Eindhoven

Düsseldorf

St Denijs-Westrem

Antwerp-Deurne

B-Grimbergen　B-Melsbroek　Asch

B-Evere　St Truiden　Köln

BELGIUM

FRANCE

Metz-Frescaty

Mannheim

JG1
JG2
JG3
JG4
JG6
JG11
JG26
JG27
JG53
JG77
V2 Flak areas
Front Line

1 January 1945

Operation *Bodenplatte* targeted key Alllied airbases in Belgium and the Netherlands, using the fighters and fighter-bombers of II.*Jadgkorps*. The airfields in question included Sint Denijs-Westrem, Eindhoven, Volkel, Brussels-Evere, Brussels-Grimbergen, Brussels-Melsbroek, Antwerp-Deurne, Sint Truiden, Asch, Le Culot and Metz-Frescaty. The German aircraft flew in at extreme low level to circumvent Allied radar, and managed to achieve almost total surprise. Some of the flight paths and targets chosen, however, took the *Luftwaffe* pilots into areas of intense *Flak*, and once the Allies managed to scramble their fighters the Germans were overwhelmed with sheer numbers.

JG11 (1 JANUARY 1945)

This representation of the force put into the air by *Jagdgeschwader* 11 during Operation *Bodenplatte* shows a mixed unit of Focke-Wulf Fw 190s and Messerschmitt Bf 109s. The specific models used were the Fw 190A and Bf 109G, the latter being one of the most advanced fighter aircraft of the Bf 109 series. JG11's commander for the operation was *Major* Günther Specht, a much-respected fighter ace. He was killed during *Bodenplatte*, most likely by heavy enemy anti-aircraft fire, and he was replaced by *Major* Jürgen Harder.

Operational aircraft – 30 x Fw 190A, 35 x Bf 109G

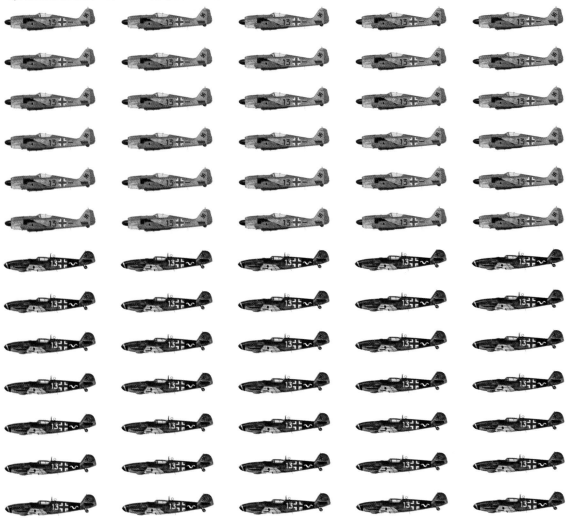

Maritime Operations: 1939–45

As a largely land-locked country, Germany was slower than many other nations in developing a naval arm to its air force. Maritime aviation, however, became more important as conquests opened up new fronts bordered by seas.

The crew of an Fw 200 Kondor undergo an operational briefing before a maritime patrol sortie.

A t the beginning of World War II, Germany's coastal areas were limited squarely to the north, bordering the North and Baltic Seas. The development of a specifically maritime force within the *Luftwaffe*, therefore, took a low priority when compared with other nations. Britain, for example, had its Fleet Air Arm and the United States had a large carrier-based establishment, but Germany did not develop a truly equivalent force. Partly this was to do with the fact that Germany's surface fleet, apart from several capital vessels, was never seriously utilized as a strategic force, nor had the strength to be so used. Furthermore, although Germany made several abortive attempts to

produce aircraft carriers, the fact that none of these were ever launched limited the incentives to develop specific maritime aircraft types.

Another restraint on maritime aviation was doctrinal in nature. Göring largely viewed *Luftwaffe* maritime operations as an improvised add-on rather than an integral part of operations, in contrast to *Luftwaffe* direct-support relations with the army. Essentially, the *Luftwaffe* would remain terrestrial in thought and outlook, and this would forever limit its relevance in a maritime context. This being said, enough *Luftwaffe* units were diverted into maritime roles to be worthy of our consideration.

Organization

Germany began World War II with a small dedicated maritime force known as the *Seeluftstreitkräfte* (Naval Air Arm). This organization operated several groups of maritime aircraft arranged in *Küstenfliegergruppen* (KüFlGr).

While Admiral Raeder wanted a specific air arm under dedicated control of the *Kriegsmarine*, Göring retained maritime aircraft under the jurisdiction of the *Luftwaffe*. In doctrine developed between 1935 and 1939, the *Luftwaffe* maritime forces were allocated to reconnaissance duties and combat support for *Kriegsmarine* vessels that were engaging the enemy.

Changes in structure
Up to April 1939, the *Seeluftstreitkräfte* operated 14 *Küstenfliegerstaffeln* (coastal aviation squadrons), plus one *Bordfliegergruppe* (BFGr; ship-based aviation group). At this point, however, the *Seeluftstreitkräfte* was disbanded with the approach of war, and instead German maritime aviation was arranged under *Fliegerdivision Luft West* and *Fliegerdivision Luft Ost*, both of these formations falling under the umbrella structure of the *General der Flieger beim Oberbefehlshaber der Marine*, at the time commanded by *Generalmajor* Hans Ritter. The two *Fliegerdivisionen* were associated with the *Kriegsmarine*'s *Marineoberkommando West* and *Marineoberkommando Ost*,

FLIEGERDIVISION LUFT WEST (AUGUST 1940)				
Luftwaffe Unit	Base	Type	Str	Op
FLIEGER-DIVISION LUFT WEST				
Stab/KüFlGr106	Norderney	?	?	?
1.(M)/106	Norderney	He 60	10	10
2.(F)/106	Norderney	Do 18	12	12
3.(M)/106	Borkum	He 59	10	10
3.(M)/706	Norderney	He 59	12	12
Stab/KüFlGr306	Hörnum/Sylt	Do 18	?	?
2.(F)/306	Hörnum/Sylt	Do 18	12	11
2.(F)/506	Hörnum/Sylt	Do 18	12	11
2.(F)/606	Hörnum/Sylt	Do 18	12	9
Stab/KüFlGr406	List/Sylt	Do 18	?	?
1.(M)/406	List/Sylt	He 115	8	8
2.(F)/406	List/Sylt	Do 18	12	10
3.(M)/406	List/Sylt	He 59	9	9
1./BFGr196	Wilhelmshaven	He 60	12	12

the former roughly responsible for waters to the west of Denmark, while the latter looked eastwards through the Baltic and up into Arctic waters. It should be noted, however, that the highest command level rested with the *Luftwaffe*, not with the commanding officers of the relevant *Marineoberkommandos*. This structure formed the foundation of German maritime aviation, with additional commands being added in new theatres.

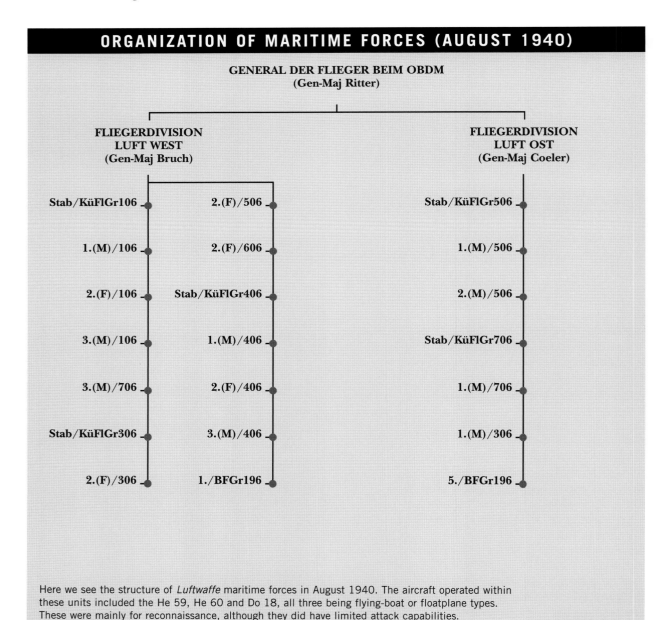

ORGANIZATION OF MARITIME FORCES (AUGUST 1940)

GENERAL DER FLIEGER BEIM OBDM
(Gen-Maj Ritter)

FLIEGERDIVISION LUFT WEST (Gen-Maj Bruch)		FLIEGERDIVISION LUFT OST (Gen-Maj Coeler)
Stab/KüFlGr106	2.(F)/506	Stab/KüFlGr506
1.(M)/106	2.(F)/606	1.(M)/506
2.(F)/106	Stab/KüFlGr406	2.(M)/506
3.(M)/106	1.(M)/406	Stab/KüFlGr706
3.(M)/706	2.(F)/406	1.(M)/706
Stab/KüFlGr306	3.(M)/406	1.(M)/306
2.(F)/306	1./BFGr196	5./BFGr196

Here we see the structure of *Luftwaffe* maritime forces in August 1940. The aircraft operated within these units included the He 59, He 60 and Do 18, all three being flying-boat or floatplane types. These were mainly for reconnaissance, although they did have limited attack capabilities.

Battle of the Atlantic

The battle of the Atlantic quickly provided the rationale for effective maritime aviation support for the U-boat arm plus dedicated anti-shipping and minelaying sorties. By 1940, long-range *Luftwaffe* aircraft were operating in these roles.

With the fall of France to Germany in mid-1940, it became apparent that *Luftwaffe* maritime operations would of necessity become more important – from now on, the English Channel, the North Sea and the Atlantic were major war zones. A new, specifically maritime force was developed for reconnaissance, minelaying and surface vessel interdiction roles.

This was X.*Fliegerkorps*, under the jurisdiction of *Luftflotte* 5, within which 9.*Fliegerdivision* provided the main operational unit. Initial operations consisted primarily of minelaying, with some torpedo attack actions. Control of operations was multilayered, involving *Luftflotte* 2, *Luftflotte* 5 and *Marineoberkommando West*, the aircraft being assigned to operations through coordinated tasking. As operations intensified in the Atlantic by the early months of 1941, and X.*Fliegerkorps* was transferred to the Atlantic in December 1940, a new command system was required.

Fliegerführer Atlantik

To complement *Luftflotte* 5, which took responsibility for maritime operations over Norwegian and Arctic waters, a new maritime force was formed in the early months of 1941. *Fliegerführer Atlantik*, commanded at first by *Oberstleutnant* Martin Harlinghausen, was created in March, and from the start showed all the signs of overworked command structure for which the Germans were notorious during World War II. *Fliegerführer Atlantik* was part of *Luftflotte* 3, and was headquartered in Lorient, France. It was moulded from parts of IV.*Fliegerkorps*, to which it still bore a command relationship. Yet the formation was designed primarily to support *Marineoberkommando West* and the *Befehlshaber der Unterseebooten* (BdU; Commander-in-Chief U-boats).

Therefore, tasking for the aircraft of *Fliegerführer Atlantik* was a convoluted process involving four major command centres. Such a tangled system meant that if

a *Luftwaffe* reconnaissance flight spotted an Allied convoy, then by the time the information had been relayed up the command structure to the U-boat commander, it was often already too late to act upon. This problem stemmed essentially from the fact that the

FLIEGERFÜHRER ATLANTIK BASES (1940–42)	
Luftwaffe Unit	**Base**
FlFü Atlantik	Lorient
Stab/KG40	Bordeaux
I./KG40	Bordeaux
II./KG40	Cognac
III./KG40	Bordeaux
Stab/KüFlGr106	Amsterdam
3./KüFlGr106	Amsterdam
Stab/KüFlGr406	Brest
2./KüFlGr506	Brest
1./KüFlGr906	Brest
Stab/KüFlGr506	Westerland
1./KüFlGr506	Westerland
3./KüFlGr506	Westerland
2./KüFlGr906	Westerland
Stab/KüFlGr606	Lannion
1./KüFlGr606	Lannion
2./KüFlGr606	Lannion
3./KüFlGr606	Lannion
Stab/KüFlGr906	Aalborg
1./KüFlGr706	Aalborg
3.(F)/122	Amsterdam
1./BFGr196	Wilhelmshafen
5./BFGr196	Brest

Luftwaffe was reluctant to relinquish its operational control over any of its aircraft, and hence the *Kriegsmarine* was unable to control a specified body of aircraft as it saw fit.

Furthermore, the redeployment of many maritime bombers to conventional bombing raids over Britain and the siphoning-off of air resources to the Mediterranean meant that *Fliegerführer Atlantik* never developed the potency of which it was capable. From June 1941, the Eastern Front added a further draw on aircraft numbers. For example, in the winter of 1942/43, significant numbers of Fw 200 Condor aircraft were transferred from operations in the West to airlift duties over Stalingrad, an appalling misuse of the type

that simply added to the attrition of maritime-capable aircraft in the *Luftwaffe* as a whole.

Atlantic operations

Atlantic operations required long-range aircraft, and the true workhorse of the maritime aviation force was indeed the Focke-Wulf Fw 200 Condor. The Condors were concentrated in KG40, headquartered from June 1940 at Bordeaux-Mérignac. An Fw 200C-0, for example, had a range of 3560km (2212 miles), and this was enough to perform the Condor's primary mission, reconnaissance sweeps between the base in Bordeaux and bases in Norway. By describing a huge operational arc, the sorties took the Condors deep into the Atlantic,

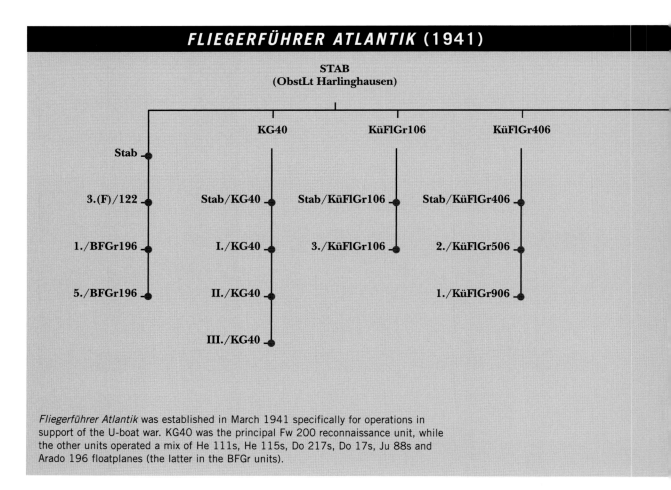

FLIEGERFÜHRER ATLANTIK (1941)

STAB
(ObstLt Harlinghausen)

	KG40	KüFlGr106	KüFlGr406
Stab			
3.(F)/122	Stab/KG40	Stab/KüFlGr106	Stab/KüFlGr406
1./BFGr196	I./KG40	3./KüFlGr106	2./KüFlGr506
5./BFGr196	II./KG40		1./KüFlGr906
	III./KG40		

Fliegerführer Atlantik was established in March 1941 specifically for operations in support of the U-boat war. KG40 was the principal Fw 200 reconnaissance unit, while the other units operated a mix of He 111s, He 115s, Do 217s, Do 17s, Ju 88s and Arado 196 floatplanes (the latter in the BFGr units).

and if a convoy was spotted, the details were radio-relayed back to U-boat stations in France, and an interception arranged.

Yet as the war progressed, the Condors became increasingly capable of delivering unilateral aggressive action in the form of bombing runs and, later, guided-missile attacks. Generally they would attack only isolated merchantmen, as their low top speed of 360km/h (224mph) made them vulnerable to the concentrated AA fire of massed escort vessels around convoys. The armament of an Fw 200C-1 included 2100kg (4626lb) of bombs carried in its underbelly gondola and on points under the outer wings, and the later C-6 and C-8 models were also capable of carrying two Hs 293 guided missiles

under the outer engine nacelles. Combine this with secondary machine-gun and cannon armaments, and the Condors were a genuine threat to lightly armed merchantmen.

In January and February 1941, for example, Condors from KG40 sank 46 ships with a total tonnage of 173,000 tonnes (170,000 tons) – the U-boats themselves only sank 12 more ships during this period.

Maritime types

The Condor was far from the only aircraft type available to *Fliegerführer Atlantik*. Operational records from the end of December 1943 list, in addition to the Condor, the following aircraft on the maritime establishment: the

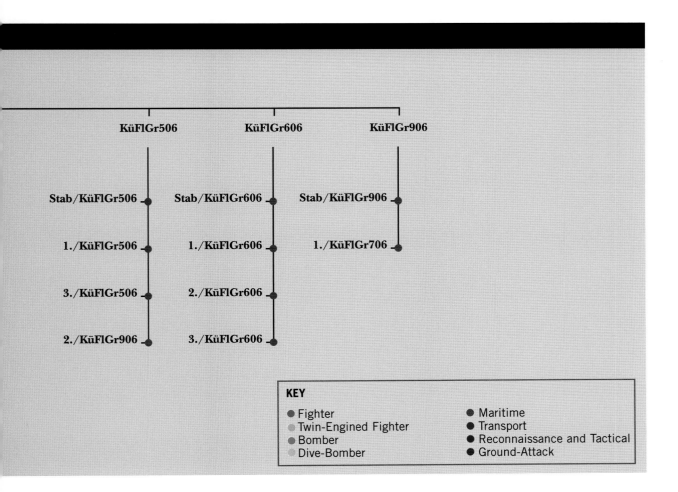

Air cover, North Atlantic, 1941–45

German airbases in Scandinavia provided strike capabilities against Allied shipping in the North Sea and North Atlantic. The map here shows the operational radius of various aircraft types.

Short-range aircraft included not only any fighter types tasked for maritime support but also seaplanes such as the Arado Ar 196 and Ar 95. For medium-range sweeps the He 111 and Do 217 were ideal, as was the He 115 seaplane. For operations requiring range in excess of 3350km (2082 miles), there were flying boats like the Bv 138, Bv 222, Do 24 and, of course, the conventional Fw 200 Condor.

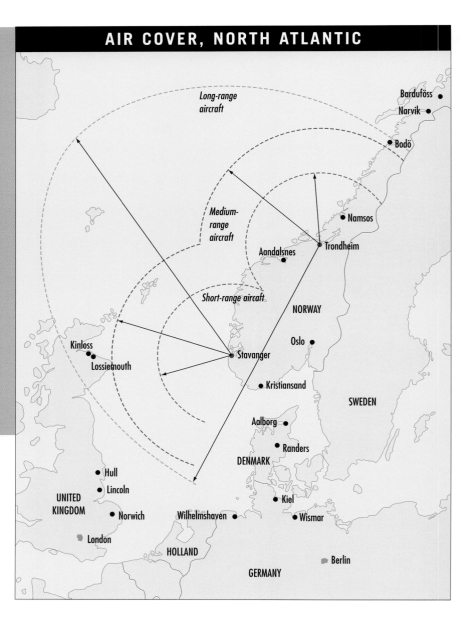

AIR COVER, NORTH ATLANTIC

He 177 'Greif' (Griffon), the Ju 290 'See Adler' (Sea Eagle), the Ju 88D-1 and Ju A-4, the Blohm und Voss Bv 222 'Wiking' (Viking), the Bv 138, the Fw 190 and the Arado Ar 196. Other aircraft employed by *Fliegerführer Atlantik* at various times included the He 111, Do 18, Do 24, Do 217 and Ju 290, the wide variety of aircraft types providing the formation with a

range of capabilities from local coastal actions through to almost transatlantic operations.

There are two main points to note about this diversity of aircraft types. First, the length of the list illustrates the German penchant during World War II for an over-proliferation of types, thereby complicating the supply and maintenance situation of the individual units.

Second, many of the aircraft used in maritime roles were not originally designed for maritime operations but were simply repurposed. The He 111, for example, was obviously Germany's premier medium bomber and the Do 217 was produced as a replacement for the Do 17, with roles that included night-fighting and night reconnaissance as well as maritime interdiction (it could carry two torpedoes in its internal bomb bay).

The problem with repurposed aircraft was that they could be turned back into non-maritime machines, something that simply wasn't possible with, say, a Do 24 or Bv 222 seaplane. This was one of the reasons why it was all too easy to divert maritime aircraft to land-based roles, and deplete *Fliegerführer Atlantik*'s capability.

Fliegerführer Atlantik faced other sources of attrition outside of force diversions. During 1943, RAF Coastal

Command increased patrols by twin-engined Bristol Beaufighter long-range fighters over the Bay of Biscay, resulting in greater German losses. In response, KG40 equipped its V.*Gruppe* with Ju 88C aircraft to provide a comparable escort force for the U-boats attempting to transit the bay.

Losing the Atlantic

During 1943, the *Luftwaffe* also produced some truly impressive long-range maritime aircraft. The Ju 290, for example, had a range of 6150km (3281 miles) and a large weapons load that included guided missiles. Yet such machines were too little too late, and the increasing numbers of Allied escort carriers meant *Fliegerführer Atlantik* was outclassed by April 1944, when its units were absorbed into X.*Fliegerkorps*.

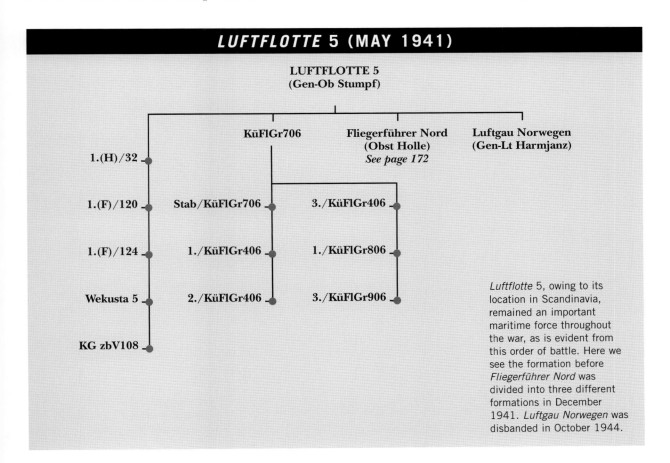

LUFTFLOTTE 5 (MAY 1941)

LUFTFLOTTE 5
(Gen-Ob Stumpf)

1.(H)/32	KüFlGr706	Fliegerführer Nord (Obst Holle) *See page 172*	Luftgau Norwegen (Gen-Lt Harmjanz)
1.(F)/120	Stab/KüFlGr706	3./KüFlGr406	
1.(F)/124	1./KüFlGr406	1./KüFlGr806	
Wekusta 5	2./KüFlGr406	3./KüFlGr906	
KG zbV108			

Luftflotte 5, owing to its location in Scandinavia, remained an important maritime force throughout the war, as is evident from this order of battle. Here we see the formation before *Fliegerführer Nord* was divided into three different formations in December 1941. *Luftgau Norwegen* was disbanded in October 1944.

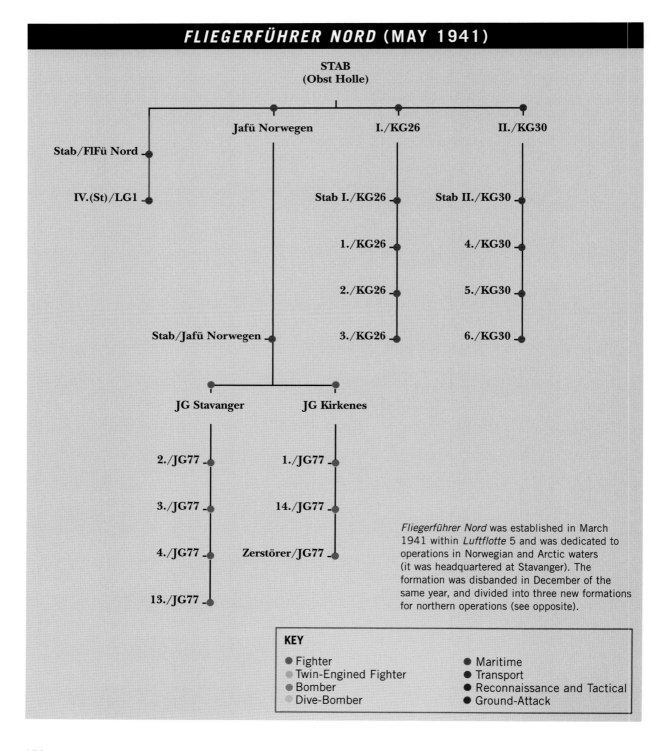

FLIEGERFÜHRER NORD (MAY 1941)

STAB
(Obst Holle)

Jafü Norwegen   I./KG26   II./KG30

Stab/FlFü Nord

IV.(St)/LG1

Stab I./KG26   Stab II./KG30

1./KG26   4./KG30

2./KG26   5./KG30

Stab/Jafü Norwegen   3./KG26   6./KG30

JG Stavanger   JG Kirkenes

2./JG77   1./JG77

3./JG77   14./JG77

4./JG77   Zerstörer/JG77

13./JG77

Fliegerführer Nord was established in March 1941 within *Luftflotte* 5 and was dedicated to operations in Norwegian and Arctic waters (it was headquartered at Stavanger). The formation was disbanded in December of the same year, and divided into three new formations for northern operations (see opposite).

KEY
- Fighter
- Twin-Engined Fighter
- Bomber
- Dive-Bomber
- Maritime
- Transport
- Reconnaissance and Tactical
- Ground-Attack

Mediterranean operations

As we have seen, control of the sea lanes was critical in the Mediterranean theatre, particularly in relation to supply shipping heading for North Africa. The *Luftwaffe* there was hence committed to a broad range of maritime operations.

Chapter Six has already explained much about the war over Mediterranean waters, but the *Luftwaffe* also invested in specialist maritime units in addition to conventional outfits targeting shipping. Ju 87 dive-bombers were integral to many anti-shipping missions, as these provided the necessary precision to hit a single vessel performing evasive manoeuvres. In January 1941, X.*Fliegerkorps* had three *Gruppen* of Ju 87R-1s, this version of the Stuka having the longer range required to make maritime sweeps.

He 111H-6s were applied as torpedo aircraft as well as conventional bombers, the crews having trained at a torpedo school established at Grosseto in Italy. The units equipped with these aircraft, which had the LT F5 and LT F5W torpedoes slung under the belly in special racks, were flown by 2./KG4 and II./KG26.

Specialist weapons

The Mediterranean theatre saw the first combat use of anti-ship guided missiles by the Germans. The Fritz-X and Henschel Hs 293 were both radio-controlled missiles (the latter was actually a glide bomb), directed to the target by an operator on board the launch aircraft using a remote control. A handful of ships were sunk, including the Italian battleship *Roma*, sent to the bottom by Fritz-Xs in September 1943, and many more were damaged in the Mediterranean, but the missiles were never widely enough deployed to have greater significance in the theatre.

Ultimately, the Allies' conquest of North Africa and their use of Malta as an island airbase yielded Allied air supremacy over the Mediterranean, and consigned a shrinking *Luftflotte* 2 mainly to operations over Italy.

USSR and the Baltic: 1939–45

In total, some 78 Allied convoys sailed between the United States or the United Kingdom and the Soviet ports of Murmansk and Archangel between August 1941 and the end of the war, convoys that the *Luftwaffe*'s northern units tried to stop.

The organizational picture of the *Luftwaffe* over Arctic waters and the Baltic Sea is complex but governed for the length of the war mainly by *Luftflotte* 5. In terms of maritime operations, the chief formation from March to December 1941 was *Fliegerführer Nord* commanded by *Oberst* Alexander Holle. At the end of 1941, *Fliegerführer Nord* was repackaged into three different units, each with sharper territorial jurisdictions. These formations were *Fliegerführer Nord (West)*, headquartered at Trondheim, *Fliegerführer Nord (Ost)*, headquartered at

Rovaniemi and then Kirkenes, and finally *Fliegerführer Lofoten*, with its command at Bardufoss.

All went through name and command changes in mid-1944, when the Allied invasion of Normandy dramatically altered the status of *Luftwaffe* units operating in the West. *Fliegerführer Nord (West)* became *Fliegerführer* 4, which in turn was transformed into *Kommandierende General der Deutschen Luftwaffe in Norwegen* in September that year. As an indication of the chaos gripping the *Reich* at this point, the last-

FLIEGERDIVISION LUFT OST (SEPTEMBER 1939)				
Luftwaffe Unit	**Base**	**Type**	**Str**	**Op**
FLIEGERDIVISION LUFT OST				
Stab/KüFlGr506	Pillau/Ostpreussen	He 60	?	?
1.(M)/506	Pillau/Ostpreussen	He 60	12	10
2.(M)/506	Pillau/Ostpreussen	He 59	10	9
Stab/KüFlGr706	Kamp/Pommern	He 60	?	?
1.(M)/706	Nest/Pommern	He 60	12	11
1.(M)/306	Nest/Pommern	He 60	12	11
5./BFGr196	Kiel-Holtenau	He 60	10	10

mentioned formation became *Stab/Luftgau-Kommando* XV by the end of the year. *Fliegerführer Nord (Ost)* was redesignated *Fliegerführer Eismeer* in March 1944, then *Fliegerführer 3* in June 1944, this formation being disbanded at the end of the year. Finally, *Fliegerführer Lofoten* became *Fliegerführer 5*, in turn subordinated to *Kommandierende General der Deutschen Luftwaffe in Finnland* for the last quarter of 1944.

In the Baltic, the picture was somewhat different. In June 1941, to coordinate with the German invasion of the Soviet Union, *Fliegerführer Ostsee* was formed,

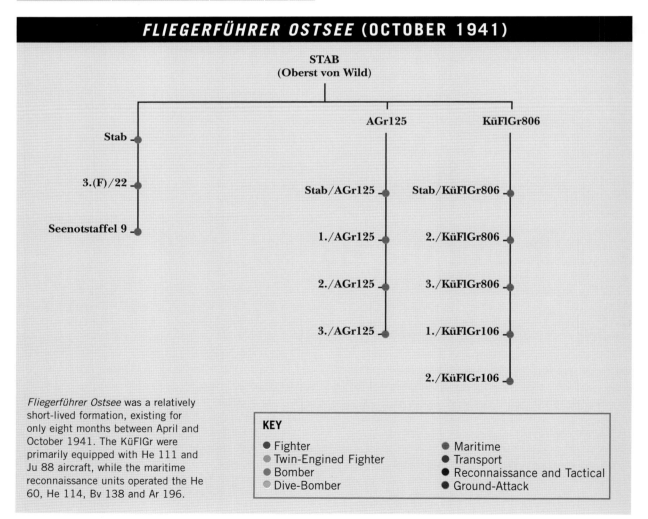

FLIEGERFÜHRER OSTSEE (OCTOBER 1941)

STAB
(Oberst von Wild)

Stab
3.(F)/22
Seenotstaffel 9

AGr125
Stab/AGr125
1./AGr125
2./AGr125
3./AGr125

KüFlGr806
Stab/KüFlGr806
2./KüFlGr806
3./KüFlGr806
1./KüFlGr106
2./KüFlGr106

Fliegerführer Ostsee was a relatively short-lived formation, existing for only eight months between April and October 1941. The KüFlGr were primarily equipped with He 111 and Ju 88 aircraft, while the maritime reconnaissance units operated the He 60, He 114, Bv 138 and Ar 196.

KEY
- Fighter
- Twin-Engined Fighter
- Bomber
- Dive-Bomber
- Maritime
- Transport
- Reconnaissance and Tactical
- Ground-Attack

operating Ju 88A, He 60, He 114 and Ar 95 aircraft types. *Fliegerführer Ostsee* survived until 27 October 1941, when it was used to create *Fliegerführer Süd*, which in turn became *Seefliegerführer Schwarzes Meer* (*Seefliegerführer* Black Sea) in December 1942 prior to being disbanded in September 1944.

Cold water operations

The *Luftwaffe* had a maritime involvement in northern waters even before it turned itself against the Artic convoys from 1941. In the prelude to Operation *Weserübung* in 1940, *Küstenfliegergruppen* made reconnaissance sorties around the Scandinavian coastline to plot naval invasion routes and airborne landing zones. Similarly, in Baltic waters maritime aircraft kept watch on Polish naval units, and provided transport flights around the Polish territories.

The convoluted coastlines of the north made dedicated maritime float- and seaplanes essential features of *Luftwaffe* operations in the theatre. The Heinkel He 115 floatplane was a versatile twin-engine workhorse, having a useful service range of 3350km (2082 miles) while carrying a bombload of 1250kg (2756lb), which made it suitable for both reconnaissance and maritime strike operations.

On a larger scale, the Bv 138 flying boat had a range of 5000km (3107 miles), and could carry six 50kg (110lb) bombs or four 150kg (331lb) depth charges. KG26 and KG30 also equipped He 111 and Ju 88 aircraft as torpedo-bombers, the latter utilizing the FuG 200 *Hohentweil* surface-search radar.

Early successes

All these air assets worked in tandem with each other and with U-boats and navy surface vessels to make the Arctic convoys a precarious duty. After detection and possibly strikes by the longer-range Condors and Bv 138s, the shorter-range aircraft would then make their assault as soon as the convoys came into range. The results could be impressive. Between 26 April and 7 May 1942, Convoy PQ15 lost three ships to torpedo aircraft, and in June/July 1942 the sinkings of eight ships (out of 24 in total) were attributed to air attack.

Such results were promising, but were not one-sided. Aircraft losses to heavy naval AA fire were significant,

KÜFLGR406 BASES (1940–42)		
Luftwaffe Unit	**Date**	**Base**
KÜFLGR406		
Stab	-	Brest Sud
1. Staffel	Jul 1940	Stavanger
	Jan 1941	List
	Apr 1941	Tromsø/Søreisa
2. Staffel	May 1940	Stavanger
	Oct 1940	Trondheim
	Feb 1941	Hörnum
	May 1941	Trondheim
3. Staffel	May 1940	Stavanger
	Jul 1940	Hörnum
	Aug 1940	Norderney
	Aug 1940	Vlissingen
	Sep 1940	Schellingwoude
	Feb 1941	Trondheim
	Nov 1941	List
	Dec 1941	Tromsø/Søreisa

SEEFLIEGERVERBÄNDE (EASTERN FRONT 1942)			
Luftwaffe Unit	**Type**	**Str**	**Op**
SEEFLIEGERVERBÄNDE			
1./906	He 115	9	4
GrSt125	He 114	3	2
	Ar 196	?	?
1./125	Bv 138	9	5
3./125	Bv 138	10	3
15./AFGr127(Estl)	He 60	19	5

and the atrocious weather over Arctic waters frequently meant that aircraft remained grounded as convoys sailed through. By the end of 1942, the Allies were using escort carriers in greater numbers, and the Hurricanes launched from these were a real handful for the slow-moving maritime aircraft. As in so many other theatres of war for the *Luftwaffe*, it was essentially the drip-drip effect of constant losses and too many commitments that undid northern operations.

End of the Reich: 1945

Even had the *Luftwaffe* been developed as a truly strategic air force earlier in the war, it is hard to see how the outcome of the air war would have been different once Germany had committed itself to fight the combined industrial might of the UK, USA and USSR.

German workers on the underground production line of the Heinkel He 162 'Volksjäger' (People's Fighter), early 1945.

As with the German land forces, the organizational picture of the *Luftwaffe* in the last months of World War II is chaotic. The formations established during this period have some splendid-sounding titles, but the reality on the ground was critically different. While the German aircraft production figures had reached a truly impressive crescendo in 1944, the numbers completely collapsed in 1945, along with the rest of German industry. In 1945 the total outputs were 5883 fighters, 1104 ground-attack aircraft, 216 reconnaissance aircraft, but no bombers and no transport aircraft. The fighter production figures may not sound too poor, but considering that the Allies manufactured over 35,000 aircraft of all types in 1945, and the complete loss of air superiority is understandable. Total serviceable aircraft in the entire *Luftwaffe* in April 1945 amounted to about 3000 aircraft, but in the last few months 'serviceable' did not equate to 'flyable'. There had been a catastrophic diminution in pilot numbers, and the training times for individual pilots was laughably short. Furthermore, at the end of 1944 and beginning of 1945 major Allied bombing strikes against German oil production facilities resulted in virtually no new fuel output. With the Allied land forces advancing into Germany on both fronts, and with the former early-warning radar stations in France and the Low Countries in Allied hands, there was almost nothing the *Luftwaffe* could do to prevent the final downfall of the Third Reich.

Final organization

As the end approached in Germany, Hitler and his high command engaged in a final reordering of their formations even as the front lines tightened around Berlin. In April 1945, of the *Luftflotten* formations, only *Luftflotte* 4, *Luftflotte* 6 and *Luftflotte Reich* remained, all vainly attempting to hold back the Soviet juggernaut from the east and continuing Allied air attacks from the west. *Luftflotte* 2 and *Luftflotte* 3, once the powerful formations that fought the Battle of Britain, no longer existed. *Luftflotte* 2 was disbanded on 27 September 1944, and became *Kommandierende General der Deutschen Luftwaffe in Italien*, a skeleton formation with less than 70 serviceable aircraft. *Luftflotte* 3 was redesignated *Luftwaffenkommando West* at the same time. Initially this

formation came under the jurisdiction of *Luftflotte Reich*, but by April it was responsible for the southwest Germany area and was subordinated to *Luftflotte* 6. In the north, *Luftflotte* 1 had been stranded by the Soviet advance up in the Baltic, where it was redesignated *Luftwaffenkommando Kurland* (Courland). *Luftflotte* 5 had, as already noted in the previous chapter, been transformed into *Kommandierende General der Deutschen Luftwaffe in Norwegen*.

Last gasp

It was these formations, negligible as they were on paper, that breathed out the last gasp of the *Luftwaffe* in World War II. There were some notes of genuine defiance from the German Air Force. Back in 1944, the first jet fighter units, equipped principally with the Me 262, had begun engaging Allied bomber forces over Germany, as had some of the unusual rocket types like the Me 163. In late 1944 and 1945, these were joined by a batch of curious experimental aircraft, including truly eccentric machines such as the *Mistel* – typically an unmanned Ju 88 configured as a flying bomb and delivered to the target by a fighter attached to it above. Night-fighters such as the Fw 189 and Arado 234 were also pressed into service, and another jet, the He 162A-2, took to the skies alongside one of the world's fastest propeller-driven aircraft, the Do 335A-0. The latter had a push-pull dual propeller system that could take it up to speeds of 763km/h (474mph).

Yet none of these technical innovations were sufficient to change the balance of power and prevent the final defeat of Germany in May 1945. And here we come to the heart of a problem that assailed all Germany's armed forces, not just the *Luftwaffe*. Ultimately, the commander-in-chief of German forces, Adolf Hitler, did not truly understand the nature of industrial war. Declaring war on both the Soviet Union and the United States brought Germany head to head with two industrial powerhouses, and over a prolonged conflict it was almost impossible to win out against the sheer numbers of weapon systems produced. The *Luftwaffe* illustrated this problem perfectly. Its pilots, particularly in the first few years, were some of the most capable aviators ever, but it was essentially led to destruction largely by its commanders.

The collapse of production

German industry had in many ways wrought miracles in keeping the outputs of *Luftwaffe* aircraft increasing year on year. Only in the final year of the war did production finally collapse as the *Reich*'s defence crumbled.

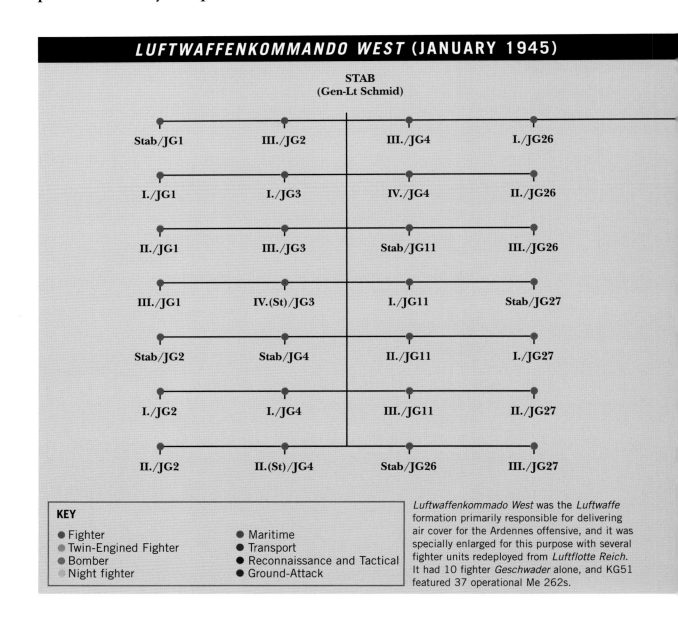

LUFTWAFFENKOMMANDO WEST (JANUARY 1945)

STAB
(Gen-Lt Schmid)

Stab/JG1	III./JG2	III./JG4	I./JG26
I./JG1	I./JG3	IV./JG4	II./JG26
II./JG1	III./JG3	Stab/JG11	III./JG26
III./JG1	IV.(St)/JG3	I./JG11	Stab/JG27
Stab/JG2	Stab/JG4	II./JG11	I./JG27
I./JG2	I./JG4	III./JG11	II./JG27
II./JG2	II.(St)/JG4	Stab/JG26	III./JG27

KEY

- Fighter
- Twin-Engined Fighter
- Bomber
- Night fighter
- Maritime
- Transport
- Reconnaissance and Tactical
- Ground-Attack

Luftwaffenkommado West was the *Luftwaffe* formation primarily responsible for delivering air cover for the Ardennes offensive, and it was specially enlarged for this purpose with several fighter units redeployed from *Luftflotte Reich*. It had 10 fighter *Geschwader* alone, and KG51 featured 37 operational Me 262s.

The German aircraft production figures for 1944 are an incredible testament to the resilience of German industry. Credit must also go in large measure to Albert Speer, who following the death of the previous incumbent, Fritz Todt, in 1942, was appointed to the position of Minister of Armaments and War Production. In this role Speer excelled, and he made genuine strides

towards building up Germany to an equal war production status to that of its enemies. Speer attempted to rationalize German industry and separate it from its interservice rivalries to make it more efficient. He was not entirely successful in achieving the latter objective, but he undoubtedly drove the manufacture of the weapons systems and aircraft to unexpected heights. For

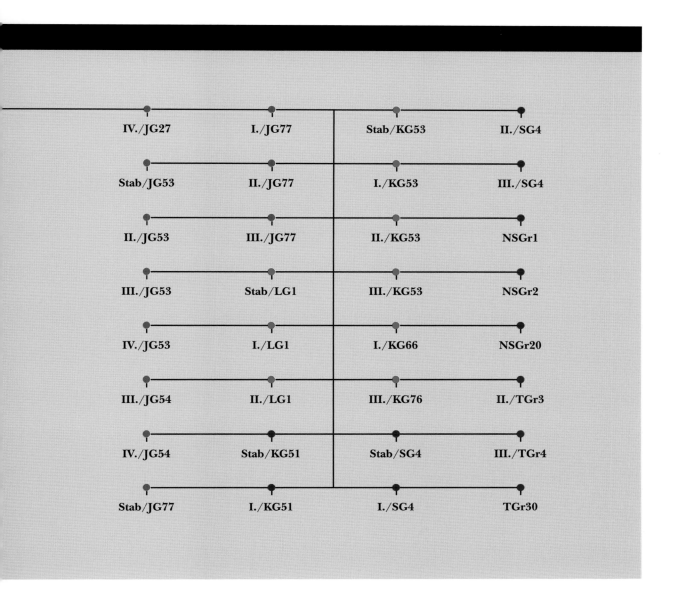

IV./JG27	I./JG77	Stab/KG53	II./SG4
Stab/JG53	II./JG77	I./KG53	III./SG4
II./JG53	III./JG77	II./KG53	NSGr1
III./JG53	Stab/LG1	III./KG53	NSGr2
IV./JG53	I./LG1	I./KG66	NSGr20
III./JG54	II./LG1	III./KG76	II./TGr3
IV./JG54	Stab/KG51	Stab/SG4	III./TGr4
Stab/JG77	I./KG51	I./SG4	TGr30

LUFTWAFFENKOMMANDO WEST (JANUARY 1945)			
Luftwaffe Unit	Type	Str	Op
Stab/JG1	Fw 190	5	4
I./JG1	Fw 190	27	22
II./JG1	Fw 190	40	30
III./JG1	Fw 190	40	35
Stab/JG2	Fw 190	4	3
I./JG2	Fw 190	28	23
II./JG2	Fw 190	3	2
III./JG2	Fw 190	19	6
I./JG3	Bf 109	31	22
III./JG3	Bf 109	32	26
IV.(St)/JG3	Fw 190A	35	24
Stab/JG4	Fw 190A	2	1
I./JG4	Bf 109	41	33
II.(St)/JG4	Fw 190A	25	18
III./JG4	Bf 109	13	10
IV./JG4	Bf 109	26	17
Stab/JG11	Fw 190	7	6
I./JG11	Fw 190	23	20
II./JG11	Bf 109	37	31
III./JG11	Fw 190	42	26
Stab/JG26	Fw 190	3	3
I./JG26	Fw 190	60	36
II./JG26	Fw 190	64	26
III./JG26	Fw 190	56	28
Stab/JG27	Fw 190	2	2
I./JG27	Bf 109	33	24
II./JG27	Bf 109	25	20
III./JG27	Bf 109	28	23
IV./JG27	Bf 109	24	22
Stab/JG53	Bf 109	4	1
II./JG53	Bf 109	46	29
III./JG53	Bf 109	39	25
IV./JG53	Bf 109	46	34
III./JG54	Fw 190D	47	31
IV./JG54	Fw 190	50	39

LUFTWAFFENKOMMANDO WEST (JANUARY 1945)			
Luftwaffe Unit	Type	Str	Op
Stab/JG77	Bf 109	2	1
I./JG77	Bf 109	43	24
II./JG77	Bf 109	32	20
III./JG77	Bf 109	10	7
Stab/LG1	Ju 88A	1	1
I./LG1	Ju 88A	29	25
II./LG1	Ju 88A	34	29
Stab/KG51	Me 262A	1	0
I./KG51	Me 262A	51	37
Stab/KG53	He 111H	1	1
I./KG53	He III/V.1	1	1
II./KG53	He III/V.1	37	25
III./KG53	He III/V.1	30	24
I./KG66	Ju 88A	29	17
III./KG76	Ar 234A	12	11
Stab/SG4	Fw 190F	49	17
I./SG4	Fw 190F	29	24
II./SG4	Fw 190F	40	36
III./SG4	Fw 190F	34	24
NSGr1	Ju 87D	44	37
NSGr2	Ju 87D	39	26
NSGr20	Fw 190	28	21
II./TG3	Ju 52	50	48
III./TG4	Ju 52	51	46
TGr30	He 111H	10	5

example, not only did German factories produce over 26,000 fighters during 1944, but also 19,002 tanks. So why did the production figures drop so precipitously in 1945? The key reason was a massive plunge in outputs or acquisitions of raw materials. Crude steel production was almost eradicated, and fuel became ultra-scarce. For instance, in 1945 12,000 tonnes (11,800 tons) of aviation fuel was acquired, but consumption was 114,000 tonnes (112,000 tons). Such an imbalance bled away reserve stocks and grounded aircraft, and without fuel the rationale for aircraft production was gone.

I./KG51 (JANUARY 1945)

In January 1945, I.*Gruppe* of *Jagdgeschwader* 51 had a total of 51 Me 262 jets as its establishment of aircraft, which were used in ground-attack roles. At this stage in the war, *Major* Fritz Losigkeit was the *Geschwaderkommodore* (*Geschwader* commander) and the commander of the *Gruppe* was *Hauptmann* Günther Schack. Miraculously, both men would go on to survive the last few chaotic and bloody months of the war. Although these aircraft were applied in the ground-attack role, such employment was actually a waste of the Me 262's speed, and 12 aircraft from I./JG51 were lost in just two weeks of operations.

I.*Gruppe* strength – 51 x Me 262s (37 operational)

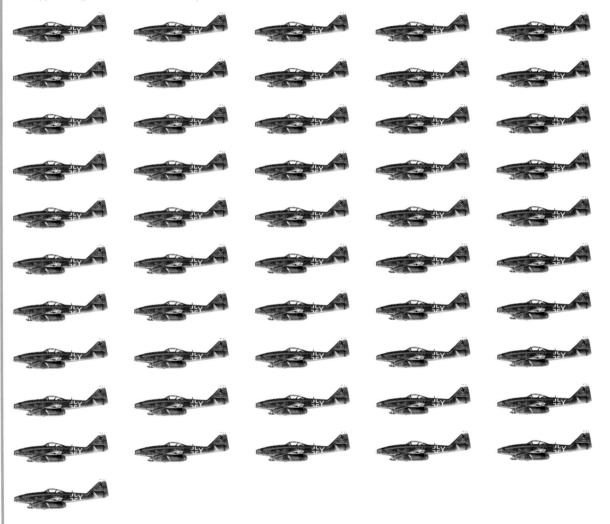

New technologies, last days

The *Luftwaffe* fought to the bitter end in World War II, and sought every means to take back the skies from the numerically superior Allies. This included putting into service cutting-edge jet aircraft that shocked, but could not defeat, the enemy.

It is one of the ironies of the German war machine that although its air force was ultimately defeated, it nonetheless flew some of the most technologically advanced aircraft in the world. German wartime advances in rocket and jet propulsion expressed themselves in genuinely capable fighting machines in the last years of the war, and many of these went on to form the research bedrock for postwar jet aircraft.

Early efforts

German exploration of jet and rocket aircraft technologies actually began during the days of victory.

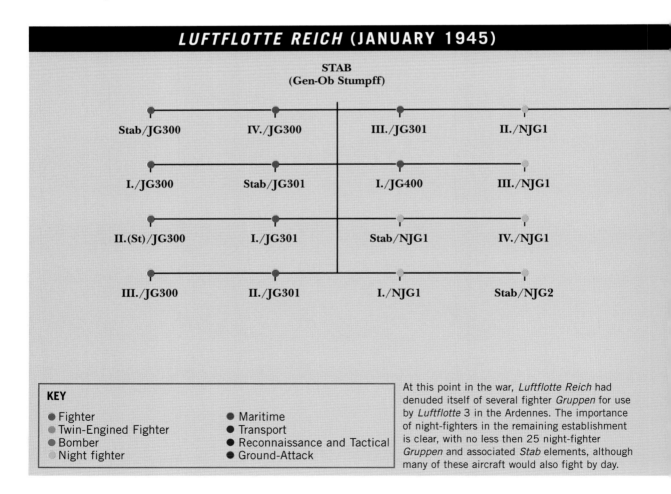

LUFTFLOTTE REICH (JANUARY 1945)

STAB
(Gen-Ob Stumpff)

Stab/JG300	IV./JG300	III./JG301	II./NJG1
I./JG300	Stab/JG301	I./JG400	III./NJG1
II.(St)/JG300	I./JG301	Stab/NJG1	IV./NJG1
III./JG300	II./JG301	I./NJG1	Stab/NJG2

KEY

- Fighter
- Twin-Engined Fighter
- Bomber
- Night fighter
- Maritime
- Transport
- Reconnaissance and Tactical
- Ground-Attack

At this point in the war, *Luftflotte Reich* had denuded itself of several fighter *Gruppen* for use by *Luftflotte* 3 in the Ardennes. The importance of night-fighters in the remaining establishment is clear, with no less then 25 night-fighter *Gruppen* and associated *Stab* elements, although many of these aircraft would also fight by day.

Heinkel led the way in the late 1930s with the He 178, the world's first turbojet-powered aircraft, which actually flew successfully in 1939, just days before the invasion of Poland. The He 178 did not attract more than passing interest from the authorities, however, but, undeterred, Heinkel demonstrated the twin-engine He 280 fighter in 1941. This aircraft had an impressive burst speed of 900km/h (559mph), but structural failures once again led to its never reaching production.

The year 1943 appears to have been the tipping point in the use of jet aircraft within the *Luftwaffe*. Jet types would never attain anything close to the production figures of regular prop-driven aircraft, but from the mid-point of the war Hitler was increasingly interested in any

technological marvel that could tip the balance in favour of Germany, particularly in its struggle against the sheer mass of Allied air power. Thus in 1943 and 1944 a number of new jet and rocket types appeared on the *Luftwaffe* establishment, albeit on a minor scale. These included the Arado Ar 234, a twin-engine jet aircraft that originally entered service as a long-range reconnaissance type in late 1944 but was later given ground-attack and night-fighter capabilities. Then there was the He 162 'Salamander' (or 'Volksjäger'), with a single turbojet mounted on top of the fuselage amidships and a heavy cannon armament in the nose. This aircraft came much too late in the war to be relevant, with the first of 275 production examples

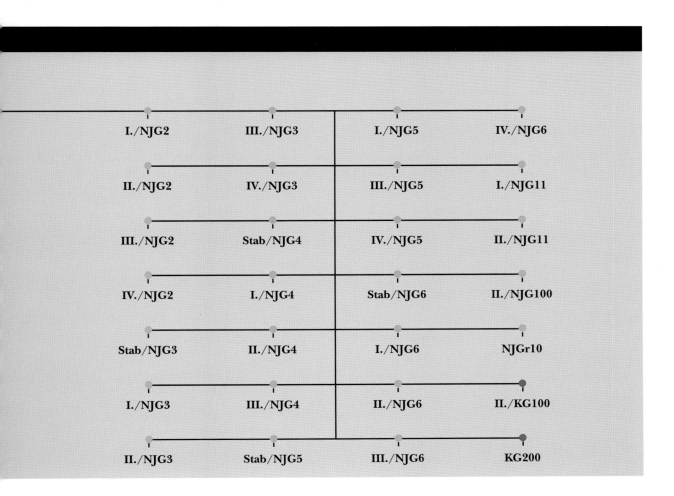

I./NJG2	III./NJG3	I./NJG5	IV./NJG6
II./NJG2	IV./NJG3	III./NJG5	I./NJG11
III./NJG2	Stab/NJG4	IV./NJG5	II./NJG11
IV./NJG2	I./NJG4	Stab/NJG6	II./NJG100
Stab/NJG3	II./NJG4	I./NJG6	NJGr10
I./NJG3	III./NJG4	II./NJG6	II./KG100
II./NJG3	Stab/NJG5	III./NJG6	KG200

emerging only in February 1945, shortly before its bases and production facilities were swallowed up by the Allied advance. Then there were the projects that bordered on the bizarre. The Bachem Ba 349 'Natter' (Viper), for example, was an expendable interceptor, intended to be launched up into the Allied bomber stream to deliver a burst of twenty-four 7.3cm (2.87in) rockets, before the fuel ran out and the pilot drifted back to earth in the parachute-retarded nose section. Only 20 were produced and were not tested in combat,

but the principle of a rocket interceptor found greater fruition in the Me 163 'Komet' (Comet). The Komet operated in a similar way to the Natter but was more airworthy, and hence was intended to glide back to earth once its fuel was expended. Tactically, its attack pattern began with an extremely fast climb to around 9144m (30,000ft); the aircraft would then fall on the Allied bombers below at high speed, attacking with its twin 30mm (1.18in) MK 108 cannon. Three hundred of the types were produced, and they had their first combat

LUFTFLOTTE REICH (JANUARY 1945)			
Luftwaffe Unit	Type	Str	Op
LUFTFLOTTE REICH			
Stab/JG300	Fw 190	6	4
I./JG300	Bf 109	57	37
II.(St)/JG300	Fw 190A	41	28
III./JG300	Bf 109	44	38
IV./JG300	Bf 109	53	39
Stab/JG301	Fw 190	5	5
I./JG301	Fw 190	38	2
II./JG301	Fw 190	40	38
III./JG301	Fw 190	26	20
I./JG400	Me 163A	46	19
Stab/NJG1	Bf 110G	20	18
	He 219A	–	–
I./NJG1	He 219A	64	45
II./NJG1	Bf 110G	37	24
III./NJG1	Bf 110G	37	7
IV./NJG1	Bf 110G	33	26
Stab/NJG2	Ju 88G	8	7
I./NJG2	Ju 88G	41	26
II./NJG2	Ju 88G	28	20
III./NJG2	Ju 88G	49	26
IV./NJG2	Ju 88G	36	29
Stab/NJG3	Ju 88G	6	3
I./NJG3	Bf 110G	48	40
II./NJG3	Ju 88G	30	23
III./NJG3	Ju 88G	37	22

LUFTFLOTTE REICH (JANUARY 1945)			
Luftwaffe Unit	Type	Str	Op
LUFTFLOTTE REICH			
IV./NJG3	Ju 88G	37	19
Stab/NJG4	Ju 88G	5	5
	Bf 110G	–	–
I./NJG4	Ju 88G	34	17
II./NJG4	Ju 88G	23	18
III./NJG4	Ju 88G	28	19
Stab/NJG5	Ju 88G	10	8
I./NJG5	Ju 88G	43	29
III./NJG5	Bf 110G	66	60
IV./NJG5	Ju 88G	51	24
Stab/NJG6	Bf 110G	29	23
I./NJG6	Bf 110G	26	12
II./NJG6	Ju 88G	26	18
III./NJG6	Ju 88G	23	19
	Bf 110G	–	–
IV./NJG6	Ju 88G	37	29
	Bf 110G	–	–
I./NJG11	Bf 109G	43	20
	Ju 88G	–	–
II./NJG11	Bf 109G	41	23
	Ju 88G	–	–
II./NJG100	Ju 88G	25	18
NJGr10	Ju 88G	17	14
II./KG100	He 177A	44	32
KG200	Various	295	206

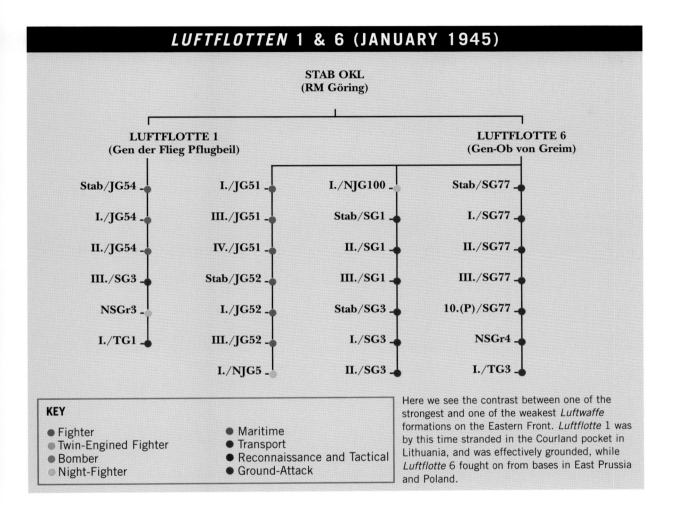

LUFTFLOTTEN 1 & 6 (JANUARY 1945)

STAB OKL
(RM Göring)

LUFTFLOTTE 1
(Gen der Flieg Pflugbeil)

LUFTFLOTTE 6
(Gen-Ob von Greim)

Stab/JG54	I./JG51	I./NJG100	Stab/SG77
I./JG54	III./JG51	Stab/SG1	I./SG77
II./JG54	IV./JG51	II./SG1	II./SG77
III./SG3	Stab/JG52	III./SG1	III./SG77
NSGr3	I./JG52	Stab/SG3	10.(P)/SG77
I./TG1	III./JG52	I./SG3	NSGr4
	I./NJG5	II./SG3	I./TG3

KEY
- Fighter
- Twin-Engined Fighter
- Bomber
- Night-Fighter
- Maritime
- Transport
- Reconnaissance and Tactical
- Ground-Attack

Here we see the contrast between one of the strongest and one of the weakest *Luftwaffe* formations on the Eastern Front. *Luftflotte 1* was by this time stranded in the Courland pocket in Lithuania, and was effectively grounded, while *Luftflotte 6* fought on from bases in East Prussia and Poland.

LUFTFLOTTE 1 (JANUARY 1945)			
Luftwaffe Unit	**Type**	**Str**	**Op**
LUFTFLOTTE 1			
Stab/JG54	Bf 109G	20	16
	Fw 190A	1	1
I./JG54	Fw 190A	35	32
II./JG54	Fw 190A	41	40
III./SG3	Fw 190F	39	35
NSGr3	Go 145	34	26
	Ar 66	–	–
I./TG1	Ju 52	45	42

outings in August 1944 with I./JG400. (By the end of the year, JG400's two other *Gruppen* were equipped with the Me 163.) In total, JG400 downed nine Allied aircraft with its Me 163s, but the accident rate amongst the aircraft was high, and during the glide phase of the flight they were extremely vulnerable to swoops by Allied escort fighters. Like many other jet and rocket fighter projects, the Me 163 was a diversion of resources at a time of increasing desperation.

Jet war
There was one jet fighter fielded by Germany late in the war that actually did have the capability and potential to

alter the balance of air power. This aircraft was the famous Me 262, design of which had actually started as far back as 1938, with first flights occurring in 1942. When the Me 262A-1a emerged in late 1944, it was a genuine force to be reckoned with. Powered by two Junkers Jumo 109-004B-4 turbojets, each generating 900kg (1984lb) of thrust, the aircraft had a top speed of 870km/h (541mph) and a climb rate of 1200m (3937ft) per minute. Its armament of four 30mm (1.18in) MK 108 cannon was capable of blasting any aircraft from the sky. Allied Mustangs simply could not catch it.

Despite its promise, the Me 262 is a classic example of how Hitler's interference could hobble a truly promising project. At first, both Hitler and Göring showed little interest in the Me 262, despite its promotion by fighter luminaries such as Adolf Galland, who was gripped with enthusiasm for the aircraft from his first test flight. In late 1943, with the war swinging against Germany, Hitler showed more interest in the aircraft, but with a curious slant – he wanted the jets armed with bombs to enable them to make fast ground-attack raids against the Allies. This was certainly viable, but the carrying of bombs

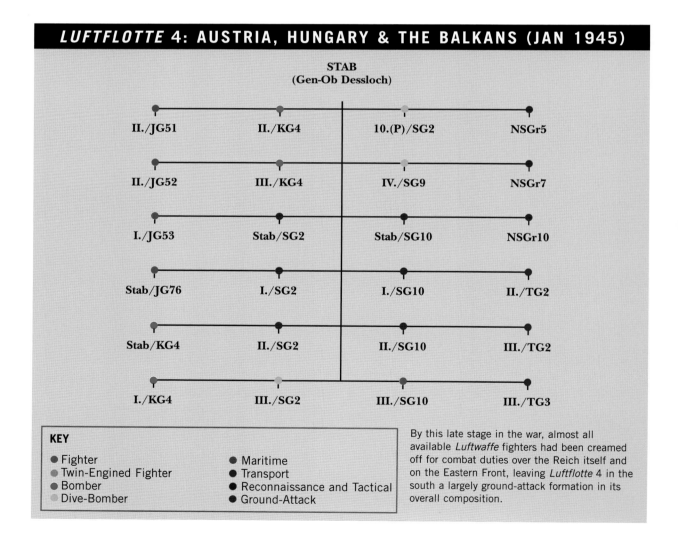

LUFTFLOTTE 4: AUSTRIA, HUNGARY & THE BALKANS (JAN 1945)

STAB
(Gen-Ob Dessloch)

II./JG51	II./KG4	10.(P)/SG2	NSGr5
II./JG52	III./KG4	IV./SG9	NSGr7
I./JG53	Stab/SG2	Stab/SG10	NSGr10
Stab/JG76	I./SG2	I./SG10	II./TG2
Stab/KG4	II./SG2	II./SG10	III./TG2
I./KG4	III./SG2	III./SG10	III./TG3

KEY
● Fighter
● Twin-Engined Fighter
● Bomber
● Dive-Bomber
● Maritime
● Transport
● Reconnaissance and Tactical
● Ground-Attack

By this late stage in the war, almost all available *Luftwaffe* fighters had been creamed off for combat duties over the Reich itself and on the Eastern Front, leaving *Luftflotte* 4 in the south a largely ground-attack formation in its overall composition.

would shave up to 193km/h (120mph) off its top speed, and speed was the Me 262's greatest strength. Arguments from combat-experienced pilots fell on deaf ears, and Me 262 fighter-bombers first appeared in action in mid-1944, the aircraft's development much delayed by Hitler's interference.

By early 1945, it became apparent even to Hitler that the Me 262 was wasted in a ground-attack role, and the aircraft were switched back to fighter duties, and even as radar-equipped night-fighters. In their original, intended role they excelled, and they were eventually formed into three main combat units: JG7, I./JG54 and *Jagdverband* 44 (JV44). Large-scale Me 262 combat fighter operations against Allied bombers began in March 1945, with promising results – in one mission alone, the jets shot down 12 US bombers and one fighter for the loss of only three of their number. One Me 262 ace, *Hauptmann* Franz Schall, downed 17 Allied aircraft in the Me 262, including 10 Mustang fighters, and other aces had similar or even better claimed tallies.

End days

In total, some 1433 Me 262s were produced before the final collapse of Germany in May 1945. However, because of Hitler's interference in their production programme only a fraction of these, around 100, were actually used in combat. Had the Me 262 been produced in sufficient quantities, and as an operational fighter from the outset, it may have had some capacity to tip the balance in the air war over Germany.

That being said, by the end of 1944 there was simply too much overall going against the Third Reich to alter the outcome of the war. Although the Allies struggled in the air to catch the Me 262, they did identify the aircraft's airbases, which were then attacked mercilessly with medium-bomber strikes. The German *Flak* crews took their toll on the attackers, but the raids nevertheless ate away at the numbers of these remarkable jets.

Ultimately, new technologies could not save Germany from its end, a fact that was finally appreciated by Göring. The man who had presided over the *Luftwaffe* for the entire war was eventually sacked by Hitler on 26 April 1945, and expelled from the Nazi Party. After the final German surrender, Göring was sentenced to

LUFTLOTTE 4 (JANUARY 1945)			
Luftwaffe Unit	Type	Str	Op
LUFTFLOTTE 4			
II./JG51	Bf 109	36	26
II./JG52	Bf 109	34	30
I./JG53	Bf 109	19	18
Stab/JG76	Bf 109	4	4
Stab/KG4	He 111H	1	1
I./KG4	He 111H	25	22
II./KG4	He 111H	23	12
III./KG4	He 111H	24	11
Stab/SG2	Ju 87D	10	7
	Fw 190F	–	–
I./SG2	Fw 190F	32	23
II./SG2	Fw 190F	34	29
III./SG2	Ju 87D	35	29
10.(P)/SG2	Ju 87G	10	9
IV./SG9	Hs 129B	59	45
Stab/SG10	Fw 190F	3	1
I./SG10	Fw 190F	22	17
II./SG10	Fw 190F	23	19
III./SG10	Fw 190F	21	20
NSGr5	Go 145	47	39
	Ar 66	–	–
NSGr7	Hs 126	54	37
	CR.42LW	–	–
NSGr10	Ju 87D	30	25
II./TG2	Ju 52	11	11
III./TG2	Ju 52	28	16
III./TG3	Ju 52	31	22

death by hanging at the Nuremberg trials in 1946, a sentence that he cheated by taking cyanide in his prison cell on 15 October.

Göring and other leaders had much to answer for. While the German air war had begun with vast fleets of the latest aircraft, piloted by some of the world's most talented and experienced combat aviators, it ended with isolated aircraft, piloted by ill-trained crews, flying virtual suicide missions over the ruins of their country.

Glossary of key abbreviations

Note: *Geschwader* is equivalent to an Allied Group, while *Gruppe* is equivalent to an Allied Wing

AG	Aufklärungsgruppe (reconnaissance group)	NG	Nahaufklärungsgruppe (short-range reconnaissance group)
BF	Bordflieger (ship-based aviation)	NJG	Nachtjagdgeschwader (night-fighter group)
F	Fern- (long-range strategic aviation)	NSGr	Nachtschlachtgruppe (night attack group)
FJD	Fallschirmjäger Division (paratroop division)	OKL	Oberkommando der Luftwaffe
FJR	Fallschirmjäger Regiment (paratroop regiment)	OKW	Oberkommando der Wehrmacht
Gen d. Flieger	General der Flieger	SAGr	Seeaufklärungsgruppe (maritime reconnaissance group)
GenFelm	Generalfeldmarschall		
GenLeut	Generalleutnant	SG	Schlachtgeschwader (close-support/assault group)
GenMaj	Generalmajor		
GenOb	Generaloberst	StG	Sturzkampfgeschwader (dive bomber group)
JaFü	Jagdfliegerführer (fighter command)	TG	Transportgeschwader (transport group)
JG	Jagdgeschwader (fighter group)	ZG	Zerstörergeschwader (twin-engined fighter group; lit. 'destroyer group')
KG	Kampfgeschwader (bomber group)		
KGzbV	Kampfgeschwader zur besonderen Verwendung (lit. 'Bomber groups for special purpose'; transport group)		
KüFl	Küsten Flieger (coastal aviation)	**Tables:**	
KüFlGr	Küstenfliegergruppe (coastal aviation group)	Str	Paper strength
LG	Lehrgeschwader (demonstration/operational development group)	Op	Operational strength
		?	Indicates that accurate figures are not available

Acknowledgements

The data in this book is collected from a wide variety of sources. Important and useful secondary sources are listed here, as are other recommended titles on the topic of the Luftwaffe in World War II.

Books
Price, Dr Alfred. **The Luftwaffe Data Book** (Stackpole Books, 1997)

Bishop, Chris. **Luftwaffe Squadrons 1939–45** (Spellmount, 2006)

Becker, Cajus. **The Luftwaffe War Diaries** (Da Capo, 1994)

Killen, John. **The Luftwaffe** (Sphere, 1970)

Murray, Williamson. **Strategy for Defeat – The Luftwaffe 1939–1945** (Eagle Editions, 2000)

Ellis, John. **The World War II Data Book** (Aurum, 1993)

Hyland, Gary and Anton Gill. **Last Talons of the Eagle** (Headline, 1998)

Websites
The listed websites constitute some of the best resources for reference on Luftwaffe data and orders of battle, and are constantly updated with new information:

World War II Armed Forces – Orders of Battle and Organizations
Dr Leo Niehorster – http://niehorster.orbat.com/

The Luftwaffe 1933–45 *Michael Holm*
– http://www.ww2.dk/

Axis History Factbook *Marcus Wendel*
– http://www.axishistory.com/

Sturmvogel *Jason Long*
– http://www.geocities.com/CapeCanaveral/2072/index.html

Luftwaffe Resource Center
– http://www.warbirdsresourcegroup.org/LRG/index.html

Feldgrau.com *Jason Pipes*
– http://www.feldgrau.com/

Unit Index

Page numbers in *italics* refer to illustrations and tables.

General Index

Page numbers in *italics* refer to illustrations and tables.

Index